THE COMPLETE IDIOT'S GUIDE® TO

The Perfect Job Interview

Third Edition

by Marc Dorio

A member of Penguin Group (USA) Inc.

ALPHA BOOKS

Published by the Penguin Group

Penguin Group (USA) Inc., 375 Hudson Street, New York, New York 10014, USA

Penguin Group (Canada), 90 Eglinton Avenue East, Suite 700, Toronto, Ontario M4P 2Y3, Canada (a division of Pearson Penguin Canada Inc.)

Penguin Books Ltd., 80 Strand, London WC2R 0RL, England

Penguin Ireland, 25 St. Stephen's Green, Dublin 2, Ireland (a division of Penguin Books Ltd.)

Penguin Group (Australia), 250 Camberwell Road, Camberwell, Victoria 3124, Australia (a division of Pearson Australia Group Pty. Ltd.)

Penguin Books India Pvt. Ltd., 11 Community Centre, Panchsheel Park, New Delhi—110 017, India

Penguin Group (NZ), 67 Apollo Drive, Rosedale, North Shore, Auckland 1311, New Zealand (a division of Pearson New Zealand Ltd.)

Penguin Books (South Africa) (Pty.) Ltd., 24 Sturdee Avenue, Rosebank, Johannesburg 2196, South Africa

Penguin Books Ltd., Registered Offices: 80 Strand, London WC2R 0RL, England

International Standard Book Number: 978-159257-827-6
Library of Congress Catalog Card Number: 2008931267

11 10 09   8 7 6 5 4 3 2 1

Interpretation of the printing code: The rightmost number of the first series of numbers is the year of the book's printing; the rightmost number of the second series of numbers is the number of the book's printing. For example, a printing code of 09-1 shows that the first printing occurred in 2009.

Printed in the United States of America

Note: This publication contains the opinions and ideas of its author. It is intended to provide helpful and informative material on the subject matter covered. It is sold with the understanding that the author and publisher are not engaged in rendering professional services in the book. If the reader requires personal assistance or advice, a competent professional should be consulted.

Most Alpha books are available at special quantity discounts for bulk purchases for sales promotions, premiums, fundraising, or educational use. Special books, or book excerpts, can also be created to fit specific needs.

For details, write: Special Markets, Alpha Books, 375 Hudson Street, New York, NY 10014.

Publisher: *Marie Butler-Knight*
Editorial Director: *Mike Sanders*
Senior Managing Editor: *Billy Fields*
Senior Acquistions Editor: *Paul Dinas*
Development Editor: *Lynn Northrup*
Production Editor: *Kayla Dugger*
Copy Editor: *Michael Dietsch*

Cartoonist: *Steve Barr*
Cover Designer: *Bill Thomas*
Book Designer: *Trina Wurst*
Indexer: *Celia McCoy*
Layout: *Ayanna Lacey*
Proofreader: *Mary Hunt*

Contents at a Glance

Contents

Foreword

How many times during a job search have well-intentioned friends or family members offered you advice on how to conduct yourself in an interview? I am willing to bet that these words of wisdom have for the most part been varied, confusing, and even contradictory.

One person tells you to "be yourself, and don't hold back," while another suggests you "play the game" and don't get "boxed in" by the crafty interviewer. Really, with all this "sage" advice it's no wonder that most job candidates approach the interview with the same enthusiasm as they would an IRS audit! There must be a better way.

Over the years, both as a corporate human-resources professional and now as an executive search consultant, I have personally interviewed hundreds of candidates for positions ranging from nonprofessional to top-level executives. These individuals have come from diverse countries and cultures. This interviewing experience has taught me two valuable lessons. The first is that preparation is key for interviewing success. What you do to get the interview in the first place, as well as preparing for it, is critical. Second, there is no pat way to interview. Each situation is unique. Flexibility and being able to correctly "read" each interviewer's style is, therefore, essential for a job seeker to hit the mark. *The Complete Idiot's Guide to the Perfect Job Interview, Third Edition*, will teach you both lessons and more.

Most books I have read on interviewing address only one issue; namely, how to conduct yourself during the interview itself. *The Complete Idiot's Guide to the Perfect Job Interview, Third Edition*, certainly does that, and much, much more. This book offers practical and proven methods and techniques for getting an interview. The techniques contained in this book will enable you to research the marketplace and discover the potential employers' needs. It will provide you with the skills to conduct a thorough job search, prepare for the interview, interview effectively, and negotiate the final offer. You will be able to do it all better than you have in the past.

Professional interviewers like myself can quickly assess a job candidate's level of preparation and confidence. This book is an invaluable tool in your job search and career management tool box. You'll enjoy reading it and refer to it often.

William Myers

Vice President, Tarnow International Executive Search Consultants (formerly Corporate Vice President of Human Resources, International Flavors and Fragrances, Inc.)

Introduction

Question: How do you measure the effectiveness of a resumé?

Obvious answer: Whether it gets you a job or not.

Try again. Because the obvious answer is wrong.

The objective of an effective resumé (or cover letter, query letter, e-mail inquiry, cold call, and all the other early steps in the job hunt) is not to get you a job. It is to get you an *interview*. The job interview is your ultimate opportunity to "sell" yourself to an employer, even as you gauge whether that employer is right for you. It is a doorway to a job and a portal to a career.

At least, that's the way it is supposed to be.

Even as we joust and jockey in quest for that interview, many of us look forward to the event as we would to any grim interrogation. We think of it as an obstacle rather than an avenue to employment. Many of us are intimidated by a process that makes us feel small, inadequate, inept—like a complete idiot.

Why a "complete idiot"?

Well we don't know what questions will be asked. Don't know if we'll be able to answer the questions when they're asked. Maybe, too, we don't know how to dress for the interview. Don't know how to negotiate salary. Don't know enough about the job. Aren't good at remembering names. Can't think on our feet. Are easily rattled and afraid of drooling.

There's plenty of *bad* to feel about interviewing—a process that *should* be filled with bright hopes and great expectations. A lot of us are afraid we'll just plain blow it. More than any other aspect of the job search, the interview is a mystery to most people. Even job hunters who are confident of their resumé-writing ability and their expertise with a cover letter often feel unsure of themselves when it comes to interviewing.

If you're leery of the interview, well, at least you're in good company. But why stay there?

How to Use this Book

The Complete Idiot's Guide to the Perfect Job Interview, Third Edition, cannot, of course, guarantee success. But reading this book will help you get excited—in a productive way—about interviewing. It will help you see the interview as an opportunity rather than an obstacle, a positive event instead of a reason for terror. *The Complete Idiot's Guide to the Perfect Job Interview, Third Edition*, is designed to take the mystery out of the interview by showing you how to "read" the employer's needs and how to present yourself as the solution to the employer's problems.

Here's what you'll find in the pages that follow:

Part 1, "Getting There," faces the fact that before you can ace an interview, you have to *get* an interview. You'll find advice on how to transform your resumé, cold calls, and online queries into interviews, and how to prepare for those interviews so that you'll come across as a winner. In this part of the book, you'll also find pointers on "looking the part"—how (and how not) to dress.

Part 2, "Being There," begins with what you need to know about interviewing online, then takes you into "real life" with valuable tips on what to do while waiting in the reception room: last-minute preparation and assessment, as well as exercises to keep you psyched up while you're trying to calm down. You won't find cut-and-dried interview "scripts" here, but far more useful tools to help you listen more effectively, to answer the most common questions, to answer the really tough questions, and to take charge of the interview and steer it in the direction *you* want to take it. All this leads up to a chapter on the bottom line: salary negotiation.

Part 3, "Do You Have Any Questions?" (You'd Better!), is devoted to the questions *you* should ask. These are designed not only to gather the information you need to evaluate an employer and an offer, but to help you "close the sale" and get that offer.

Part 4, "Special Settings and Challenging Circumstances," explores many of the less typical, but still important, interview scenarios, including the informational interview that *you* arrange, the preliminary or screening interview, and the telephone interview. You'll also find tips for handling such situations as the mealtime interview, the panel interview, the sequential interview, and the automated or computer-assisted interview.

Part 5, "On the Spot," is a special part on mastering performance and stress interviews—certainly the most intimidating and challenging of interview scenarios—and turning employers' objections into persuasive selling points.

Part 6, "To Follow Through, Follow Up," covers the all-important post-meeting phase of the interview process, beginning with the follow-up interview and what to do, say, and write after all the interviewing is finally over.

Three appendixes bring up the rear, including a glossary of interview buzz words; sources of information, both in print and online, to help you prepare for an interview; and exercises to help you conduct an inventory of your skills.

Extras

Throughout the book, you'll find loads of helpful sidebars that give you extra bits of important information. Here's the description of the different kinds of boxes:

Don't Call Us ...

Put your foot in your mouth, and a prospective employer may send you hopping out the door. Look in these boxes for advice on avoiding pitfalls, verbal and otherwise.

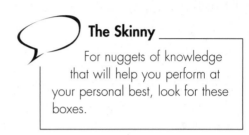

The Skinny

For nuggets of knowledge that will help you perform at your personal best, look for these boxes.

Clincher

These are tips and "extra-mile" advice on how to make your interviews more effective.

def•i•ni•tion

The path to a terrific interview is strewn with jargon, catch phrases, euphemisms, and hot-button words. These boxes will tip you off to the most important ones.

Nice Save!

Common interview mishaps—from faux pas to catastrophe—happen more than you'd like. The tips you'll find in these boxes will teach you how to overcome mishaps gracefully.

Special Thanks from the Publisher to the Technical Editor

The first edition of *The Complete Idiot's Guide to the Perfect Job Interview* was reviewed by an expert who not only checked the technical accuracy of what you'll learn in this book, but also provided invaluable insight and suggestions. Our special thanks are extended to Ron Smith.

Ron Smith is a project manager at IBM Global Services. He has published three books on application development and ten computer-related articles. Ron is also a past president of the Greensport Area Toastmasters in Houston, Texas, and enjoys racquetball.

Trademarks

All terms mentioned in this book that are known to be or are suspected of being trademarks or service marks have been appropriately capitalized. Alpha Books and Penguin Group (USA) Inc. cannot attest to the accuracy of this information. Use of a term in this book should not be regarded as affecting the validity of any trademark or service mark.

Part 1

Getting There

If you've read other interview books, you already know that a big problem with most of them is that they just plop you down in the interview and start spitting out whatever advice they have to give.

But how do you get that interview in the first place? And how do you go about preparing for it—or not just for a particular interview, but for interviewing in general?

Here is a bouquet of chapters to help you develop productive interview attitudes, to research firms and industries and acquire the "inside" knowledge you'll need, to secure the interview, and to get ready for your very next interview. You'll even find advice on dressing for the occasion.

Myths and Reality

In This Chapter

- ◆ Correcting misconceptions about interviews
- ◆ How to help the interviewer interview you
- ◆ Why most interviewers aren't sadists
- ◆ Putting the focus on the interviewer
- ◆ What employers look for

I was going to title this first chapter "Don't Screw Up," but then I thought about how, when my friends and I played baseball as kids, we used to rattle the opposing batter, poised for the pitch, by shouting similarly "friendly" advice: "Don't choke! Don't choke!" So it seemed better to me to call this chapter "Myths and Reality."

But facing an interview—the proverbial "big chance"—aren't you really thinking, somewhere in the back of your head, "Don't screw up"?

In a perfect world, you would always think of the interview not only as a job opportunity for yourself, but as a hiring opportunity for the employer— a chance for the employer to meet you, the ideal person for her needs and the solution to her problems. But in this very imperfect world, many of us face the interview as if we were the orphan Oliver Twist asking for just one more dollop of cold gruel, *please.* Some of us even see the interview more as a brick wall than as a doorway. The result? We're driven not by upbeat, hopeful energy, but by fear and loathing. On this important day, we don't feel all that good about who we are and what we have to offer.

If you feel this way about interviews, this chapter should help you to begin to change. And if you're lucky enough to feel good about the interview process, I hope this chapter will help you feel even better.

Interview Myths

Even a seasoned veteran of employment interviews tends to think of them the wrong way. She goes into each interview assuming that the interviewer holds all the cards, a deck that he has craftily stacked against her—in order to grill her, wear her down, to expose her every flaw. That is one of several interview myths. There are more.

Myth 1: Employers Always Know What They Want

Even if you could manage to show your "best," how do you know it would be good enough? How do you know that *your* "best" is *the* "best," what this particular employer is looking for?

So the real problem is that you're in the dark, and fear of the dark is a pretty common—pretty *primal*—fear.

Clincher

Don't think of the interview as something that is done *to* you, but as a collaborative project you share with the interviewer or interviewers. Cooperate with them to successfully complete the "assignment." Transform a scenario of "you versus me" into a "we" situation.

You have some choices to make. You can stumble around in the dark and feel more and more afraid as you bruise yourself on all the end tables you can't see. Or you can try to find some light.

Although you can't know for certain whether your "best" will be seen as good enough or not, you *can* go into an interview knowing quite a bit about how this employer defines "best." Appendix B supplies strategies and resources for learning about the needs, wants, desires, and problems of prospective interviewers *before* you walk in the door.

But this brings us to the crux of our first interview myth. You can research and prepare thoroughly, then brilliantly analyze the problems of an industry and the needs of a particular firm. And believe me, doing so will shift the odds very much in your favor.

Unfortunately, even doing *this* is no guarantee that the interviewer knows what the problems of his industry are or even what his company needs.

The interviewer does *not* always know what he wants. In fact, interviewers who have a clear and clearly formulated idea of what they want constitute a distinct minority. The majority are in the dark, at least more or less.

Distressingly few interviewers take the time to *think through* the specific qualities, qualifications, personality traits, and broader background that would make up the perfect widget analyst for their particular situation.

Many interviewers are precisely in the position of, say, a technically unsophisticated customer in the market for his first high-definition flat-screen TV. He has a vague idea of what he wants and how much he wants to spend, but the salesperson—as any good salesperson does—must educate and guide him. The salesperson doesn't go so far as to tell him what to buy, but does walk him through the process, in order to determine what product and combination of features will most satisfy his particular needs and budget.

Your job as the interviewee is to prepare sufficiently for the interview so that you can meet the interviewer at whatever level of preparedness you may find him. Then you have to be ready to educate and guide him. This, of course, puts you in a tremendously powerful position. You, the job candidate, will help the employer decide what he needs. In the fullest sense, you are perfectly situated to *sell* yourself.

Myth 2: Employers Are Masters of the Interview

Granted, the interviewer may not have fully explored every dimension of his firm's needs in regard to the job in question, but, certainly, a manager with the power to hire *must* know people. And this means that he *must* have substantial experience and skill as an interviewer.

In a pig's eye.

Most interviewers are full-time something else: engineers, managers, financiers, accountants, whatever. Anything but professional interviewers. They have not been trained as interviewers; in fact, they've had relatively little experience interviewing people. More often than not, interviewers feel awkward and uncomfortable in the role. They might actually consider the interview a necessary evil, at best, and, at worst, an unwelcome interruption of their "real" work. To top it all off, interviewers don't typically spend hours reviewing your resume and other documentation. More than likely, your website, MySpace or Facebook page, or paperwork is given a quick once-over a few minutes before the meeting—probably while you're waiting in the reception room.

You'd really be sweating if you walked into the interview unwilling or unprepared. Well, it's likely that the interviewer *is* unwilling and unprepared. He could use some help, and he would be most grateful for it. Go ahead, then. Help him out, and earn some gratitude.

This means walking into the interview prepared to take it over and give it direction. (You'll find out more about how and when to do this in Chapter 9.) The beauty of taking over the interview is that it does much more than transform a doomed meeting into a productive one. It instantly casts you in the role of problem solver. You see, before you walked through that door, you were just part of today's problem: "A million things to do, a million deadlines to meet, a million clients breathing down my neck, and *this* of all days is the day I've got to interview Joe Blow!" But sit down with the interviewer, assess the situation, take over, and turn it into a piece of cake for him, and you've miraculously become part of the *solution*—one of the few really good things that happened to this guy today.

Myth 3: Employers Just Love to See You Squirm

You could conceivably come up against a genuine sadist, but the prospect isn't very likely. Few interviewers are warped enough to enjoy watching the agony of the candidate, let alone set out deliberately to humiliate or embarrass the interviewee. Indeed, if anyone squirms, it's more likely to be the interviewer, who feels that the candidate is judging *him* and judging the company through him.

That said, some interviewers will use so-called *stress interview* techniques, which you'll read about in Chapter 23. A stress interview employs harsh, high-pressure techniques—long silences, deliberately offensive questions, impossibly difficult questions, a brusque questioning style—to test your mettle. Relatively uncommon, the stress interview is most often used to evaluate candidates for high-pressure jobs in which difficult or hostile customer contact is anticipated. These techniques are meant to put you on the spot, to see how you react and operate under pressure.

Nevertheless, you're far more likely to find a reasonably polite interviewer, fairly eager to make the meeting a pleasant one. Why? The reasons are pretty intuitive:

◆ Few people enjoy being party to an uncomfortable, unpleasant conversation. They do whatever they can to avoid starting such a conversation.

◆ Few people actually enjoy being mean.

◆ Most people want to be liked and to create a favorable impression.

◆ Most businesspeople understand that the world of business—in a particular community or in a particular industry—is a *small* world and that what goes around comes around. Even if this particular employer doesn't hire you, he understands that he may end up doing business with you someday. No sense in abusing you.

◆ Even if the two of you never see one another again, no businessperson wants bad word of mouth. If this interviewer treats you poorly, what will you tell the world about her company?

◆ And what if she does hire you? Why create a situation that will produce bad feelings from day one?

Interview Reality: They Don't Really Care About You

I've tried to dispel some prevalent and pervasive interview myths. Now for a dose of reality. I'll give it to you straight: *the employer doesn't really care about you.*

Before you sputter in righteous outrage, ask yourself this: do *you* really care about the employer?

Be honest now.

No, of course you don't. If you did, you'd work for free. The fact is, it's not the employer you care about, it's yourself: providing a good living for yourself (or for yourself and your family) right now, while carving out a productive and lucrative career for the long haul.

Just as you don't really care about the employer, then, the employer doesn't really care about you. She cares about herself and about her business. Insofar as you can help her and contribute positively to her business, you *do* count. Beyond that, however, you are a stranger.

This revelation isn't meant to cast a cloud over your day, but, rather, to change your focus. Naturally, gearing up for an interview, you're thinking about yourself:

◆ Will I make a good impression?

◆ Will I screw up?

◆ Will I look good?

It's only natural, but that doesn't make it all good. You need to shift your focus—*unnaturally*—to the employer, what she needs, what she wants, what problems she faces, what concerns her.

Look at it this way: one of the questions an interviewer might ask, point-blank, is "Why do you want this job?" It's possible that the answer uppermost in your thoughts is "Because I need the money." Giving voice to that answer, however, while admirably honest, will almost certainly result in a premature end to the interview and no offer of employment. Obviously, you've told the interviewer nothing she wants to hear.

But what *does* she want to hear?

Answers to all her problems. She wants to hear how you're going to contribute to her bottom line. She wants to hear how you're going to make her look good. She wants to hear about how *you* will make a positive difference for *her*.

Not only will forcing yourself to focus on what the employer cares about—namely herself—greatly improve your chances of scoring the job, the effort will also yield an added dividend: you'll be less nervous and less afraid. Veteran actors learn that stage fright comes from focusing on yourself—on how *you'll* perform, on how *you'll* feel, on how *you'll* look—rather than on your audience. If you think more about the audience and less about yourself, stage fright becomes largely a thing of the past.

Clincher

Ask not what the interviewer can do for you, but what you can do for the interviewer.

What Every Employer Really Wants

You need to prepare for an interview knowing three important things about the employer's needs, wants, and desires:

1. You can discover a lot about what an employer needs, wants, and desires by taking the time to do your homework: research the industry in general and the company in particular before you walk through the interviewer's door.

2. What you discover may very well be *more* than the interviewer knows. Be prepared to educate him about his needs, wants, and desires.

3. Each employer needs different things, but there are some major things that all employers want from their employees.

Let's explore point #3 in detail.

Clincher _____

Being prepared for an interview and being willing to take the lead not only benefits you directly—by ensuring that you deliver the information you must deliver—but also benefits you indirectly by helping the interviewer. To the degree that you make his job easier, you will be perceived as a problem solver, which is something *every* organization *always* wants and needs, regardless of any particular job description.

A Fresh Solution Instead of Another Problem

The employer wants to hire a solution, not a problem. Present yourself accordingly. This means coming into the interview prepared (see points #1 and #2 earlier), having fully scoped out the issues that concern the industry and the company. It also means working with the interviewer to make the interview itself pleasant and productive. Know when to listen and when to take the lead (see Chapter 12 for more on successfully steering the interview).

Do *not* come into the interview bristling with demands, objections, and complaints. Instead, emphasize cooperation and a willingness to strike a bargain. You can always negotiate or, if necessary, turn down an offer. But you have to *get* the offer first.

You will also probably be perceived as a problem rather than a solution if you complain about your present job or present employer, or if you complain about *anything:* the weather, the traffic, the subway—whatever. Adopt a cheerful, positive, upbeat tone.

And one more sure way to come off sounding like a problem: enter into the interview as unprepared as the interviewer probably is. Few situations are more awkward, painful, or problematic as a meeting in which neither participant has anything to say.

Someone Who Can Do the Job

While many—perhaps most—interviewers have only a vague idea of their own requirements, most do understand that they need someone who can do the job. The interviewer may not think about this beyond the dimensions of raw ability and experience as defined in some official job description, or as defined more crudely by the interviewer's generalized concept of the job: *The job is* selling. *This guy's gotta be able to* sell.

Address this "can do" aspect of the interview by ensuring that your qualifications are clearly and convincingly spelled out in your resumé, website, Facebook page, and whatever other pre-interview material you have furnished. Be prepared to back up your claims with specific examples, anecdotes, and, wherever possible, facts and figures. Prepare and make use of the "Interview Kit," which is discussed in Chapter 4.

Accent the positive, even when you're not entirely sure of your qualifications. Don't shoot yourself in the foot by expressing self-doubts or other reservations that may intrude into your consciousness during the interview:

>**Interviewer:** You'll also have to analyze widget sales on a quarterly basis.
>
>**You:** Gee, I have to admit I've never done that before … I'm not absolutely sure …

Such a response, while honest, will probably get you a one-way ticket out the door. Don't grossly deceive the interviewer with false claims of unmerited expertise, but at this point, it's best to cloak any doubts and self-doubts with a mantle of positive attitude:

>**Interviewer:** You'll also have to analyze widget sales on a quarterly basis.
>
>**You:** I look forward to that opportunity.

If the interviewer asks you point-blank if you have widget sales analysis experience, answer honestly but positively, citing related experience, as well as a willingness and capacity to learn:

>**Interviewer:** Do you have experience in widget sales analysis?
>
>**You:** I have experience in sales, and I've certainly made extensive use of analytical reports. I look forward to honing more specific expertise in widget sales analysis.

Someone Who Will Stick Around

Searching for, interviewing, relocating, training, and breaking in a new employee are all expensive propositions. Each day that a new employee is on the job represents an investment for the firm—an investment in education and development—and no employer wants to see his investment evaporate after only a few months. Be certain to convey to the interviewer an image of stability and commitment.

What happens if your resumé suggests a history of using multiple jobs as mere stepping stones? Put this in the best light possible: "One of the things that most excites me about this position, Mr. Burns, is that it is truly worth my long-term commitment. I have been searching for a job in which I can grow while developing a great program for the organization."

Don't Call Us ...

Beware of volunteering information about your political and social beliefs at an interview. You don't know whose toes you might step on. Also note that it is inappropriate (and illegal) for the employer to ask you questions relating to your religious beliefs, ethnic background, sexual orientation, age, disabilities, marital status, or plans for raising a family. See Chapter 11 for more on handling difficult interview questions.

Someone Who Will Fit In ...

Learn everything you can about the environment and "culture" of the prospective employer. This includes making an effort to find out how people dress (suits? casual wear?) and groom themselves (beards okay? long hair okay on men?), as discussed in Chapter 5. It also involves demonstrating social ease, which is most loudly proclaimed nonverbally, through body language. Check out Chapter 8 for a discussion of this.

Make an effort to discern something about the politics of the potential employer. Is the orientation conservative? Liberal?

If it becomes apparent to you, as the interview conversation develops, that you do *not* fit in—that you just don't like these people—try not to let your doubts show. It's always better to secure an offer, which you can evaluate in calm and tranquility before you reject it. For now, do everything you can to keep your options open.

... But Also Stand Out

Related to the question of whether the prospective employee will fit in is whether she stands out as likeable. In certain positions, such as sales and customer service, "likeability" is a job prerequisite, but even in positions that require little or no customer contact, it's important to be pleasant and enjoyable to be around.

Sure, you're nervous, but do your best to project a forthcoming, friendly, open image. Avoid single-sentence or one-word responses to questions. Don't chit-chat aimlessly, but do open up. Be approachable. Smile and make eye contact. Speak with enthusiasm.

Showing that you are conspicuously likeable is not the only way to stand out. Let your personality shine through. Put yourself across as cooperative and a team player, to be sure, but not as a mere follower. Show that you will fit in, but also strive to make a memorable impression.

Someone Who Will Return Their Investment

Every employer wants good value for his investment. Be prepared to speak with enthusiasm about the mission of the company, department, or division and how you intend to dedicate yourself to it. Be prepared to discuss how you will go "the extra mile" to ensure that the mission is always accomplished.

How to Present Yourself as a "Force Multiplier"

What all of this adds up to is not a vague and nerve-wracking game of guessing precisely what formula or combination of qualities an employer is looking for. It is, instead, a matter of presenting yourself as an answer rather than a question, an asset rather than a liability, a solution rather than a problem.

Military commanders always look for combat "assets" they call "force multipliers." These are weapons, tactics, and—most of all—people who add up to more than the sum of their parts. A person who demonstrates a willingness and ability to give 110 percent—to hit the ground running, but also to develop in the job for which she is initially hired—is a force multiplier. In selecting his next hire, an employer doesn't want a good bargain, he wants *more* than he bargained for: the great salesperson who has the potential to be an even greater director of sales.

If you make the goal of each of your interviews conveying the message that you are a solution for immediate problems and force multiplier for future opportunity, each interview will become less murky, less confusing, and far less intimidating. In fact, each interview will come to seem what an interview is actually meant to be: an experience in positive communication and a fair exchange of value between a prospective employer and employee.

The Least You Need to Know

◆ Think of the interviewer as your customer—someone who has some idea of what he wants, but who will greatly benefit from your guidance.

◆ Learn everything you can about the prospective employer *before* you show up for the interview.

◆ Shift your focus from yourself, from what you feel and from what you need, to what the interviewer feels and needs. Address these issues during the interview.

◆ Needs and wants vary from employer to employer, but rest assured that all employers look for employees who will solve, not create, problems and who will serve the enterprise as a force multiplier.

Chapter 2

On Your Mark

In This Chapter

◆ What are "portable skills"?

◆ Identifying your highest-level portable skills

◆ Interview preparation: why and how to use research

◆ Doing pre-interview research online

Let's start with a jolt: *Don't bother to prepare for an interview.*

Let me explain.

What's the *critical* difference between a good salesperson and a great salesperson? A good salesperson makes a sale, while a great salesperson creates a customer. The difference is one sale versus a potential infinity of sales.

Take a lesson from the great salesperson. Don't prepare for *this* interview or *that*. Don't hang all your career hopes on a one-time shot in the dark. Instead, invest your precious time in preparing yourself for the upcoming interview *and* for any number of interviews to come. Prepare to present yourself as what *every* employer, *everywhere* and *always*, desperately wants and needs: a remarkable person with skills not only specifically suited to the job at hand, but also with the manifest capability and character to manage anything thrown his or her way.

This chapter is not about last-minute cramming for tomorrow's interview, but about taking the longer view. After all, you're likely to live beyond tomorrow—and even beyond your next job.

Pack Up Your Portable Skills

In taking the longer view, then, don't focus on skills specific to a certain job; rather, put the focus where it should be: on you. The skills you carry with you matter more— to you as well as to any of your employers—than the skills that a certain job happens to require. Because such skills are yours, rather than peculiar to some job, we may call them *transferable* or, better yet, *portable skills*.

Now you probably already think you know what you're good at and what your skills are. For example, you might say of yourself, "I am persuasive," but that is a description of a trait, not a portable skill. On the other hand, declaring, "I am a salesperson" is just a job description, which likewise says nothing about portable skills. Take a step toward redefining the trait and the job description as a portable skill by transforming the adjective describing the trait into a verb: "I am persuasive" becomes "I persuade."

def•i•ni•tion

Portable (or transferable) skills are specific to you rather than to a particular job. They describe a function—that is, how *you* work with people, data, or things. For example, knowing how to write computer programs in the C++ programming language is a job-specific skill, whereas the ability to analyze and synthesize information is a skill you can carry (or transfer) from job to job.

Next, expand the narrow job description. This is rather easy once you learn that portable skills fall into three categories: skills in relation to *people*, to *data*, and to *things*. Decide whether "salesperson" chiefly involves working with people, data, or things. The answer is *people*, and your description of a portable skill becomes "I persuade people."

Climb the Ladder

Notice that "I persuade people" describes a function—that is, *doing something* with *people*, *data*, or *things*. And notice, too, that expressed as a function, it is a very powerful skill that is of tremendous value in a great many jobs.

You can, however, make the statement even more powerful and the skill yet more compelling to an employer. Portable skills are rungs on a ladder that ascends to levels of increasing complexity. *Persuading* is on a middle rung. It is a more complex "people" skill than merely *communicating*, which, in turn, is more complex than a bottom-rung skill such as *following directions*. But *persuading* is less complex—it is on a lower rung—than *negotiating*, while *mentoring* is even higher than *negotiating* on the people-skills ladder. If you can convince an interviewer that you *persuade* people, you may well get a job in sales. If you can convince her that you *negotiate* with people, you may score a position as an account executive. Demonstrate to the interviewer that you excel at *mentoring*, and maybe she'll see in you the makings of a Director of Sales.

The Higher the Better

In short, you want to identify your highest-level portable skills because …

◆ The higher your portable skill level, the more unique you are as a candidate for employment and the less competition you will face.

◆ Jobs that require higher levels of portable skills usually pay more and are more interesting than jobs calling for lower levels of these skills.

◆ Jobs requiring higher levels of portable skills tend to be careers (that is, jobs with a future).

◆ The higher your portable skills, the more control you are likely to have on the job. Positions requiring only the lower levels of portable skills are usually cut and dried, whereas higher-level positions invite and require creativity.

> **Clincher**
>
> Be prepared to present to interviewers the most complex (highest-level) portable skills to which you can legitimately lay claim.

Free-Form Exercise

So let's get started. Find three blank sheets of paper, and write "PEOPLE" at the top of one sheet, "DATA" at the top of another, and "THINGS" at the top of the third. Below these headings, on each sheet, write "I am good at …" Next, complete that sentence in as many ways as you can for each portable skill category: people, data, and things. For example:

PEOPLE

I am good at …

persuading

selling

helping people make purchase decisions

explaining how machinery works

being patient

listening

… and so on.

If you find working with a blank sheet of paper intimidating, flip to Appendix C and use the lists I've provided.

Make Yourself Marketable

Use the free-form method, the lists in Appendix C, or a combination of the two to put together a list of six to eight of your strongest and highest-level portable skills. Then, put each of these in a complete sentence, beginning with "I am good at …" If, for example, you've decided that *negotiating* is one of your top skills, you would write, "I am good at negotiating."

But don't stop now. You're on a roll. Include an object in your sentence: "I am good at negotiating *prices*." Try going another step by tacking on an adjective, adverb, or a clause that includes one of these parts of speech: "I am good at negotiating prices *that are satisfying to both buyer and seller.*"

Step by step, you should be able to identify your top portable skills and then define them in a way that not only describes you accurately and vividly, but sets you apart from the teeming masses yearning for the very job *you* want.

Do the Research

Now that you know something about yourself, you'd better find out something about the rest of the world. Research can serve three interrelated purposes:

1. It can help you identify a job/career/field suited to what you know about your portable skills.

2. It can help you locate specific job opportunities.

3. It can provide information about an industry, field, or even a particular company that will make you sound highly impressive and well informed in an interview.

Make Friends in Places High, Low, and in Between

Start with whatever is closest to you. If you are currently employed, open your file drawer and look over past projects. Identify firms and individuals who interest you as potential sources of information and potential employers. Do your best to get around and meet people in your field and in other fields that may interest you. Collect business cards and save e-mails; maintain a file of both. Also keep these contacts alive with an occasional friendly e-mail, phone call, or, if appropriate, a breakfast or lunch. Pretty soon, you'll find that you've got something a lot more meaningful than a file of names. You've got a *network*.

def•i•ni•tion

A **network** is an informal set of business and personal contacts the job hunter deliberately develops in order to acquire information and employment leads.

Joining a professional group or organization in your field is another great way to network. Not only are you likely to meet potential employers, you will usually get access to newsletters and magazines that publish industry-specific want ads. If you can't readily find an appropriate organization in your field—and even if you can—be sure to check out the following networking websites:

- **LinkedIn (www.linkedin.com):** This is the biggest networking website for businesspeople in practically every field.

- **Tribe (www.tribe.net):** This networking site takes in the world of business, but also goes beyond, reaching into many aspects of everyday life.

- **Monster Networking (www.monster.com):** The nation's most popular job-search site, Monster offers a sophisticated networking area as well.

Also consider Toastmasters International (www.toastmasters.org), a most supportive organization for the would-be networker who not only wants to make contacts, but also wants work on self-expression and self-esteem.

Your growing network serves two purposes:

1. It generates information. Each of your contacts is a potential source of news about a job, an industry, or a field.

2. Each of your contacts is a potential employer or referral to an employer.

You don't need to be currently employed to build a network. Potentially, everyone you know—friends, neighbors, old school chums, as well as contacts you make online—can be useful nodes on your network.

Former co-workers don't just vanish from the planet. They can become live-wire nodes in your employment-opportunity network. Never forget the personal and professional friends you've made in a company you left.

> **Don't Call Us ...**
>
> Review your list of contacts carefully before calling on any one for a referral. Make certain that the person you tap for good words will, in fact, have nothing but good words to offer. Beware of hidden agendas, and be aware that your contact may be a potential competitor for your target position.

Online: General Guides

In addition to using the Internet as a means of expanding your business network, you will find in cyberspace a host of general-interest job-hunting sites that will not only help you look for a job but will provide research material to help you prepare for an interview. In fact, there are so many career-related sites that it is all too easy to end up spending your interview prep time searching a plethora of websites. I have winnowed the list to a few must-check resources:

- ◆ **Job-Hunter's Bible (www.jobhuntersbible.com):** This site is a collection of articles and up-to-date information on using the Internet as an aid to job hunting and pre-interview research. It also includes a lot of hyperlinks (shortcuts) to get you to the most popular job search websites.

- ◆ **Monster (www.monster.com):** This is the best-known of all job-hunting websites. Check out the useful tools it offers, such as the Job Search Agent, which will e-mail you when it finds openings that match criteria you supply.

- ◆ **Yahoo! HotJobs (http://hotjobs.yahoo.com):** In addition to job listings, you will find a good selection of links to other online resources as well as job-hunting articles. Material here will help you research entire industries as well as individual firms.

- ◆ **CareerBuilder (www.careerbuilder.com):** An online service of three major newspaper chains, this site offers job postings from a wealth of employers plus want ads from a large number of newspapers.

> **Don't Call Us ...**
>
> Avoid relying on outdated reference material. Check the posting date on articles and listings you find online, and when you use hardcopy reference works in the library, make sure you consult the latest edition of the work available. The reference librarian can help.

Online: Industry and Company Sources

The object of networking, whether in person or online, is to transform yourself from an outsider into an insider. If you are interested in getting a job at Acme, Inc., it is obviously to your advantage to have as much inside information as possible about the company. In the days before the proliferation of the Internet, getting inside information required, at the very least, a visit to Acme, Inc. These days, however, Acme, Inc.—and hundreds of thousands of other firms—visit you. Most major—and many smaller—businesses maintain websites, which the companies use to conduct business with their current and potential customers as well as to communicate with investors, job seekers, and anyone else interested in the company.

Always thoroughly study the target employer's website before you apply for a job. Then review that site thoroughly when you are preparing for an interview.

Also make certain to research the industry of which your target employer is a part. Use any one of a number of available Internet search engines to find the websites of companies in a particular industry and to find other information relevant to the industry.

The biggest and best-known search engine is Google (www.google.com), but you should also try Yahoo! Search (http://search.yahoo.com) and Ask Jeeves (www.ask.com). An alternative to the conventional search engine is the so-called "meta-search engine," the best known and most popular of which is Dogpile (www.dogpile.com). From the user's point of view, a meta-search engine works just like a regular search engine. You just type in a keyword or combination of keywords. What happens next, however, is that your search is submitted simultaneously to more than one search engine, and you get all the results.

Google and Dogpile troll as much of the Internet as possible, often returning a staggering number of results. You may also find it worthwhile to go smaller. Take a look at the specialized search engines available on the Internet. These may well turn up more material of specific interest to you in your particular pre-interview research. Begin by checking out All Search Engines at www.allsearchengines.com, which provides a list of many specialized search engines.

Actually using most search engines is relatively straightforward and intuitive: you simply type a keyword or keywords that relate most directly to your search. If you are interested in the publishing industry, you might use such keywords as "publishing industry," "book publishers," "publishing industry outlook," and so on. All of the major search engines include help pages, which provide directions, advice, and tips on conducting effective searches and using keywords effectively, so there is no reason to get stuck. If you want more help, log on to www.askscott.com/tindex.html or University of South Carolina: Basic Search Tips, at www.sc.edu/beaufort/library/pages/bones/lesson7.shtml, which furnishes primer-level instructions to help you avoid frustrating web search experiences.

Get a Library Card

When you take a break from the computer or while you are looking around your office (if you have one) for the names of folks to induct into your network, be sure to comb through those stacks of trade journals and newsletters that you've been meaning to read "when you have the time." They contain valuable industry talk that not only will expand your knowledge of the issues and trends current in your field, but may also alert you to job opportunities and the needs and desires of specific firms.

If you don't have an office, or your desk isn't cluttered with periodicals and newsletters, or you want to look beyond your current job, career, or field, go to the nearest public library and get yourself a library card. Then, consult the following:

◆ *National Trade and Professional Associations of the United States* (Washington, D.C.: Columbia Books). This reference lists not only the associations that are relevant to your industry, but any publications those associations may produce.

◆ *Reader's Guide to Periodical Literature* (Bronx, NY: H. W. Wilson Co.; available in most library reference departments). Use this reference to look up a subject and find magazine and journal articles relevant to it.

Don't scan trade and business periodicals just to find the want ads. Also look for …

◆ Articles that tip you off to hot firms and solid opportunities.

◆ Articles that inform you about industry trends and developments, and that identify growth and opportunity areas.

◆ Names of article authors (if they are industry professionals) and the names mentioned in the articles; these are potential job contacts and sources of inside information.

◆ News about promotions, executive moves, retirements, and, yes, even deaths; such information will help you identify possible openings at specific companies.

Clincher _____

Appendix B gathers some of the most useful printed and electronic sources of employment-related information. Check it out.

◆ Product and service ads; these may tip you off to companies that are producing hot new merchandise and trend-setting services.

The public library is also a great place to access the Internet if you don't own a computer or don't otherwise have ready access to one, or if you aren't otherwise connected to the Internet.

Learn to Leverage Everything You Learn

You get a phone call. XYZ, Inc., wants to interview you. Great! What's even greater is that you've done the research and you can now walk into the interview with an insider's knowledge of the needs, goals, and problems *specific to XYZ, Inc.* All you have to do is filter the information you've already obtained. Thoroughly review XYZ's website. If the company's annual report is posted there, terrific. Read it, and read any annual reports from prior years that may also be posted. If this document is not available online, do your best to get hold of it. Call the company and ask for it. Also look for company brochures and other published material. Cross-reference these with whatever general industry research you've turned up; then, you can specifically identify:

◆ **Company issues.** Do your sources emphasize certain themes or issues as critical to the firm?

◆ **Industry issues.** Do your sources emphasize certain themes or issues as critical to the industry as a whole?

◆ **Relevant current events.** What's going on in the world, nation, community, or neighborhood that affects the company or the industry?

You want to walk into the interview armed with plenty to say about …

◆ **The business of the company.** What does it do or make?

◆ **The scope of the company.** How large is it? Where does it do business?

◆ **The competition.** Who are they, and what is the target company's standing among them?

What, Me Worry?

Here are my final words—for this chapter, anyway. You'll need days, weeks, or months to find a job. You can spend that time just looking, or you can invest it—leverage it—in order to acquire knowledge that will make you look like an insider when the interview finally comes. The explosion of Internet company and industry resources has made research faster and easier. But also be aware of this: the universal availability of these resources has raised the bar. Potential employers now expect the candidates they interview to come to the table fully informed and well prepared. Make yourself as savvy as possible. It's your time. It's your call.

The Least You Need to Know

- ◆ Prepare for *interviewing* rather than cramming for a particular interview.

- ◆ Become intimately familiar with your "portable skills" by taking a thorough inventory of them.

- ◆ Invest in research time online, through your network, in the library—it will make you a knowledgeable (and therefore compelling) interview candidate.

- ◆ Build a network, starting with friends and colleagues, making use of the appropriate professional organizations in your field, and using networking sites on the Internet.

Chapter 3

Making an Interview Happen

In This Chapter

- Being proactive: *making* interviews happen
- A more effective approach to the resumé
- Turning Internet postings and want ads into interviews
- Getting interviews through unsolicited "cold calls," "cold letters," and e-mails
- Uses and limitations of employment agencies

I know there are other how-to-interview books out there. And my publisher is eager for me to assure you that this particular one is the best of them all. Fortunately (because I don't like to lie), that happens to be true. You see, most interview how-to's just plop you down at the interview, as if the interview were a given, something that just magically materialized. The fact is that if you *wait* for interviews to *materialize*, you'll probably be unemployed for a very long time. Take some advice from the first line of a classic recipe for rabbit stew: "First, catch your rabbit." First, make the interview happen.

Set Your Sights Both High and Wide

Capitalism! The free job market! Ain't it grand? Hey, it works like this: you need a job. You've got certain skills, education, and experience. An employer out there—somewhere—needs an employee with your skills, education, and experience. You find one another. She interviews you. You're hired!

In your dreams.

It's true that most employers aren't stupid enough to actually *hide* the jobs they have. But that's about all the reassurance I can give you concerning the American employment system. *System?* It's hardly that organized. You'd think that because companies desperately need talent, they would employ full-time talent scouts. Well, very few do; most, however, do not. It's up to you not only to make your presence and availability known, but to appear before an employer as the perfect fit, the key to his lock, the answer to his prayers.

Those Old Resumé Blues

It's important, first, to know who you are, what you have to offer, and who may be looking for it. That's the business of Chapter 2. Once you've done your homework, tradition dictates that you present yourself in the form of a resumé, either online or on paper. Now everyone knows what a resumé is: a document that summarizes your experience. But here's something else everyone *should* know. Back in 1995 (on the cusp of the Internet revolution, when almost all resumés were still typed on paper and sent via snail mail), for every 1,470 unsolicited resumés mailed hopefully to the nation's employers, 1,469 ended up in the wastebasket. These days employers are flooded with even more unsolicited resumés via e-mail and through the portals they provide on their own websites. Has this resulted in more resumés finding more willing employers? Hardly. It has just meant that the trip from physical desk to physical wastebasket has become, more often than not, an even faster trip from on-screen "desktop" to iconic "wastebasket" via the old click and drag.

I'm not saying you should abandon the resumé, either on paper or online. After all, employers do need summary information about you. But this book is about interviewing, not resumé writing. (For help on resumé writing, check out *The Complete Idiot's Guide to the Perfect Resume, Fourth Edition*, by Susan Ireland; Alpha Books, 2006.) That said, it's important to make a critical point here: the problem is not that employers are uninterested in resumés; rather, it's that they are far less interested in your *experience* than in your *qualifications*. Here's the difference: *experience* is what you've done in the past, whereas *qualifications* are experience *plus* the qualities, skills, and abilities that make you (in the words of the fourth edition of *The American Heritage Dictionary of the English Language*) "suitable for a particular position or task."

Obviously, the qualifications you want to present in your resumé are the qualifications for the job at hand. But this is precisely where most resumés fail to generate an interview. Most resumés concentrate on the needs of the applicant rather than on the requirements of the job—that is, the *needs of the employer*. Avoid the resumé blues by focusing on what the employer—not you—wants:

Clincher _____

Job hunting can be discouraging. You *will* suffer rejection. But it is a mistake to be discouraged by rejection. Use each rejection as an opportunity to learn about yourself and about your approach to the employment process. Rejection is a valuable opportunity to learn. Exploit it.

- ◆ Describe abilities instead of job duties.

- ◆ Include indications of performance that tell just how well you do your job.

- ◆ List accomplishments instead of responsibilities.

- ◆ Begin by asserting your "objective"—a statement about how you will address the needs of the employer.

Let's talk about the last point for just a moment. Many resumés don't even begin with a statement of objective, and those that do usually do so with an *ineffective* statement of objective—one that fails to make clear how the applicant's objective will benefit the employer. Here's an example of a typical narrowly stated objective:

OBJECTIVE: Quality Assurance Engineer

This tells an employer nothing beyond the fact that the applicant wants a position, and unless the employer has a position with this precise title available, it's not likely that he or she will pursue the applicant's candidacy.

Here's a broader statement:

OBJECTIVE: Seeking an opportunity to utilize my skills, education, and energy in a working environment that offers a good, solid career path.

Great—for the applicant. But why should the employer care? What's in it for him or her?

Here are three progressively more effective statements of objective:

> **OBJECTIVE:** To obtain a position where my 15 years of material, production, and inventory control experience will be a company asset.

This one says something about what the applicant brings to the employer's table. But try transforming *experience* into *qualifications:*

> **OBJECTIVE:** To obtain a position where my 15 years of creating innovative and cost-effective systems for material, production, and inventory control will be a company asset.

The Skinny

According to one prominent authority, 78 percent of resumés "fail to do justice to the people they describe." Reason: they describe *experience* rather than what employers are really interested in—*qualifications*.

The phrase "creating innovative and cost-effective systems" transforms passive experience into active qualifications. Notice the use of the verb form *creating*. Well-chosen verbs—*creating, developing, inventing, marketing, selling*—always energize a description of qualifications. They are your best shot at prompting the target employer to take his or her feet off the desk and call you for an interview. But let's not stop here:

> **OBJECTIVE:** To be a member of a team that needs my 15 years of experience creating innovative and cost-effective systems for material, production, and inventory control.

In this objective, the applicant goes beyond merely stating his or her qualifications. Instead of concentrating on the simple fact that he or she has skills to offer, the applicant focuses on how this set of qualifications fits with the employer's particular needs and wants. Suddenly, the employer is no longer considering a job application, but an answer to what his or her *team needs*.

The Awful Truth About Want Ads

Even a strong, employer-focused resumé is a long shot if it's entirely unsolicited. For this reason, most job hunters scour want ads online (using Monster and other web-based employment sites), in newspapers, and in trade journals (online or in print) rather than just roll the dice. But a recent Department of Labor survey reported that only 6 out of every 100 American job holders got their positions through newspaper or online want ads, and other surveys have placed this figure as low as 2 out of every 100. Worse still, if these surveys had been restricted to upper-level employees, the numbers would have practically evaporated. The overwhelming majority of want ads, whether in print or online, are for entry-level or lower intermediate-level positions.

The Skinny

The major online job search sites segment postings by salary range, offering everything from entry-level postings to executive searches. Recently, sites such as The Ladders (www.theladders.com) have emerged to target positions at the "$100k+" level exclusively. In the past, this territory has been largely reserved for professional "head-hunters," but, if you are after big game, check out the online sites that specialize in the stratosphere of the job market.

Don't get too depressed. After all, responding to want ads does increase your chances of getting the job you want by 2 to 6 percent (over simply sending unsolicited resumés or relying exclusively on employers finding you through your Monster or other online listing). Better yet, in responding to want ads placed in special-interest, professional, and trade publications or websites, your "hit rate" should be higher—and the jobs more attractive. Just don't make the mistake of building your job search entirely on the classifieds section and its online equivalents.

Do, however, maximize your chances of transforming a response into a call for an interview. You'll sharpen your edge once you understand the dual purpose of a want ad: it is both a *net* cast to snare likely candidates, and a *screen* used to sift out and discard 95 (or more) resumés out of every 100 received.

To get by the screen, follow these tips:

- Respond quickly. Employers expect to receive most resumés within 96 hours of the ad hitting the streets or the date of an online posting. Day three is the peak, and by day four or day five, the employer starts going through the pile in earnest.

- Respond concisely. Your cover letter or online document should be short and to the point.

Don't Call Us ...

It can be tough to confine your response to the parameters of the ad or posting. Resist your natural tendency to give the employer a little "something extra." That something extra could end up convincing the employer that you don't quite fit in.

◆ If you are replying to a print ad or to an online posting that does not include a direct reply link, mention the source and date of the ad or posting in the first sentence of the cover letter and state that you are interested in the position because it is such a great fit with your qualifications: "Your advertisement for a widget analyst in the May 18th *Widget World* intrigues me because my qualifications so closely match what you are looking for."

◆ In the next part of your cover letter or document, paraphrase the qualifications asked for in the ad or posting, and address only those.

◆ Present your qualifications in a bulleted list rather than in sentences within paragraphs. Your cover piece must "sell" you *at a glance*. Don't make the reader work to find out who you are.

◆ Don't ignore criteria you don't meet. Invent some way to address them. For example, if an ad or posting asks for "experience with database design"—experience that you lack—respond that you are "interested in database design."

◆ If you are not asked to state your salary requirements, don't. Pick the wrong target figure, and you may get screened out.

◆ Even if you are asked to state salary requirements, don't. Difficult as it may be, just ignore this request. If you absolutely must respond to a query about salary needs, compromise. Don't pinpoint a figure; just allude to the subject of salary: "As I have moved upward from position to position, my salary has increased commensurably." Or respond with a range. If you're looking for $35,000, but would settle for $30,000, set your range at $30,000–$40,000, adding the phrase "depending on the scope of my responsibilities."

Web Dreams and Internet Illusions

The Internet is a rich source of employment information, but it is a mistake to rely exclusively on want ads posted online. Many job hunters use the Internet as nothing more than an online version of the traditional newspaper want ads. What's wrong with this approach? Internet want ads are neither more nor less effective than want ads posted in newspapers, professional or industry journals, or elsewhere. In other words, the Internet is not a magic carpet to a job.

Getting Serious Online

"We're in an Internet revolution," the pundit says. To which we answer, "Thank *you*, Paul Revere."

It's very old news, and the phrase "Internet revolution" is worn out precisely because it expresses something so obviously true. During the past decade or so, we have come to rely on the Internet to transact more and more of our business, both personal and professional. The web is a library, a communications device, a news source, a bank, and the mother of all mega-malls. No wonder we believe that a really great job is just a few mouse clicks away.

It is high time to see the Internet for what it is, at least as far as getting a job interview goes. It is a tool—a powerful and very useful tool, to be sure, but a tool first and last.

The Internet is a place to look for job postings or want ads, and it is also a place where you can post your resumé, but, for the truly serious job hunter, the Internet is even more important as a tool for research and for networking. Research can help you make career decisions and is also indispensable to preparing for an interview. As I explained in Chapter 2, networking will help you to get an interview in the first place.

The Mega Job Search Engines: Monster and the Rest

The mega job search sites include:

◆ Monster (www.monster.com)

◆ Yahoo! HotJobs (http://hotjobs.yahoo.com)

◆ America's Job Bank (www.ajb.dni.us)

◆ CareerBuilder (www.careerbuilder.com)

All of these sites list job openings—a *lot* of job openings—but you should not stop with these. Some of the big sites provide many other useful features and tools, including networking options and, in the case of Monster, an interactive virtual interview feature (http://interview.monster.com/virtualinterview/campus), which gives you an opportunity to practice your interview skills. Take advantage of everything the mega-sites have to offer.

Supply Side: Using Facebook, MySpace, and Craigslist

One of the most fascinating dimensions of the "Internet revolution" is the emergence of blogs. *Blog* is a contraction for "web log," essentially an online diary, journal, or scrapbook in which the owner of the blog can write about whatever he or she wants. Some blogs are general diaries, but most are based on a specific interest or theme, including (among many, many more) job hunting and networking.

The Internet has spawned a number of "social networking sites" especially for bloggers. The two best-known social sites are Facebook (www.facebook.com) and MySpace (www.myspace.com). Add to these two Craigslist (www.craigslist.org), an online community on which people post all manner of information, ranging from advice on where to get the best brunch in Cleveland to an ad selling a carburetor for a 1967 Chevy Malibu. Craigslist also makes it possible for job hunters to post resumés, and it is also a good place to look for temporary local work to fill the gap while you search for something more permanent or more closely related to your career.

Don't Call Us ...

Be extremely careful what you post online. Post nothing you do not want a prospective employer to read.

Facebook and MySpace are good places to post a blog and personal profile, which tell people—including potential employers—something about who you are, what you are interested in, and what you may have to offer them.

Consider creating pages on MySpace and Facebook. Doing so will get your name out there. But observe these do's and don'ts:

- ◆ DO create a page specifically related to your job search. Include your resumé, appropriate samples or a portfolio, as well as any special credentials or certifications you may have.

- ◆ DO create a blog related to your career interests. Include material you *want* potential employers to see. If you are interested in a career in widgets, start a blog that discusses widget research and industry trends. Show that you are interested, committed, savvy, and really competent in everything widget.

- ◆ DON'T include a link to your blog on your Monster or other resumé if it is irrelevant to the career field or position for which you want to interview. If you are looking to get into widget sales, don't include a link to a blog that talks about a career in financial planning.

- ◆ DON'T post material impulsively or thoughtlessly.

 ◆ DON'T post material critical of your job or current or past boss.

 ◆ DON'T post intimate personal material.

 ◆ DON'T post anything embarrassing, immoral, or illegal.

Drilling Deeper Down

Anybody can create a blog, and anybody can create pages for MySpace, Facebook, and the like. Skilled job searchers looking to turn a resumé or a response to a want ad into an interview take the opportunity to drill deeper.

Get more of yourself on the web by linking the resumés you post on such sites as Monster to your MySpace or Facebook page or to your own website—*provided that* the page or website contains material that adds valuable and marketable dimensions to you as a person and a professional and does not contain material that might prompt an employer to think twice before hiring you.

For example, let's say you are seeking a position as a corporate publicist. In your posted resumé you mention some pro bono work you did to publicize a community charity. You cannot take much space in the resumé to go into vivid detail about this work, but you can provide a link to the part of your Facebook page that includes the whole story, including wonderful photos.

The great thing about the Internet is that it can liberate you from the one or two dimensions of the printed page. It can reveal you as a multidimensional being. Despite what you might have been told, potential employers are not looking for a faceless cog to feed into their profit machine. They are looking for a person—a person who thinks, feels, cares, and creates. These dimensions can be difficult to convey in a concise resumé, unless that resumé is linked to the dimensions of your life and experience that you put on display elsewhere on the Internet.

Turning a Cold Call into a Warm Reception

You needn't rely exclusively on sending unsolicited resumés or responding to want ads. After researching the job market and the suitable firms in your field, try some cold calls. A *cold call* is an unsolicited employment query/application over the phone. The target employer doesn't know you and hasn't asked you to call. You could make cold calls based on a Yellow Pages search, but you'll more likely make a meaningful connection if you do some research on your target employer and industry first (see Chapter 2 for more help).

If the prospect of calling a stranger to ask for a job seems daunting, don't be too intimidated. The object of a cold call is nothing so momentous or terrifying as actually *getting a job*. The goal of a cold call is to generate sufficient interest to get you an interview—or, second best, a receptive reader of the resumé you will send.

Don't Call Us ...

Some authorities advise sending a want ad reply in an envelope marked "Personal and Confidential." This may well ensure that the intended target opens the letter, but it could also irritate the employer, who will feel deceived. The same goes for marking as "high priority" an e-mail response to a want ad.

Make an End Run Around Human Resources

So who do you talk to? When you contact larger companies, the Personnel, or Human Resources (HR), department is the obvious target. Obvious, but not the best. In many—perhaps most—organizations, the function of HR, so far as recruitment is concerned, is to eliminate unsuitable candidates from the pool of applicants. Why talk to a screen? The more effective strategy is to speak directly to a person with the authority and power to hire you.

Follow the Clout

Your research may tell you who that person is, or you could call HR now and tell them that you are researching careers in X field and that you would like to talk to a senior staff member in the X department: "Could you give me the name of that person?" Emphasize that you are not applying for a job, but only seeking information. Once you have the name of the contact person, you might indeed start with a request for an informational interview, as discussed in Chapter 17. Just tell the cloutmeister that "your Human Resources department recommended I speak with you." If you decide to bypass the informational interview and proceed directly to the cold inquiry, warm it up a bit by mentioning that "your Human Resources people suggested I contact you."

Phone It In

Chapter 19 is all about the telephone interview, but you can use some quick advice about the cold call now.

Make your call with one primary and three fallback objectives firmly in mind:

- ◆ **Primary objective:** To arrange a meeting.

- ◆ **Fallback #1:** To arrange a time to talk further on the phone.

- ◆ **Fallback #2:** To secure a receptive reader for your resumé. This may be combined with Fallback #1, to discuss your resumé.

- ◆ **Fallback #3:** To secure a lead on a job possibility elsewhere or to seek information on future prospects for employment at the target company.

Keeping these objectives in mind will prevent you from suddenly going blank when the voice answers on the other end of the line.

Clincher

Beware the "voice of fear"—the thin, tight, quavering, high, breathless, and utterly unpersuasive voice that comes out when you're scared or nervous. Combat the voice of fear by breathing deeply and always pushing your voice into a deeper register. Male or female, you command more respect if you speak in a relatively deep voice. And slow down! Take your time. Give value to each word.

Stamp Out Spontaneity!

No law dictates that a telephone conversation has to be spontaneous. You wouldn't "wing" *any* major presentation, would you? So why not script the cold call? Here are the parts:

1. Greet the recipient and identify yourself. If you're calling on someone's recommendation, make this the third thing you say: "Good morning, Mr. Smith. My name is Joseph Billing. Your client Pat Mitchell strongly recommended that I give you a call."

2. Reel out your "hook," a statement designed to appeal to the recipient's self-interest. For example: "As you know, the new government regulations have created a climate of crisis. But, Mr. Smith, I see them as a challenge and an opportunity."

3. Now that you've got him hooked, develop the recipient's interest: "I'm assistant to the Director of Regulation Compliance at Acme Widget, Inc., and I've been part of a team that's been achieving cost-effective compliance."

4. Then, transform interest into desire: "I'd welcome an opportunity to sit down with you and share some of the cost-saving strategies I've been a part of. I'd like to explore how my work might benefit your firm."

5. Prompt the recipient to take action—or take action for him: "I'll call you next week to determine a time when we can get together."

The Hardest Sales Letter You'll Ever Write

While the cold call is generally more effective than an unsolicited letter—a "cold letter"—you may feel more comfortable sending one of these. As you would with the cold call, research your target employer before writing a cold letter; don't just take a shot in the dark. The letter can be structured identically to the cold call; start with a *hook* (in this context, an appeal to the employer's self-interest), then write a few sentences to create *interest*, and continue the discussion to generate *desire*. The letter should end with a call to action.

Clincher

Use the cold letter as a cover letter to accompany your resumé. Just as you tailor your letter to the individual employer, so you should modify your resumé. The resumé is not carved in stone, and its content should detail the highlights you give in your letter.

The Letter-Call Formula

Why think in terms of a cold call *versus* a cold letter? Combine the two, beginning with a cold letter and following up with a cold call designed to underscore the points made in the letter.

If the cold call yields an interview and there will be more than a two-week lag between the call and the meeting, follow the call with a letter thanking the recipient for agreeing to the interview, underscoring how much you are looking forward to it, and briefly recapitulating the benefits—to the employer—you outlined in your phone conversation.

E-Mail vs. Snail Mail

Some people believe the classic "business letter" is an endangered species—that it has been pushed out by e-mail. After all, why compose, print out, stamp, and physically mail a paper letter when you can just send a digital one? Here's the answer: while there is no law against sending a cold letter via e-mail, it is almost certainly wasted effort. Anyone behind a desktop computer screen gets flooded on a daily basis with e-mail messages. A good many potential employers look upon unsolicited job-seeker appeals as just so much spam.

Of course, there is no guarantee that your paper letter won't be tossed into the waste-basket, but the very fact that you have chosen to compose a real letter, commit it to real paper, put it in a real envelope, affix upon it a real stamp, and then actually mail it sets you apart. These days, a snail-mail paper letter does not exactly demand attention, but it does appeal for it, increasing the odds that your message will at least be read.

Working with an Agency

Only 5 of every 100 job hunters who walk into an agency actually get a job through the agency. It's not that the agencies are incompetent; rather, while you may believe the agencies are working on your behalf, they are well aware that they're really working for the people who pay their bills: the employers. Think of the employment agency as a combination talent scout and screening service. First and foremost, the agency's mission is to find suitable employees for its clients—not a job for you. So, in working for the employer, the agency may or may not also be working for you—it all depends on the agent's judgment.

Presenting Yourself

In many ways, presenting yourself at an employment agency interview is no different from presenting yourself at an employment interview, but there are a few key differences:

♦ **Be clear about what you want.** Don't define yourself and your needs so broadly that you waste everyone's time getting called for jobs you'd never even think of taking, but do define yourself and your needs broadly enough so that you are not eliminated from consideration for jobs that might actually be a good fit.

♦ **Don't use the agent as an employment counselor.** That's not his job. Remember, he works for the employers, not for you.

Don't Relax Yet

The employment agent works for the employers, not for you. Don't put your professional life in the hands of an employment agency. It's fine to sign up with several agencies, but pursue the job hunt on your own as well. Regard the agency as nothing more than an adjunct to your primary employment campaign. At the very least, your encounter with the employment agency is valuable as an opportunity to practice your interview skills.

Is This the Best Place for You?

Courtesy pays. Treat the people at the employment agency with respect, and exhibit good manners. But don't take your chivalry to an extreme. If you ever begin to feel that you are being unfairly pigeonholed, bullied, or just plain ignored, don't stick around out of courtesy. Walk away and go on to the next agency. There are plenty of them.

And because there *are* plenty of them, you don't have to confine yourself to a single agency. Sign up with several. Your chances of getting "placed" by any one agency are about 1 in 20, so registering with a few of them betters these long odds at least to some degree. Don't feel guilty.

The Least You Need to Know

♦ Interviews rarely "just happen"; you need to proceed vigorously and proactively in order to *produce* them.

♦ Take a long, hard look at your resumé. Is it focused on the needs of the *employer?*

♦ All of the traditional approaches to job hunting (including the "new" traditions online) have limitations, so don't rely solely on any one approach.

♦ Don't count out snail mail. A hardcopy letter packs a punch e-mail cannot touch.

♦ Never lean too heavily on an employment agency; the agency works for the employer, not for you.

Chapter 4

Get Set

In This Chapter

- ◆ How to respond to a request for an interview
- ◆ Developing and deploying your "interview kit"
- ◆ Creating an effective interview "E-kit"
- ◆ Rehearsing for the "performance"
- ◆ Logistics: getting there on time
- ◆ The night before …

You've landed an interview. You should feel just great—rarin' to go. Right?

Well … maybe. And maybe not.

Jubilant excitement, high anticipation, second thoughts, out-and-out doubt, and naked fear—all are part of the pre-interview emotional stew. Well, don't just simmer. Your time—now—is a precious asset. Here's how to use it best.

Go!

The big news may come to you in a letter, but more than likely you'll hear by phone or e-mail. However the invitation comes, answer promptly. Before you rush headlong into a response, check and double-check your calendar to make certain that you have no conflicts. Once you set a date and time, it's important that you don't make any changes. The last thing you want is to annoy the interviewer right off the bat by making her rearrange her schedule for you.

> **The Skinny** _____
>
> According to *What Color Is Your Parachute?* (Ten Speed Press, 2007) by Richard Nelson Bolles, on average, 48 of every 100 job interviews result in a job offer.

It's possible that your first telephone contact will itself be a preliminary screening interview rather than a request for a face-to-face interview. See Chapter 19 for a discussion of the telephone interview.

Responding to the Big Call (or the E-Mail of Destiny)

These days, a request for an interview will usually come by phone or e-mail. If you get a phone call, respond with pleasant enthusiasm, but don't go wild. Be certain to …

◆ Speak loudly enough to be heard.

◆ Use correct grammar.

◆ Speak in complete sentences whenever possible.

◆ Avoid long pauses.

◆ Focus your voice, pitching it somewhat lower than normal.

◆ Smile when you speak. Even though the caller cannot see you, smiling will often naturally inject warmth into your voice.

What to Ask Now

Your first assignment is to listen. Don't hang up until you have obtained the following:

◆ The caller's name and title

◆ The name of the company

◆ The address of the company—or wherever the interview will take place

◆ The date and time of the interview

◆ The names and titles of the person(s) with whom you'll be meeting

◆ The telephone number of the caller and of the key person with whom you'll be meeting

If the interview location is familiar to you, great! But if you need directions, ask for them: "I'm not familiar with that part of town. Can you tell me the best way to get there from such-and-such street?" It's better to ask now than to get lost later.

You *should* have your calendar and date book by the telephone, but if you don't and you're not certain whether the proposed date and time are free, it's better to ask to call back. Be sure to promise to call back at a specific time: "I need to check my schedule. It's 10:30 now. Can I call you back in a half-hour, at 11?" Then be certain to call back at exactly that time.

If you *know* that you have an irreconcilable conflict (such as another job interview, you lucky dog), reply that you can't make it at the time proposed. Don't explain why, and don't invite discussion of the issue. But do offer an alternative: "Any time Wednesday or Friday would work well for me."

Clincher

You've sent out X number of query letters and therefore, you have some right to expect a call or two for an interview. Why not tack up a note by the phone with a checklist of the information you need to obtain from a would-be interviewer?

What to Say (and Not Say) to Your Present Employer

If you are currently employed, you need to decide what to tell—and what not to tell—your employer. Perhaps he or she knows that you are looking for another job and is even supportive of your efforts. Wonderful. More likely, though, you're conducting your job search without your boss's knowledge. If this is the case, you need to practice discretion at your place of work.

Being discreet begins with how you handle the phone call summoning you to an interview. Take the call, and greet the caller. Then ask for a moment to shut the door. Just say, "Can you give me just a moment? I need to shut my door." You don't have to say why. The caller *knows* why, and he understands.

Don't Call Us ... _____

Although it is generally acceptable to include your work phone number on your resumé or job application, you should avoid disclosing your work e-mail. All e-mail sent and received at your place of business is the property of your employer. If you use the company's computer, network, and e-mail account, you have no right to privacy. An employer can legally monitor your e-mail communication; therefore, furnish only your personal e-mail address.

If you don't have a door to shut, try to get the essential information without betraying the nature of the call. Should your caller begin to transform the call into a telephone interview, you will have to stop him: "Mr. Smith, I'm in a high-profile, high-visibility position here, and I can't discuss this matter with you now. May I call you back this evening at six when I'm at home?" Or just say, "I'm sorry, Mr. Smith, but I'm not in a position to discuss this matter with you now. Can I call you back this evening at six?"

If you know you can't take job-hunt–related calls at work, plan a way to handle them elsewhere, but make sure you return calls *before* the end of the day. If you have a cell phone, make sensitive calls from a private area, such as your (parked) automobile.

As a ploy to get a raise or a promotion, you may be tempted to do away with discretion and actually start dropping hints around the office that so-and-so wants to interview you. This is almost certainly a bad move. Instead of getting what you really want with your present employer, you'll more likely persuade him that you are disloyal. In the end, you might want (or need) your current position for quite a while. The best policy, then, is to avoid talking about your job search with anyone at your present workplace.

Don't Call Us ... _____

Do *not* express fear to the prospective employer: "My boss would can me in a heartbeat if he found out I was interviewing." Nor should you imply that you are skulking around behind your boss's back; after all, you'll be interviewing with your potential *new* boss. Just ask that the interview be kept confidential. That is all that needs to be said.

It's a Small, Small, Small World

You've just hung up the phone. An interview! Great!

Then, a persistent little thought wraps its icy claws around your medulla oblongata: what if this *prospective* employer blabs (inadvertently or otherwise) to your *current* employer?

You try to dismiss the notion as mere paranoia. But in truth, you're not paranoid. It could happen. In most cases, it's a fairly remote possibility, but the smaller and more tightly knit a particular industry is, the greater the likelihood of a "security breach." It would be wise, therefore, to stress to the prospective employer that you would prefer to keep the upcoming interview in strict confidence.

Present a Tidy Little Bouquet of Graceful Lies

You will need time for the interview. And that means taking time away from your current job. If you have a flexible lunch hour, plan to take an early or late "lunch" so that your interviewer can keep her regular lunch hour—you don't want her going hungry just to interview you.

Of course, squeezing an interview into a lunch hour can be uncomfortably confining. The better strategy is to tell your current boss a graceful lie that will allow you maximum flexibility.

◆ As part of your general job-hunting strategy, hoard a cache of vacation days. Deploy these as necessary to leave an entire day free for an interview.

◆ If you are entitled to personal days, use them. You have a "dentist's appointment," a "doctor's appointment," "a parent-teacher conference," "automobile trouble," a "visit from the plumber." Any of these should free up, at minimum, a morning or afternoon.

◆ Keep your lie simple. The best lies are the most basic. Elaborate stories are usually too flimsy to stand up for long.

> **Don't Call Us ...**
>
> Don't let your clothes betray you. If you usually wear a casual shirt and khakis to work, nothing will broadcast, "I've got an interview!" more loudly than your suddenly showing up in a spanking-new suit and tie. Make up an excuse: "Boy, I *hate* wearing a tie. But I've got to talk to Johnny's teacher this afternoon, and I don't want to look like a bum."

Best Time for an Interview

If you have any choice in the matter, schedule your interview at the optimum time—neither on Monday nor Friday. The middle of the week is best, because it's apt to be less hectic than the start or end of the week.

◆ Ten o'clock in the morning is a great time for *any* meeting, including an interview. The interviewer(s) will have settled in for the morning, alertness and attentiveness are usually at their peak, and lunchtime (with growling stomachs and accompanying impatience) is still in the comfortably distant future.

◆ Avoid late-afternoon meetings. Your energy level, as well as that of the interviewer, tends to be at its lowest.

◆ Avoid hectic times (such as the day or two before a big sales conference) and hectic seasons (for example, Christmastime in the retail industry).

Resolving Scheduling Conflicts

The best way to resolve conflicts is to prevent them altogether: don't forget to consult your calendar. If a conflict does develop, first try to resolve it without involving the potential employer. Always move your schedule around to accommodate his. If that proves impossible, call the employer immediately. Put the conflict—and the consequent need to reschedule the interview—in the best light by explaining that an "urgent professional commitment" or "urgent professional emergency" has suddenly come up. Then continue, "I am really sorry to cause you inconvenience, Mr. Smith, but I just can't let the rest of my team down." Putting the matter this way at least testifies to your ethical character and high degree of professional commitment.

Life, of course, is uncertainty. Illness, accident, and family emergencies do arise and force you to change your plans. Inform the prospective employer immediately. Describe *briefly* the nature of the emergency, apologize, and—if possible—reschedule immediately. If you can't, give the best estimate that you can. Never fabricate personal crises or family emergencies as an excuse for rescheduling an appointment.

"Trust, But Verify"

When you make an appointment, you must trust the potential employer to keep it. However, if more than a few days will elapse between the phone call and the appointment, telephone the employer the day before the interview to confirm: "I was just calling to confirm our ten o'clock meeting tomorrow at your office."

How to Build an "Interview Kit"

Your prime objective in approaching a prospective employer is to appear to her as *the* answer to her needs. Come to the interview as part of the solution rather than just another part of the problem. And the interviewer's problem at the moment is how to get through the interview comfortably and productively.

So how can you be part of the solution? Come prepared with thorough research and great questions. Part 3 will tell you more about what questions to ask. Finally, come prepared with one very handy prop: the interview kit.

> **Don't Call Us ...**
>
> Be careful *not* to include in your interview kit anything that may be construed as trade secrets or confidential or proprietary material that belongs to your current employer!

What It Is

The interview kit is a kind of scrapbook, which may contain such items as additional copies of your resume (three should be enough; avoid carrying around a sheaf, which makes you look desperate) and, perhaps, a half-dozen copies of an executive briefing, which hits the high points of your resume in a single narrative paragraph. Your interview kit should also include letters of commendation, awards, copies of business presentations you have made, photos of equipment you have worked with, and so on.

If the work you do—or want to do—involves creating ads, artwork, and so on, don't try to stuff samples of everything into an interview kit. Instead, prepare a full-scale portfolio of your work. Your portfolio may be a big, bulky thing, or you may be able to put it on a CD-ROM or DVD-ROM and present it on a laptop/notebook computer you bring to the interview. You might also use your computer to link to your website (if you have one), your Facebook or MySpace page, or any other relevant site.

How to Use Your Interview Kit

The purpose of the interview kit is not only to exhibit some of your wares and highlight your qualifications and accomplishments, but, quite literally, to serve as a conversation piece: something to look at, something to spark comment, something to prevent awkward silences.

It is best, however, not to let the interview kit become the object of rapt attention; use its contents as springboards to further comment and discussion:

> **You (as you and the interviewer look through the interview kit):** I received this letter after I completed a project that saved my client $40,000.
>
> **Interviewer:** Oh. Tell me something more about that.
>
> **You:** Well, this was the client's situation as I saw it …

Each item you select for inclusion in the interview kit should have a strong, positive, compelling story to go along with it.

Stay in Control

It is important to remember that *you* control the interview kit. You may give the interviewer one of the copies of your resumé—especially if he has failed to bring in the copy you sent by mail—but the interview kit itself always stays in your hands. Don't give it over to the interviewer, but merely let him or her look. Your objective is to convey that the work it contains is yours, is of great value, and is not up for grabs.

Presenting an "E-Kit"

In most interview scenarios, a hardcopy interview kit is a safe bet. But consider supplementing it with a digital version, which you can exhibit on a laptop computer you bring with you. Also think about preparing a presentation using Microsoft's ubiquitous PowerPoint program or a similar AV program from another vendor. Essentially, a PowerPoint presentation will enable you to present a kind of slideshow featuring you and your key achievements.

Keep your presentation concise. Hit the highlights only, but do have available documents and examples that go into further depth and detail, if an interviewer wants to pursue something you touch on in the PowerPoint-style presentation.

Your Life on a Laptop

When you make an E-kit part of your interview kit, always bring your own means of showing it. That requires toting along a laptop with a good color display. A 15-inch display is better than 12, and 17 is better still.

If you intend digital material to be a significant part of your interview presentation, respond to the interview invitation by asking if the target employer has facilities for projecting a PowerPoint (or similar) presentation. If the answer is yes, bring your laptop, along with whatever adapter you need to connect it to the projector. If the answer is no, be prepared to present the material on your laptop. In either case, do not depend on the interviewer having the appropriate equipment, and, if at all feasible, back up your digital presentation with a hardcopy portfolio you can present instead.

Burn That CD or DVD

Although you should maintain control of your interview kit, whether it consists of hardcopy material, a digital E-kit, or includes both hardcopy and digital components, be sure to burn CDs or DVDs of your digital presentation, along with whatever supporting materials you want to include. Leave the CDs or DVDs with the appropriate people, so that they can review your material.

Do You Have a Website?

Consider investing in a website. If you are confident of your ability to put together a good one yourself, do so. Most of us, however, can benefit from the services of a professional web designer. Type the keywords "website design" into your favorite search engine, and review the results. If you like someone you see, make contact.

MySpace? Facebook?

If you do not want to lay out the time and cash to create a standalone website, consider developing a page or blog on one of the popular social websites, such as MySpace or Facebook. See Chapter 3 for more on this option.

Some interviewers will have the capability and willingness to log on to your website or MySpace or Facebook page, either on a computer in the office in which you are being interviewed or using your own laptop and wireless network—if wireless network access is available.

Obviously, you should not depend on the interviewer either wanting to go online or being able to at the moment, so don't make access to your website or other online presence an essential aspect of your interview presentation. Nevertheless, do ensure that the interviewers have the information they need to log onto the relevant sites at their leisure.

Rehearse It and Nurse It

Few things are scarier than relying on spontaneity, especially if your career, your very livelihood, depends on it. No wonder most of us dread job interviews! The fact is that a job interview does not have to be conducted under the tyranny of spontaneity—*if* you stop thinking of the interview as an event over which you have little or no control. Instead, conceive of it as a *performance*—more like a speech or presentation than an interrogation.

Once you start thinking this way, your next step becomes obvious: Rehearse.

Gather Ye War Stories

After you have thoroughly researched the employer and industry you're aiming to join (see Chapter 2), you should review your own "war stories"—the achievements, accomplishments, problems encountered, and problems solved that relate to what you have determined to be the needs and requirements of the prospective employer.

- ◆ Select three or four concise, solid war stories that show you off at your best and relate to what you believe the employer needs.

- ◆ Structure your war stories. They need a beginning, middle, and end. This structure effectively corresponds to statement of problem, analysis of problem, and solution to problem.

- ◆ If possible, coordinate your war stories with the contents of your interview kit or E-kit. It should include letters and other documents that illustrate your narratives.

Don't Call Us ...

If you're reviewing and memorizing your strengths, shouldn't you do the same for your weaknesses? Yes, you certainly should. A favorite interview question is "In what areas do you feel you could use improvement?" Just remember *not* to initiate discussion of these issues yourself. If the interviewer asks, respond. If not, pitch your strengths only. See Chapter 10 for tips on turning negatives into positives.

Review Your Research

You've done all the research, organized your interview kit, put together an E-kit, and memorized your war stories; you're ready, right? Wrong. Now you need to review and rehearse the rest of your "lines":

◆ Conduct an intensive review of your research about the target employer. Bone up on three or four major industry issues, problems, and trends that you will want to discuss at the interview.

◆ Review your personal information as well. Know your skills, qualifications, achievements, and interests. These constitute your basic, general sales pitch. Know them cold.

◆ Adapt your general sales pitch to meet the needs of the target employer. It's like a game of connect-the-dots: certain dots represent your skills and qualifications, while others represent the employer's needs; you should be able to link all the dots to form a complete picture.

When you rehearse alone, consider video recording yourself. This is a great method for zapping nervous tics, bad posture, fidgeting, wild gesticulations, or jittery hands. If the person you see on your screen is not smiling, you'd better make a conscious effort to do just that. (You'll find a concise body-language primer in Chapter 8.)

You might also ask a friend or family member to role-play with you by acting the part of the interviewer. You can prime your costar's pump by furnishing a list of some questions, but also invite her to invent questions of her own.

Questions, Questions, Questions

Now is a good time to skip ahead to Chapters 10 and 11. Take time to anticipate the most likely questions and prepare answers. You should write these out.

Once you have the answers to the tough questions you're anticipating, go ahead and read the chapters in Part 3 about questions *you* should ask. Prepare a short list of questions to ask. These should raise issues that put your skills, qualifications, interests, and accomplishments on display.

Interview Logistics

Don't become so immersed in the Theater of Interview that you neglect logistics—you've got to get to the interview site, and you've got to get there on time. Plan your route in advance. If possible, make a trial run over the route at the same time of day that the interview will be taking place, so that you can better estimate travel time. And be sure to give yourself plenty of extra time, especially if the office is in a city where traffic can be a problem.

Online or "IRL"?

The hiring sequence used to be a matter of routine: The job seeker applies for a job or answers an ad, the potential employer calls to set up an interview, and the job seeker travels to the employer's office. These days, we would say that such an interview takes place "IRL," *in real life*. For most jobs, IRL interviews are the way the employer likes it. But, increasingly, employers are extending their reach by arranging online interviews, using such Internet-based telephone connections as Skype, often combined with a webcam so that the interviewer(s) and the interviewee can both see and hear each other.

Prepare as fully for an online interview as for an interview IRL, and strive to perform at the same high level. See Chapter 6 for a full discussion of the art of the online interview.

Travel: Who Arranges and Who Pays?

If you are interviewing IRL out of town, you should clearly establish who will be arranging your travel. Typically, it's your responsibility to book a flight, but the employer will often make the hotel arrangements. That said, don't assume anything. Always ask. If you're expected to reserve a hotel room yourself, ask for advice on the most conveniently located hotel— not the "nicest" or "best," but the "most conveniently located."

In most industries, the employer pays for your travel and accommodations, including meals. However, what if *you* are asked to foot the bill? Then you're faced with a tough decision. Should you stake travel costs on the interview? What does this say about the prospective employer? How serious is she about considering you for a job? Should you suggest an online interview as an alternative?

Clincher _____

When should you arrive? If your appointment is early in the day, be careful that a premature arrival doesn't intrude on your host's morning routine. Four or five minutes before the scheduled time is acceptable. If you arrive even earlier, tell the receptionist that you're early and would rather not disturb Ms. Whomever yet. Could she announce you in five minutes?

And don't just ask these questions of yourself. Talk to the employer: "I am not accustomed to paying my way to an interview. Is this usual with your company?" Or: "I have to tell you, Mr. Johnson, that I don't ordinarily pay my own way to an employment interview. Before I commit to this investment, can you tell me how many others you are interviewing for the position? Where do I stand?"

The Night Before

Here's this chapter's hardest piece of advice: relax. Devote the night before your interview to relaxation. Free your mind to prepare for the day ahead. Don't allow family problems, financial worries, or other events and personal crises to intrude on this time. If they're eating at you right now, take out a pad and pencil, make a list of your worries, and then promise yourself that you will deal with them—*after* the interview.

See a Show, Walk the Dog

Distract yourself with something mindlessly pleasant. Go to a movie. Have a nice dinner. Don't stay out late, and, if you can avoid it, don't drink.

Living with Jet Lag

If you're traveling substantial distances to get to the interview, especially if you are traveling overseas, reserve your arrival day as a day of rest. Don't try to hit the airport in the morning and rush to an interview. You'll probably run out of steam. Jet lag is a harsh reality and can hit you with the sandbagging impact of the flu. Allow time to sleep. Definitely arrange for a wake-up call, and back this up with your own alarm clock. Jet lag wreaks havoc on your body's internal clock.

Into the Land of Nod

Do what you can to get a good night's sleep. It's a bad idea to force yourself to go to bed early, since you'll probably wake up in the wee hours and may not be able to fall back to sleep. Retire at your usual time. Avoid unpleasant discussions. Remember to set your alarm. Congratulate yourself on having landed the interview. Now have a good night.

The Least You Need to Know

- Don't fly to pieces when you are called for an interview. Obtain all the information you need, and consult your calendar before committing to a time.

- Be discreet about the interview; it is important to protect your current job. Avoid using the interview as a ploy to improve your situation with your current employer. You could end up losing your job.

- Make good use of the days before the scheduled interview: review your skills and qualifications (as well as your weaknesses); anticipate the interviewer's questions and prepare answers; prepare questions of your own; rehearse; and assemble your interview kit.

- Consider assembling an E-kit to present your career and samples of your work on a laptop computer you bring with you.

Chapter 5

Clothes Call

In This Chapter

- ◆ Wearing the company or industry "uniform"
- ◆ "Appropriate" and "safe" interview dress defined
- ◆ Travel tips
- ◆ Dressing for an online interview
- ◆ Wardrobe guidelines for men and women

Doubtless, your mother or father or somebody who was supposed to know better told you something to the effect of "It's what's inside a person that counts, not what's outside." Or maybe you got the "don't judge a book by its cover" version.

Right.

The truth is, whether we like it or not, appearances are *very* important. Although dressing a certain way will not magically produce a job for you, poor, indifferent, or inappropriate grooming may very well get you screened out of a job before a single word is exchanged. This chapter gives you some dressing strategies to show you at your best.

Evaluating Your Employment Wardrobe

Now—*before* you are called in to an interview—is the time to take stock of your "employment wardrobe." You need to ask yourself two questions:

1. Do you have clothing appropriate to the position, industry, company, and department in which you are seeking a job?

2. Is this clothing in excellent condition: clean, neat, in impeccable repair, and not obviously "dated"?

The second question is self-explanatory, I believe, but the first could benefit from some discussion. "Appropriate" dress: What is it? I mean, this is a free country, right? You're not applying for a military career. You don't have to wear a uniform.

Nice Save!

A rainy day. You've gotten off the bus and are walking to the interview. A car speeds around the corner, tires churn into a mud puddle, and you are splattered head to foot. What do you do?

Let's face it. There's no way that this is a desirable event. However, you can turn this disaster to your advantage. If possible, duck into a restaurant or other place that has a public restroom, and tidy up as best you can, particularly your face and hands, if they were splashed. If you can't find a place to do this, try to find a public washroom at the interview venue. You might explain to the receptionist what happened to you and secure from her a key to a washroom.

Looking as clean as you can under the circumstances, walk into the interview and announce: "A funny thing happened to me on my way down here ..." Narrate the incident, then conclude: "I apologize for my appearance, but this meeting is important to me, and I didn't want to postpone it or cause you the inconvenience of rescheduling. I hope you'll bear with me. This *was* a good-looking suit, up until a few minutes ago!"

Handled this way, the incident won't make you look foolish. The interviewers will be treated to your healthy sense of humor, your unflappable nature, your ability to put matters into their proper proportion, and your professionalism: *nothing* could stop you from getting to this interview.

You're not joining the army. But don't be so sure that this gets you out of wearing a uniform. You're probably already well aware that many career fields and professions have unspoken dress codes. If you walk into an interview dressed right—that is, wearing the appropriate "uniform"—you broadcast that you understand at least something about the job, without even uttering a word. If hiring were 100 percent fair and logical, you'd get job offers based strictly on your abilities. In the real world, however, an employer's decision to hire is to a significant degree influenced by *feelings*—and one of those feelings is that you will "fit in." So go ahead: walk in the door already suited up as a member of the team.

But how do you know what to wear? Scan the "Careers" and the "Style" sections of any large bookstore or search the online booksellers, and you will most likely find a variety of "dress-for-success" books. The problem with consulting these is that fashions change, and none of the available books explores the dress codes of specific industries, let alone how those dress codes may be influenced by regional preferences and individual corporate cultures.

So where do you get the lowdown on the right "uniform"? Well, the best place to get any information is straight from the horse's mouth: as a company's "dress code" is on public display every day, just pay a visit to the target company in advance of the interview and take a look around. If you can't do that, or if the nature of the company's business is such that it does not allow for a casual visit, check out any newsletters or other literature the company publishes, and log on to the firm's website; look for photos showing staff members. How do they dress? Plan your interview wardrobe accordingly.

On Diversity

Okay, so you've scoped out the wardrobe style of an industry or a particular company. Should you then strive slavishly to emulate that style?

The truth is that you probably cannot go very wrong doing just that; however, you may find doing this difficult or even personally offensive. After all, our clothes are, among other things, an expression of who we are—or who we want others to think we are. Dress in a manner that is utterly foreign to you, and it is likely that you will feel uncomfortable. If you feel uncomfortable, you will probably act and speak in ways that betray your discomfort.

As we will see, the most effective interview wardrobe is personal yet fits into the environment of which you seek to be a part.

For some of us, however, what we like to wear expresses not only aspects of individual personality, but ethnic, lifestyle, or even age-related issues of identity. Today, in America and Canada (among many other places), it is common to see people in clothing characteristic of Africa, Asia, and various Hispanic regions and cultures. Religious beliefs may also enter into the choice of attire, including (for example) head scarves worn by Muslim women and yarmulkes worn by some Jewish men. Clothing may also reveal an affinity with hip-hop culture, with various aspects of youth culture, or with gay culture.

Federal law strictly prohibits employers from discriminating against job applicants on the basis of race, ethnicity, national origin, gender, and sexual orientation. Moreover, a growing number of businesses have come to regard diversity—high-profile, highly visible diversity—as an asset. After all, most businesses function in a diverse society, so why not acquire a diverse staff in order to maintain an edge on the competition?

Having said all of this, anyone preparing for an interview needs to be aware that ethnic looks, or clothing associated with lifestyles some deem as out of the mainstream— or even a style that is perceived as overly or aggressively conservative—may not appeal to people from different demographics. You take a risk when you stray too far from the current mainstream. This goes for ethnic clothes and grooming as well as overtly regional looks, such as the Texan who wears his bolo tie, cowboy boots, and Stetson to an interview with a Wall Street financial services firm.

I would never advise anyone *not* to dress as they like. But I do insist that an interview is about striking a balance between demonstrating that you are an individual *and* showing that you intend to fit into the organization. I also suggest that the most effective interviewees always tip the balance slightly away from the theme of individuality and toward a demonstration of fitting in.

Diversity is a personal, cultural, and business asset. Nevertheless, as a newcomer, deliberately setting yourself apart from what you believe or perceive that the target employer considers the norm will, at the very least, contribute nothing to your prospects for landing the job. At worst, it may compromise those prospects.

Dress Codes

Effective interview dress is a combination of what makes you comfortable, what expresses how you feel about yourself and (perhaps) your cultural and ethnic background, *and* what is appropriate to the field or industry in which you are seeking employment.

Everyone knows what "comfortable" means, but just be aware that what is comfortable at home—say jeans and a T-shirt—will make you very *un*comfortable at an interview for an investment banking position. Remember that comfort has physical, emotional, and cultural dimensions. Consider all three in choosing your interview wardrobe.

And what about "expressing how you feel about yourself"? This is fine, dandy, and wholly positive—as long as what you feel about yourself is appropriate to the position you're seeking. Dressing with a generous serving of panache may send the right signals if you're angling for a job as art director of an illustrated magazine, but, no matter how you *really* feel about yourself, donning something more conservative will almost certainly give you a better shot at that accountant slot with Dewey, Cheatham & Howe.

Clincher _____

Sales professionals make it a practice to dress just a little better than their customers. Apply this thinking to your interview attire by dressing up from the interviewer just a bit.

I Gotta Be Me (You Gotta Be Kidding!)

Here's a short and sweet prescription for interview dress and general grooming: male or female, the best interview look is the *safest* look—mildly conservative and recognizably traditional or, if you prefer, *classic*.

Accept this as the base on which you can build a more individual look, if you wish.

The "safe" look extends to personal grooming as well as wardrobe:

◆ **Avoid dousing yourself in perfume, cologne, or after-shave.** The sense of smell is highly charged emotionally. If you flood the office with too strong a scent, you may be perceived as annoying and intrusive—or, at best, inconsiderate. You should also be aware that some people suffer allergic reactions to perfume and could become ill from it. The last thing you want is to make an interviewer sick!

◆ **Do feel free to use your favorite scent sparingly.** A hint of perfume or cologne can create a pleasant, inviting, clean, and polished aura. Just remember, the scent should be *barely* perceptible.

◆ **Reevaluate your hair.** Hair length—especially for men—was a downright inflammatory issue during the 1960s and 1970s. These days, the social controversy has died down, but it hasn't disappeared. Very long hair on men is still widely perceived as a token of rebellion or, at least, a hang-loose kind of sloppiness. Mullets and ponytails on men also tend to send the wrong signals. On the other hand, some people associate excessively *short* hair (the "buzz cut") with hyperconservatism or "skinhead" attitudes. (Women don't have to be as concerned about hair length. Just be aware that some interviewers may find a severe "mannish" cut intimidating.)

◆ **If you have a mustache or beard, ensure that it's neatly trimmed.** In some corporate cultures, however, beards—and even mustaches—are frowned upon. If you have any misgivings, scope out the situation through a pre-interview office visit or a look at photographs from inside.

Nice Save!
Employment in the United States is regulated by some excellent laws barring hiring practices that discriminate on the basis of age, gender, or race. However, no law can regulate the emotions, including those associated with humanity's uglier sentiments. Although a growing number of employers not only accept but positively encourage ethnic and cultural diversity in the workplace, you may want to reconsider "ethnic" hairstyles that represent significant departures from what is generally perceived as the cultural mainstream. Just as it is illegal to discriminate on the basis of race or ethnicity, so it is unlawful to do so on the basis of age. Nevertheless, employers continue to place a premium on youth or, at least, the appearance of youthful vigor. You will have to decide for yourself whether gray hair is an advantage—conveying an aura of experience and wisdom—or a disadvantage, suggesting that you are older than your years.

From Executive Assistant to VP

Don't get carried away with all of my conservative advice. *Dress appropriately for the position you are seeking, not for the position you currently have.* For example, if you are an office assistant accustomed to wearing a sport jacket, shirt, tie, and jeans, you should invest in the best conservative suit you can afford before you interview for the position of assistant account executive. If you're an assistant account executive now, don't look like one when you interview with the "creatives" for an advertising copywriter position.

Remember that fashion is a powerful form of communication. Just as you shouldn't open your mouth to speak without something to say, so you shouldn't put on your interview clothes without knowing what you want them to "say."

The First Commandment: Be Thou Sharp and Clean

It matters little how carefully you select your wardrobe and how much you pay for it if what you wear fails to be sharp and clean. This, above all, is what an interviewer will notice. Suits—for men and women alike—should be dry-cleaned or (if the garment is not soiled) professionally pressed immediately prior to the interview. Shirts and blouses should be freshly laundered; light to medium starch is best.

The New Normal

In the press, on TV, and on the Net, we hear, see, and read stories about "the new normal" in the workplace, which may include not just "casual Fridays," but casual everydays, and which also (we are told) encourages more personal expression and allows flextime and telecommuting, with employees doing some, most, or even all of their work at home.

The truth is that there is no *new* normal, but, rather, an expanded definition of plain old normal. The majority of businesses still require some form of traditional business dress, which, depending on the nature of the business, may be a coat and tie for men and a business suit for women or some form of "business casual," which, typically, is a somewhat dressed-down version of more traditional business dress: a jacket without a tie, a more casual suit, or a fairly conservative skirt and blouse combination.

Don't Call Us ...

Be careful about visiting the firm on a Friday. In many offices, Friday is "casual day" and does not reflect the prevailing dress code. Don't be misled if the prevailing look is casual on that day.

Only in a select group of enterprises—generally, "creative" or youth-oriented industries, such as advertising, web design, and computer programming—have dress codes significantly loosened up.

As you prepare for an interview, avoid hasty assumptions about the "new normal." Do a little research to discover what people really do wear; then, for the interview, wear something a notch more conservative.

Traveling Clothes

Even in these days of online interviewing, most businesses prefer to see candidates in person, at least those who have made the final cut. Often, this involves travel, and travel is hard on clothes.

Fold and pack everything neatly and carefully. The days when you could hang a garment bag in a closet at the front of an airliner are long gone. You will have to fold your garment bag in half. Your suits, shirts, and blouses will survive this torture with fewer wrinkles if you keep them in the plastic bags the dry cleaner delivers them in. Professionally laundered shirts are best transported in the boxes cleaners provide if you order your shirts folded rather than on hangers. If you fold suit jackets in a suit-case instead of a suit bag, fold them in half, lengthwise, *away from* the lining—that is, so that the lining shows. This fights wrinkles.

> **The Skinny** _____
>
> A 2007 study revealed that U.S. airlines "mishandled" 6 of every 1,000 items of checked luggage during the prior year, and more than 1 in 6 airline passengers who participated in a recent *Consumer Reports* poll reported some problem with checked baggage. Pack a change of clothes—at least a fresh shirt/blouse and underwear—in your carry-on.

A Webcam Wardrobe

Dressing for an online interview, in which you focus a webcam on yourself as you sit in front of your computer keyboard and monitor, need not be radically different from dressing for an in-person interview. Prepare yourself by scoping out the company's prevailing "dress code," and then clothe yourself accordingly. Observe these additional guidelines:

- Dress from head to toe. Even if the webcam shows you only from the chest or neck up, there is always the possibility that, in the course of the interview, you'll have to step away from the webcam and reveal a long shot.

- Favor neutral shades and solid colors rather than patterns. These show up best on web broadcasts. Be aware that the color of your shirt or blouse may reflect and thereby tinge your complexion. Avoid reds and greens.

For Men Only

In general, dress to communicate an impression of reliability and attention to detail. Don't allow any single article of your outfit to become the subject of attention or discussion. (*You*, not your clothes, should be the focus of the interview.)

- Be aware that dark colors suggest authority, and that dark blue conveys the greatest degree of authority. (Why else is a police officer's uniform dark blue?) Black certainly qualifies as dark, but wearing a black suit may strike the interviewer as funereal. Avoid it. (Very dark colors should not be worn for webcam interviews.)

◆ Don't bother with synthetic fabrics. They generally have a sheen and texture that make them look cheap—even if they aren't. Also they don't "drape" as attractively as natural fibers do, and they tend to retain body odors stubbornly. For your interview, wear natural fabrics only.

Suit Yourself, Sir

Dark colors convey authority, and, except in webcam interviews, dark blue does it best. Solids and subtle patterns are fine. Be aware that "banker stripes"—muted, narrow pin stripes—are associated with conservative finance and power politics. If that's the message you want to deliver, fine; some interviewers will be impressed, while others might find it mildly pretentious.

You're on safe ground limiting your choice of fabric to 100 percent wool. Even if you are interviewing in the summer, you'll be better off in a summer-weight wool suit than a light-colored linen or linen-blend suit. Linen wrinkles quickly and badly.

It pays to monitor prevailing fashion and to go, more or less conservatively, with the prevailing trend, always staying slightly *behind* the cutting edge, unless you are interviewing in a very style-conscious industry (fashion design or clothing retailing, for example).

> **Don't Call Us ...**
>
> Avoid loud checked patterns that conjure images of disreputable hucksters. That designer-logo tie you paid a bundle for—chuck it (or at least, don't wear it to your interview). Many interviewers feel that designer ties broadcast insecurity, as if you needed a designer's imprimatur to certify your good taste.

If you have a slender build, the smart European cuts can look great, especially if you are interviewing in a "young" industry (such as communications or advertising), but you are generally safest wearing a more generous—and conservative—American cut.

Keep Your Shirt On

Wear only long-sleeved shirts. Period. Wear a white or very pale blue shirt. Avoid patterns and stripes. As with the suit, natural fabrics are best for the shirt. Since cotton wrinkles more readily than polyester blends, it is absolutely essential that you get your shirts *professionally* laundered with light starch.

Fit to Be Tied

It's up for debate whether the first thing the interviewer will notice is your tie or your shoes. Some authorities insist that the eye naturally goes to the tie, others say that the shoes make the first impression. What is safe to assume is that the tie makes at least *one* of the initial visual impressions. For this reason, the tie is important. The wrong one can make an expensive suit look cheap, while the right one can lift even modest attire a notch or two.

There is only one acceptable choice of fabric for ties—100 percent silk. Linen wrinkles instantly, wool is too casual, and synthetics don't knot well and always look cheesy.

If your suit is patterned, don't wear a tie with a pattern that competes with it. Tie widths expand and contract with the tides of fashion, but the width should always be in proportion to the suit lapels: a reasonable rule of thumb is that the width of the tie should be approximately equal to the width of the lapel.

Don't Call Us …

How about a bow tie? Nope. Not at an interview. And don't even *think* of clip-on *anything*.

Go with the traditional patterns: foulards, stripes, and muted paisley prints, in addition to solids. Broad, solid "power stripes" are fine. Just be sure you shun polka dots, pictures (the heads of hunting dogs, the bodies of naked ladies, and the like), and silly sporting images (golf clubs, polo mallets). Ditch the tie with the Bart-and-Lisa-Simpson print.

Shoes and Socks

Black shoes are safest, especially with a dark-blue or gray suit; however, well-made brown shoes can be made to work well with anything but a black suit. The shoes should be well polished, with heels that are in good repair.

Especially if you choose a slip-on shoe with a low vamp, you must be attentive to your socks. The color of your socks should always complement your suit and should be long enough to permit you to cross your legs without showing hairy, bare skin.

All Accessories Included

You may equip yourself with the following:

◆ **An attaché case.** Carry a simple and slim attaché case or a neat portfolio, if this is more appropriate to your profession.

- ◆ **A handkerchief.** Use a plain white cotton or linen handkerchief.

- ◆ **A belt.** Make sure that it's leather and that it matches or complements your shoes. Avoid bizarre or oversize buckles—the cavalry look (Union *or* Confederate), the cowboy look, or the Hell's Angel look.

- ◆ **Suspenders (or braces).** They reached the height of their popularity in the late 1980s as tokens of "manly" financial achievement. They are seen somewhat less frequently these days; be aware that some interviewers may find them pretentious.

- ◆ **Jewelry.** Restrict yourself to simple cuff links (if your shirt has French cuffs) and a wedding band (if you're married). Shun necklaces, stick pins, bracelets, and pinky rings.

> **Don't Call Us ...**
>
> For some years now, earrings have graced the lobes of many an unlikely male wearer. Like most bold cultural statements, however, they turn off as many people as they impress and should never be worn to an interview.

For Women Only

While women have a greater range of interview dressing options than men, they are also under greater economic pressure to invest in current fashions. A man can wear a three-year-old suit without raising any eyebrows—provided, of course, the suit is in impeccable condition—but a woman's interview attire must be more current. This is, without doubt, a blatant double standard. It's also simply the way things are in most business environments.

The Suit du Jour

A suit is appropriate for most white-collar interview situations. The good news is that your suit doesn't have to be a severely cut imitation of a man's two piece. Although a charcoal-gray suit with a white blouse is perhaps the safest interview combination, solids, pinstripes, and muted plaids in a variety of colors are all acceptable.

In contrast to men's wear, all-natural fabrics may not be the wisest choice for a woman's suit. Garments woven of wool or linen wrinkle readily; therefore, consider natural-synthetic blends. If you are committed to an all-natural fabric, however, choose wool.

Clincher

Make-up for an interview is governed by one simple rule: Less is more. In this situation, the best look is *natural*. This means minimal make-up carefully applied. If you're comfortable without lipstick, avoid it. If you do use it, apply a subdued shade sparingly.

Hemlines rise and fall from season to season. The "career women" you see on most television shows typically wear skirts that are way too short and sexy for the real-world office. You and the interviewer will be most comfortable if you opt for a skirt that's longer than one you would wear on a social occasion.

Until fairly recently, pantsuits created some controversy among business dressing authorities. This is no longer the case. Savvy, powerful, high-profile women from Condoleezza Rice to Hillary Clinton have made the stylish pantsuit a safe and acceptable alternative to the skirt.

Blouses and Neckwear

Long-sleeved blouses are most desirable, and it is a good move to show a quarter- to a half-inch of cuff beyond your jacket sleeve; this is typically interpreted as a token of professionalism and authority. Avoid short-sleeved blouses, and shun sleeveless blouses entirely.

For the blouse, a natural fabric is best, especially cotton or silk. Women may choose from a spectrum of colors, but white and pale blue are the most universally accepted colors in the business world. A fresh variation on this conservative theme is pearl gray or the deeper shades of blue.

Simple styles are best. While a front-tie bow is always appropriate, a button-down collar, though a bit severe, appeals to interviewers in conservative companies or industries.

Feel free to accent your interview outfit with a scarf. Wear something you love, but avoid the matching scarf-and-blouse look or oversize polka dots (small ones are fine). Ideally, choose pure silk in a color and pattern that complement your suit.

Heels and Hosiery

A closed-toe pump with a 1-inch heel is the safe choice for an interview. Avoid very high heels, which may make your walk less self-assured. Choose shoes that complement your suit and accessories.

When it comes to hosiery, the key word is *unobtrusive*. Wear neutral or skin tones. You know that your stockings will run at the most inopportune moment, so keep an extra pair of pantyhose or stockings in your briefcase or purse.

And the Accessories ...

Attaché case or purse? You may carry one, not both. A smart attaché projects more professionalism and authority than a purse. Why not put the essential contents of your purse in a small clutch bag, which you can store in the attaché? Also consider carrying an attaché that doubles as a carrying case for your laptop—if you are bringing one to the interview. This will avoid the necessity of carrying two cases to the interview.

As with just about every other item of dress, women can choose from a wide range of belts, belt materials, and belt styles, as long as they match or complement the shoes. Be aware that although snakeskin, alligator, and lizard belts may be attractive, you might come up against an interviewer who feels strongly about certain environmental issues. Wear the skin of an endangered or near-endangered species, and you'll lose before you've uttered a word.

With jewelry, less is more. Wedding bands and engagement rings are always fine, but avoid wearing rings on multiple fingers. Shun thumb rings, and while small, discreet earrings are quite acceptable, jewelry that pierces any other part of the body is taboo.

There's nothing wrong with accenting your ensemble with a fine necklace, but don't wear fake pearls or gaudy costume jewelry. The same is true of bracelets. Don't wear charm bracelets or jewelry with your initials engraved on it. Many interviewers find charm bracelets too "cute" or juvenile, and with engraved jewelry, women run the same risk as men who wear monogrammed shirts: Some find it vulgar. And never wear an ankle bracelet to an interview.

Don't Call Us ...

Long, dangling earrings make distracting jangling noises, swing around, tickle your neck, and may even catch on clothing. Avoid them.

The Least You Need to Know

◆ An important part of interview preparation is discovering the "uniform" prevailing at the target employer.

◆ Dressing "comfortably" for a job interview requires, in part, dressing appropriately for the field or industry. Be aware that dressing effectively for a job interview may require some compromise of individual expression.

◆ In general and for most industries, dress *a little* conservatively, aim a notch above how you expect the interviewer to be dressed, and dress appropriately for the position you seek, not the position you currently have.

◆ Dress for an online interview as you would for an interview in person, but avoid busy patterns and very dark colors, which do not show up well at low resolution.

◆ Good personal grooming and hygiene are just as important as the perfect outfit.

Part 2

Being There

I'll leave it to the reader to judge whether this book has "heart," but I can tell you that it does have *a* heart—and the chapters in this section are it. No book can give you a set of *effective* cut-and-dried interview scripts to memorize, but you can develop and hone the intellectual, expressive, and emotional tools you'll need to excel in the employment interview. This is precisely what this section is designed to help you do.

Look here for advice on how to make use of the precious minutes just prior to the interview; for guidance on making the most of the crucial opening moments of the meeting, including how to become fluent in positive body language; for ways to become a dynamic listener; and for strategies to help you answer many interview questions—both the usual and the unusual. You'll also find ways to take control of the interview, together with strategies for negotiating salary effectively and profitably.

Chapter 6

Meet Me in Cyberspace

In This Chapter

◆ The online interview—what it is

◆ Surviving the gatekeeper interview online

◆ Nailing the "canned" (prerecorded) interview

◆ Technical requirements

◆ Delivering a winning performance

The past-tense verb "revolutionized" has been so brutally overused that, as an expressive tool, its edge is worn duller than a butter knife. Nevertheless, it's awfully difficult to avoid the conclusion that the Internet has revolutionized just about everything we do, especially anything involving research. Moreover, no area of research has been more revolutionized by the Internet than that of searching for a job and preparing for a job interview.

In Chapters 2 and 3, I spent a good deal of time discussing how to use the web to prepare for an interview. No question about it, when it comes to nailing an interview, the greatest value of the Internet is as a doorway to insider knowledge. But during the past several years, the Internet has also come to play a growing role in the actual interview itself. An increasing number of firms conduct at least some form of the pre-interview or actual interview online, sometimes via e-mail and instant messaging, sometimes through web-based interactive questionnaire or interview forms, and, more and more, through real-time audio-video conferencing. With each passing day, for any job hunter, the odds of interviewing online increase. Better start getting comfortable with these odds.

The Art of the Online Interview

Typically, an online interview is a face-to-face interview conducted over the Internet using some form of communications software (Skype is a popular example) that provides real-time audio-video conferencing. All videoconferencing software systems are *VoIP* solutions. This stands for "Voice Over Internet Protocol" and is a means of transmitting both voice and video over the Internet; the interviewer(s) as well as the interviewee see and hear one another. Whereas the dedicated hardware videophone, called the Picturephone when it debuted to the public back in 1970, failed to gain widespread acceptance, PC- and Mac-based videoconferencing has become commonplace.

The Skinny

Learn more about Skype at the official website, www.skype.com. While Skype is certainly the best-known software VoIP (Voice Over Internet Protocol) solution, there are a number of alternatives worth investigating. Check out Amicima (recently acquired by Adobe: www.adobe.com/special/amicima/), Google Talk (www.google.com/talk/), and SightSpeed (www.sightspeed.com).

What's the Use?

Employers conduct online, videoconference interviews for two main reasons.

First, they use them to screen potential candidates. Check out Chapter 18 as well as very next section in this chapter for a discussion of the gatekeeper or screening interview and how to transform it from an obstacle into an event you can use it to your advantage.

The second reason for an online interview is distance. Cross-country and international travel is expensive and time-consuming. Online interviewing gives a lot of companies an easy way to reach out beyond the local pool of job candidates without making a major investment of money or time.

Gatekeeper, Let Me In!

Now is a good time to jump ahead to Chapter 18 for the 411 on the gatekeeper interview. The bad news is that the function of this interview—also known as a screening interview—is not so much to identify the best job candidates from a group of submitted resumés as it is to *screen out* candidates who, for one reason or another, are judged less than optimal. Many, probably most, employers view the initial stage of the selection process not as a true process of selection (inclusion), but as one of culling (exclusion).

Because online interviewing is cheap and easy, the medium naturally lends itself to screening interviews. The gatekeeper interview may take place in real time between you and the interviewer(s) or you may be asked to participate in a canned (prerecorded) interview, which is a net employers use to troll for new hires.

Clincher

Don't wait for a company to invite you to an online interview. Most of the mega job-search sites (Monster and the others mentioned in Chapter 3) will link you selectively to *recorded* online interviews, and a vigorous search of the websites of companies that interest you may also turn up invitations to interview online. Be proactive.

A number of web-based service companies have sprung up to facilitate prerecorded online interviewing, especially at the gatekeeper stage. A good example is Interview On Demand (www.interview-on-demand.com), which is in business to help employers set up interviews. It works like this: the employer creates an interview consisting of either his own questions or questions selected from a readymade template the service company provides. This prepared interview is posted on the Interview On Demand website, and the employer invites candidates to log on to "take" the interview. The candidate answers the prepared questions while he or she is recorded via a webcam. The resulting video is available for the employer's hiring team to review over the Internet.

Whether you find yourself in a real-time gatekeeper interview or a recorded one, devote the same care and consideration to the occasion as you would to a live, in-person interview. You are performing. You will be seen and heard. In the gatekeeper situation, keep your answers concise and to the point. Don't give the interviewer more than she has asked for, and don't give her less. Remember, your main job at this stage is not to get hired, but to avoid being screened out. By keeping your responses relatively brief and tailoring them precisely to the questions asked, you reduce the risk of saying something that might get you screened out.

Don't Call Us ... _____

Don't confuse an online interview, whether in real time or recorded, with submitting a video resumé. Some job candidates put their resumés on CD or DVD or post them online. Whatever the electronic format, this is essentially a recorded verbal version of a resumé. You should not attempt to deliver such a presentation in an online interview anymore than you would pull out your printed resumé and read it to interviewers at an in-person interview. The online interview is an unscripted, interactive video performance, not a recitation.

Getting Technical

Online interviewing requires special equipment and a fast Internet connection. As little as five years ago, the technical requirements for videoconferencing would have left many candidates—and a fair number of employers—in the dust. Today, the computer equipment and connectivity that most of us either own or have ready access to are quite adequate for online interviewing.

Equip Yourself

For videoconferencing, you will need a computer capable of running Windows XP or Vista or Mac OS X. All these operating systems include software capable of basic videoconferencing, but you may also need additional videoconferencing software, such as Skype or an alternative. (There is a wide variety of free or inexpensive videoconferencing software available online for download.) The employer may make things much easier by setting up the conference through a dedicated website or through a third-party online interviewing service. In these cases, you will be required to do no more than sign on to a website.

Clincher _____

If you don't own the proper software, hardware, or high-speed Internet connection—and you cannot afford to get these in time for the online interview—use a friend or relative's equipment.

In addition to an up-to-date computer, you will need a webcam and a microphone. You don't have to spend a small fortune on either of these. The class of webcams and microphones sold through the large office supply stores (such as Office Depot, Office Max, and Staples) or through their websites are just fine. A webcam priced between $30 and $80 should be more than adequate, and a microphone in the $25 to $35 range will also serve you well.

The key to trouble-free videoconferencing is a reliable and fast high-speed Internet connection, via cable, DSL, or satellite Internet service. The minimum requirement is a 128kB connection, but the faster the better.

Lights, Camera, Sound!

Set up your lighting, webcam, and microphone well in advance of the interview. Thoroughly familiarize yourself with the hardware and be sure to test everything.

Lighting should be diffuse rather than harsh or glaring. It should not cast strong shadows. The amount of light should be adequate to illuminate your face fully. You do not want to come across as a literally shadowy figure. As in an in-person interview, it is especially important that the interviewers see your eyes; therefore, make eye contact via the webcam, ensure that there is enough light to make your eyes highly visible but not so much that you have to squint.

Set up the webcam to frame you from the chest up when you are positioned to make comfortable eye contact with the camera. If you fail to make eye contact, you may end up showing the interviewer mostly the top of your head. Be sure you frame yourself effectively.

Test your microphone before your interview. Both the Windows and Mac operating systems allow you to access a sound module through which you can adjust the volume of your microphone. Make sure you can be heard.

Consult the owner's manual that came with your microphone for advice on where to position it. If you do not have a manual, try 12 to 18 inches for a self-standing mike. If you are using a headset instead of a self-standing microphone, the microphone portion of the headset should be about 1½ inches from your lips.

> **Clincher**
>
> Most third-party online interview providers (such as Interview On Demand) furnish a means by which candidates can test their equipment and connection before going online to take an interview. Always take advantage of any test opportunity offered.

Set the Scene

When you accept an invitation to a live, in-person interview, you have no control over—and bear no responsibility for—the setting in which the interview takes place. It may be in the offices of the employer, a conference room, or even a hotel suite.

Whatever the setting, it is the interviewer who calls the shots. In an online interview, the setting is all yours. It is your responsibility to provide a quiet, orderly, businesslike environment from which your end of the interview will take place.

Plan ahead. Usually, you will be seated at your computer, at home, at the house of a friend or relative, or perhaps in a college dorm or an apartment shared with any number of roommates. Whatever the setting, arrange with those you live with to steer clear of you for the span of time in which the interview is scheduled. If possible, others should be in another room, preferably on another floor. The optimum set-up? Everyone evacuates the building and leaves you alone.

Don't Call Us ...

It is almost always a very bad idea to conduct an online interview from your current employer's place of business, using the company's computer and network. In the first place, even if you have a very private office, it may be difficult or impossible to control interruptions—including interruptions from your boss or from (possibly jealous, backstabbing) colleagues. In the second place, all communications conducted using your employer's computer, network, and phone lines are the property of the employer. He can listen in, and he can record everything. Your job and your privacy—as well as that of the people and firm interviewing you—are at grave risk.

Clear all distractions from the interview area. You want all attention focused on you. For this reason, try to set up a solid background—at the very least a background that conveys a businesslike attitude. Eliminate clutter.

There is visual "noise," and there is *noise* noise—literal noise. Both types of noise can thoroughly sabotage an online interview. Therefore, in addition to providing a mostly neutral, neat, and clean visual setting, eliminate potential sonic distractions.

As I mentioned, ensure that friends, family, and roommates are at a safe distance away—the farther the better. The same goes for children and pets. Turn off your telephone, including your cell phone and pager. If you cannot disable the telephone ringer, unplug the phone for the duration of the interview. Just be sure that you do not unplug your Internet connection from your computer. Check for other sources of noise: alarm clocks, e-mail alerts, computer calendar alerts, open windows, buzzers, the television in the next room, and so on.

It is true that you will be seated throughout most of the interview, and if you have planned and positioned everything properly, only your head and upper torso will be in the webcam frame. Indeed, you should try to keep yourself in that framed area throughout the entire interview. Yet it is possible that you will have occasion to stand up or stand back, showing more of yourself. For this reason, wear a complete outfit—not just the upper half of one. If you don a suit jacket, dress shirt, and tie, don't throw on a pair of tattered jeans (let alone nothing but your boxers) below. If you stand up, the interviewer(s) will see you in full-length.

Snafus and How to Survive Them

Asked to inventory the horrors they fear most, a majority of people put "public speaking" at the head of the list, *followed* by "death" in the number-two spot. Unfortunately, most people would put "interviewing for a job" in the same class as public speaking—that is, just above death.

While it is true that many of us find online interviewing somewhat less intimidating than interviewing in the flesh, the online interview is still an anxiety-provoking experience, and anxiety produces a number of physical effects, including dry mouth.

To avoid discomfort or the onset of a coughing fit—the proverbial "frog in the throat"—keep a glass of water nearby. It should be positioned outside of the webcam frame, but within easy reach.

Dry mouth, throat clearing, and coughing are the most common interview snafus, whether you are in person or online; the online situation, however, also introduces the possibility of what television broadcasters like to call "technical difficulties." Computers go down, Internet providers experience outages, nervous people press the wrong key, people trip over wires, liquids get spilled on keyboards. Sometimes, the Internet just gets so busy that slowdowns take place, which may interfere with real-time or even recorded audio-video transmission. As the saying goes (more or less): *stuff happens.*

Your best defense against technical glitches is to be prepared for them by thoroughly familiarizing yourself with your computer equipment and peripherals—DSL or cable modem, router, webcam, and microphone. Know how they work and how they can fail and, even more important, what steps you can take if there is a failure.

You should have a backup phone number to enable you to reach the interviewer in case equipment or connections suddenly go south. If the interviewer has not supplied you with a backup number, you should begin the interview by saying, "I can see and hear you just fine, but do you want to give me a phone number—just in case?" When you get the number, say, "Thanks. My number here is 555-555-5555." Then get on with the show.

If you do experience a glitch, and it is on your end, endeavor to fix it. "Sorry. I need to turn up the volume on my speakers. There. That's better."

Whatever happens, display calm efficiency. Don't panic. Don't swear. Never confess your ignorance of technology. Doing so will not elicit sympathy. It will merely suggest that you are helpless, deficient in resourcefulness, and generally incompetent. At worst, it will give the interviewer(s) a reason to eliminate you, to screen you out.

Do your best to fix the problem—if it is on your end—or to suggest a solution the interviewer might try, if the difficulty is on his end. Make it your business to know as much about online communications as possible. Remember, whatever specific skills and qualifications an employer is looking for, what every employer always wants is a person who solves problems. A technical glitch is a problem. If you can solve it, it becomes a wonderful opportunity.

Nice Save!

If a technical difficulty proves insurmountable, ask the interviewer what he wants you to do—provided, of course, you can still communicate. Follow his lead. If he does not know what to do, make a suggestion: "What if we both log off completely, and I attempt to reestablish the connection? If this fails, I will call you on the 555 number you gave me." Even if your solution fails, at least you have offered one. That alone speaks eloquently of your attitude, your competence, and your approach to difficulties and frustrations. If necessary, be sure that you agree on a new date and time to try the interview again.

Being There While Being Here

Let's face facts. A remote interview, even if the digital gods shine upon it and all the audio-video elements work flawlessly, is no substitute for real life. A face-to-face, in-the-flesh interview not only shows more of you and allows for fuller interaction than an interview mediated by distance, digits, and pixels, it also represents a greater investment in you on the part of the potential employer. By inviting you into her house, as it were, and, if any great distance is involved, paying for your transportation and accommodations, she has already put money on you. Once a person puts money on something, the natural tendency is to protect and promote that investment.

So that's the real news—and the disappointing news—about online interviewing. Generally speaking, it comes in a distant second to an interview "in real life."

Put Yourself Across

"Generally speaking." Fortunately, we don't have to speak generally.

These days, much of our business is conducted remotely, often over the telephone and, increasingly, via videoconference. For all its shortcomings, the online interview has one big advantage over the live interview. It allows the candidate to demonstrate how she performs in a realistic business scenario: not live and in person, but from a distance, over wires and cables. It allows the interviewer to audition the candidate in a real-world situation.

This said, the art of communicating remotely is the art of putting yourself across *as if* you were right there, in the same room.

Doubtless, your mother and father spent a lot of time telling you, begging you, ordering you to *stop watching TV!* Forget what your parents told you. Start watching TV now. Look at the way professional newscasters and others present themselves. TV personalities are sometimes called "talking heads," but the fact is that those who appear on TV for a living move heaven and earth to ensure that they never come across as a mere "talking head." They need to present themselves as vivid, flesh-and-blood people. Their object is to come across as guests in their viewers' living rooms.

How do they achieve this effect? It starts by learning how to treat the camera as if it were a person. Watch the professional carefully. He looks at the camera, and he talks at the camera, but you feel that he is looking at you and talking to you. There is no stiffness in his body language. It is calmly animated. If his hands are visible, he uses his hands to express himself.

Is all of this hard to learn? Not really. Just pretend—convince yourself—that the webcam into which you are looking is a person, not a hunk of electronics-stuffed plastic. Convince yourself of this and behave accordingly. To create the illusion that you are in the same room as the interviewer, behave as if the interviewer is in the same room as you are.

And don't be a talking head. Use your hands to help convey your meaning. When you are not using them this way, make sure that they are out of sight or folded on your desk. Do not play with a pen or pencil. Do not twiddle your thumbs. Do not wring your hands or crack your knuckles. Raise your living presence a notch by smiling as much as possible.

Clincher _____

Just as you need to appear lively and animated when you speak, make sure you don't go stiff and dead when you are listening. Watch that webcam as well as the image of the interviewer on your monitor screen. Allow your facial expressions to reflect what the interviewer is saying. Smile. Show that you understand. When you agree with something that is being said, nod your agreement.

Dramatize the Data

If your interview involves presenting data—numbers, charts, and the like—be prepared with the appropriate exhibits. In some digital conferencing scenarios, you may have access to a so-called whiteboard, which allows you to transmit images and documents and even underline, circle, and otherwise draw on them. If such capability has been arranged _by the employer_, great. Make use of it.

But even if your online interview consists of nothing more than your presence transmitted via webcam and microphone, you can still dramatize your data with appropriate props.

Prepare any necessary charts or tables in a form sufficiently large and legible to be easily captured by the webcam and transmitted. Rehearse this. Look at your monitor. Can you read your own charts? If not, neither can an interviewer.

You can just hold up a chart next to your face and simply use your finger to point to the significant data as you discuss it. As with any other exhibit you may present in a flesh-and-blood interview, it is important that you retain control of the prop—that you don't simply offer the exhibit to view, but that you physically point out whatever you wish to emphasize and accompany your visual presentation with a running verbal explanation.

Practice Electronic Etiquette

Now keep watching TV.

Tune to any national newscast and watch when the anchorperson talks to a reporter halfway around the globe. We've grown accustomed to the electronic miracle of seeing and hearing conversations between a person based in a New York City studio and a reporter standing in a Baghdad street. We've also become used to the slight delay between the question the anchorperson asks and the response from the remote reporter. It takes some time for signals to pass from satellite to satellite, from relay point to relay point, and then through any number of microprocessors along the way. The TV professionals take the delay into account and are careful to avoid stepping on one another's lines.

Videoconferencing in an online interview scenario often introduces delays similar to those we see professional TV personalities cope with. Take a lesson from the pros. Provide extra time to accommodate the delays. This means …

- Ask questions clearly and concisely. Then wait for the response before chiming back in.

- When answering a question, don't be in a hurry to jump right in. Be certain that the interviewer has the whole question out and has stopped speaking before you begin your answer.

- Avoid interrupting the interviewer. In a live interview situation, this is impolite, which is bad enough. In an online interview, interruptions can become highly confusing and distracting, badly damaging comprehension on both sides.

- Be sure to *show* that you are listening. Let your facial expressions mirror the interviewer's remarks. Exhibit enthusiasm. When you agree with a point the interview makes, nod. Such visual cues serve to reassure the interviewer that she is coming across clearly to you.

- If something an interviewer says is garbled or unclear, do not pretend that you understood. Ask the interviewer to repeat himself: "I'm sorry. That last question did not come through clearly. Can you repeat it, please?"

- If you are asked to repeat an answer, do so—and do so cheerfully, without betraying the least sign of anxiety, impatience, or irritation. You are there, after all, to solve problems.

Getting to Real Life

The process of getting happily employed can seem overwhelming. Veteran job seekers—and, remember, you can expect to change jobs on average seven times during your working life—learn to make the process more manageable by breaking the whole thing down into separate objectives rather than starting out by going for the ultimate goal: getting the job. Thus, making a cold call has as its objective a request for a resumé—not the offer of a job. Similarly, the objective in submitting a resumé is not to get a job, but to get an interview, even if it is only a first-stage gatekeeper interview.

The object of a gatekeeper interview? To avoid being screened out.

So what is the object of an online interview? In part—especially if it is a first-stage, gatekeeper interview (and most online interviews are just that)—your objective is the same as it is in any gatekeeper interview. You want to avoid being dumped. But the online interview has another, more positive objective as well: to get a real-life interview.

Your objective, in the online interview, is to put yourself across so vividly that the interviewer wants to see you *in real life*. He's beheld you in two dimensions via your resumé. Next, via a videoconference, he's seen something like two and a half of your dimensions. Put yourself across effectively online, and he'll be hungry to see that final half a dimension. To get you live and in person in his office, the prospective employer must make an investment in you, and that means he has already gone a long way from "I'm interested" to "I gotta have you."

The Least You Need to Know

◆ Online interviewing is becoming increasingly common, as employers seek simultaneously to reduce interviewing costs while also extending their reach beyond the local talent pool.

◆ Most online interviews are gatekeeper, or screening, interviews rather than selection or final interviews; therefore, the best interview strategy is one that avoids getting screened out.

◆ Many firms use third-party online interview providers to set up prerecorded interactive interviews rather than real-time videoconferences. To come across most effectively, treat the "canned" interview as you would a live interview.

◆ Plan ahead for online interviews. Make sure you have the right equipment and an adequate high-speed Internet connection and that you are prepared to put yourself across on-camera and over the Net as if you were appearing "live and in person."

Chapter 7

Reception Room Savvy

In This Chapter

- The importance of punctuality
- What to do if the employer is late to the interview
- Conducting "reception room research"
- The receptionist as ally and resource
- Coping with nerves

It is *the* longest elevator ride. Up, up, up, with many painful stops before you reach your floor. "Killing Me Softly" (ca. 1971) hums irritatingly from an unseen loudspeaker somewhere in the elevator. At last, the doors glide open. The reception desk peeks out from behind a huddle of limp potted plants. A corporate logo stands in relief against the wall behind the receptionist. You announce yourself to her, then take a seat on a chrome-frame chair upholstered in a nubby material that is even more irritating than the elevator music.

You wait.

You're not looking forward to this.

You're still waiting.

There *must* be something to do with this 10-minute span besides keeping tabs on the butterflies in your stomach. This chapter offers some ideas.

"Punctual": That Means On Time

Interviews go sour for any number of reasons. You can bet that there's *one* thing even the vaguest and most vacant employer wants: his or her employees to show up on time. Either you're there on time or you're not. Chapter 4 stressed the importance of knowing where to go, how to get there, and how long it will take. Move Heaven and Earth to arrive on time.

Clincher

> *Use* this time. If there's some company literature in the reception area, read it (see "Reception Room Research" later in the chapter). If you have any work-related reading material stuffed in your attaché, review that. As a last resort, peruse other reading matter available in the reception area, but pick up something related to your field: if you're in business, go for the *Fortune* instead of that two-year-old *People*.

Is Early Bad?

Aim to arrive 10 minutes before your scheduled interview time. If you get there earlier, use your extra time to scope out the reception area resources. We'll look at this in a later section called "Reception Room Research."

When the Employer Is Late

"I'm here. Where is *she?"* you say to yourself, smoldering, then stewing, then finally steaming.

What should you do when the employer is late?

First, be certain your appointment knows you've arrived. If a receptionist is present, check in. If there is no receptionist, wait until precisely the appointed minute, and then knock on the office door. If the receptionist is away from his or her post, wait no more than a minute past the appointed time. If a door is available for the knocking, knock. If a phone is within easy reach, dial your party's extension. If you don't know it, dial "0." Never go behind the receptionist's desk to use the phone. Use it only if it's clearly meant to be available to visitors. Don't use your cell phone—yet.

Of course, "late" is a relative term. For you, it means a minute past the agreed-on hour. For the employer, it's a matter of opinion—and yours doesn't count for much.

Here's what I would do:

◆ At seven minutes past the scheduled hour, ask the receptionist (if there is one) if she's had any word from Mr. Smith: "My appointment was scheduled for 10. Have you had any word from Mr. Smith?" This will confirm that the receptionist has, indeed, announced you. It might also move the receptionist to buzz Mr. Smith with a reminder. If the answer is "No. No word. He'll call you when he's ready," say thanks and return to your seat.

◆ At 10 minutes past the scheduled time, and assuming there is no receptionist and no door to knock on, use your cell phone to call your contact.

◆ At 17 minutes past the mark, *ask* the receptionist to check in with your appointment: "He's really pretty late. Would you mind checking in with him?" If there is no receptionist or waiting-room telephone, try your cell phone again.

◆ If a half hour goes by without the employer having materialized, take out a sheet of paper from your attaché—or ask the receptionist for one—and write a polite note: "Dear Mr. Smith: It's 10:35, and I assume that you've been unexpectedly and unavoidably detained. Perhaps we'd better reschedule our meeting. My cell phone number is 555-5555. I'll check in with you later this afternoon." Sign the note, fold it in half, inscribe it clearly with Mr. Smith's name, and hand it to the receptionist. In a polite voice that betrays absolutely no trace of irritation, ask him or her, "Please be certain that Mr. Smith gets this note. We'll have to reschedule our appointment. Thanks very much."

Keep this situation in perspective. Forgive, forget, and get on with the interview. That said, you may want to keep this incident in the back of your mind as *you* decide whether to accept an offer from a boss who thinks nothing of keeping you waiting.

Clincher

Don't assume that the receptionist, the low person on the corporate totem pole, couldn't possibly have any company wisdom to impart. He or she sees everyone who comes and goes and, in many offices, handles most of the phone traffic. Make use of this asset by treating him or her with utmost courtesy.

The Receptionist: A Friend Indeed

Want a friend on the inside? Make an ally of the receptionist. This is not difficult. Receptionists, alas, are accustomed to being treated like waiting-room furniture. Your approach should be different. Try this:

You: Good morning! Sarah Livingston to see Mr. Thomas.

Receptionist: Please have a seat. I'll tell him you're here.

You: Thanks. And your name is …?

Receptionist (pauses a beat, slightly surprised by the question): Jane Reynolds.

You: Hi, Jane. I'm interviewing with Mr. Thomas. How's he doing this morning?

Receptionist: Oh … he's okay. You know, always rushed. Pressured.

You: Oh. Anything unusual?

Receptionist: Well, I know they're all uptight about the big sales meeting. Happens every year. Always a crunch … Look, I'd better tell him you're here.

You: Thanks, Jane. Nice to meet you.

Receptionist: Well, good luck!

A brief exchange like this may accomplish three things:

1. It encourages the first gatekeeper to help you. This help might be nothing more than a pleasant voice announcing you to Mr. Thomas. A polite "Ms. Sarah Livingston is here for your meeting" will put Mr. Thomas in a more receptive frame of mind than a barked, "Your 10 o'clock is here." Moreover, if Mr. Thomas doesn't answer when buzzed, a friendly receptionist may help track him down.

2. You might obtain a sliver of inside information, at least something that could help you adjust the pitch of your presentation to Mr. Thomas's mood. Even more important is a tidbit that makes you look *really* on the ball: "Mr. Thomas, I'm so pleased that you set up this meeting— especially when you're so busy with your sales meetings. I know what *that's* like." What a great way to begin an interview!

Don't Call Us …

Avoid anything that looks or sounds flirtatious, patronizing, or condescending. You are a professional, and the receptionist is a professional. Speak and act accordingly.

3. If the receptionist knows who you are, he or she is that much more likely to expedite your subsequent follow-up calls: "Hi, Jane. This is Sarah Livingston. Could you put me through to Mr. Thomas?"

Reception Room Research

Isn't it great when things work out in the organized and orderly way I've described it in this book? You decide to send a cover letter and resumé to Acme Widgets, so you do your research online or at the library (see Chapter 2 for suggestions), and when you're called for an interview, you're 100 percent prepared—fully versed in the who, what, and where of Acme Widgets.

Things *can* work out this way. And then again, what if this happens: it's 9:30 on Wednesday morning, and a company you just sent a shot-in-the-dark cold letter to calls you for an interview. They want you there at 11:30. Today.

Without time to prepare, do you:

A. Wing it and hope for the best?

B. Say you have another appointment and try to reschedule?

C. Just say no?

Out of these three, B is probably your most productive choice. But what if the employer replies that he's in a hurry? "We need somebody right away. I've got a lot of candidates waiting in line, and I just don't know if I can squeeze you in any later." Or what if this is just too great an opportunity to risk putting off?

Then skip A through C and proceed directly to Plan D: tell the employer that you'll reschedule your other appointment and that you'll be there at 11:30 sharp. Get any necessary directions, and be certain to ask if the office has a reception area (because you'll have to use it for quick research): "Is there a reception area I'll be going to?" Thank the employer, then hang up and use whatever spare moments are left to do some

Don't Call Us ...

Be careful about how you deploy your research knowledge, whether it's based on long-term study or reception-area cramming. Don't just trot out the facts; doing so may make you sound overly rehearsed and insincere or may quickly get you in over your head. Work the information into the conversation as naturally and as seamlessly as possible.

super-fast online research. If the company has a website, start there. If not, use your favorite search engine to get whatever information you can on the company and its industry.

Now—if the employer has answered that you will be reporting to a reception area—rush like mad to get to the office at least 20 minutes before the appointed time. A half hour is even better, particularly if your online search has yielded little or nothing. Survey the lobby or waiting area for such company literature as …

- ◆ Annual reports
- ◆ Monthly newsletters
- ◆ Product catalogs
- ◆ Product/service brochures or leaflets

If you don't see anything on the end tables and brochure racks, ask the receptionist, "Do you have any brochures that give a capsule description of Acme Widgets? Anything I could read while I'm waiting?" And while you're talking to him or her, be sure to say that you are very early for the appointment. You don't have to explain why you're so early, but do ask not to be announced just yet: "Please don't announce me yet. I don't want to interrupt Mr. Thomas."

Now use your time to sit down and read. Fill in any gaps left by your kamikaze online search. Look for precious hooks to hang the upcoming conversation on:

- ◆ **Major products or services.** Scan the literature for these. What are the firm's "flagship" products or services? What makes them special?

- ◆ **Big events.** Newsletters may mention recent sales conferences, conventions, and the like. What products, services, or issues were key in these events?

- ◆ **Hot trends.** Look to the literature for identification and discussion of hot-button topics.

- ◆ **Pressing problems.** The literature may cite industry problems, regulatory difficulties, and the like.

Butterflies Are Free

Just about every how-to-interview book you'll come across admits that fear and nervousness are part of the picture, but, usually, the upshot of the discussion is, in effect, *you'll just have to live with the feelings:* "Everybody feels nervous. You're not alone."

True enough, but not much help when your heart is pounding, your mouth is as dry as old cotton, and you feel like you're going to puke.

Let's not gloss over the sensations of fear. You probably remember reading about the "fight-or-flight" response in a high school health or biology class—how, faced with a threat to survival, the organism gears up for combat or escape: the heartbeat accelerates, the digestive system shuts down, the muscles tense up, the senses become more narrowly focused. Now as a civilized human being living in the twenty-first century, you can tell yourself that you aren't really facing a life-and-death situation: no saber-toothed tiger is about to storm your cave.

And you'd be right. But will this knowledge calm you down? Probably not. Although it's true that you're not fighting for your life, you *are* fighting for your livelihood. Face it: a lot *does* ride on a job interview. Whatever any particular interview might mean to you—a step up the career ladder, a raise in pay, or the ability to make next month's rent—it's always about getting something you need or something you want (not to mention something your family needs or wants as well). No wonder you're scared.

But don't just *tolerate* or *live with* the fear. Do what champion athletes, great musicians, top-flight race-car drivers, and star actors do. *Use* your fear. Feel it, harness it to energize you, to sharpen your mind, reflexes, senses, and sensibilities.

How do you do this? Follow the example of the pros in any field. Prepare as fully as you can. They make it their business to learn how to take the hurdles, how to hit C above high C with the clarity of crystal, how to speed through to the groove at Indianapolis, how to find the heart and soul of Prince Hamlet. Do the same in your field.

Afraid Because We Run

The great American philosopher and psychologist William James declared that we do not run because we are afraid, but that we are afraid because we run. Likewise, much of the fear you feel in an interview situation comes not from actually being scared, but from your interpretation of your physical reaction to the interview. Sound confusing? Well, when the anxiety and stress of the interview (just like the stress of running) kick in, your heart beats faster, your muscles tense up, and—voilà!—you feel fear (or at least you think you do). And as a result, your heart beats faster still, your muscles grow even more tense, and butterflies beget yet more butterflies.

Nice Save!

Unfortunately, whether due to anxiety or some other cause, you may feel too ill to perform effectively at the interview. If at all possible, call in and reschedule the interview. If the employer is seriously interested in you, he will comply. But, in any case, it's usually better to risk losing this particular interview at this particular time than it is to create a bad impression that may remain with this employer permanently, barring you from ever getting hired by him.

If you become ill just before or during the interview, excuse yourself and go to the restroom. If you cannot compose yourself, return to the interviewer and explain that you have been fighting the flu (or some other common ailment), that you thought it would go away, but that you feel too ill to continue the interview: "I don't want to expose you to the risk of catching my flu. I would greatly appreciate it if we could reschedule, so that I can be at my best."

Heroics will not be appreciated at an interview. No employer wants to have a meeting with a ghostly apparition who is obviously suffering. Nor does an interviewer wish to be closeted with someone who is sneezing and hacking. Your most effective move is to bid for a new interview date.

Getting a Handle on Nerves

Here are six little exercises to help you ease your nerves just *before* an interview:

1. The first piece advice most people give about calming yourself down is to take "deep breaths." Actually, this is counterproductive. Instead, try taking in a shallow breath and then *exhaling* deeply, letting out more than you took in. Repeat a few times. This tends to reduce or prevent panic.

2. Grab the sides of the seat of your chair and pull up while silently counting to five. Repeat as often as you like.

3. Put your hands together at right angles to one another, the thumbs gently interlocking. Now press your palms together as tightly as you can. Repeat as necessary.

4. Close your eyes and concentrate on relaxing each muscle in your body. Start with your toes and work your way up, moving on to the next set of muscles only after the previous set is relaxed. Focus on your back last. Relax it. Lay your head back and relax your neck muscles.

5. Once you are physically relaxed, visualize a peaceful natural scene: a waterfall, waves lapping at a beach, tall pines waving against a blue sky.

6. Take the focus off yourself. Think about your "audience"—the interviewer—and how you will help him by sharing your knowledge and offering him a chance to hire you—which would, in turn, greatly improve his department or his company.

Faking It with Body Language

These exercises work. Try them. But if it is true that we are afraid because we run, by far the wisest thing to do is to stop running. In the next chapter, we'll explore the subject of body language. For now, be aware of the kinds of body language that signal fear:

- Leg swinging, foot tapping, or "piston leg"—poising your foot on your toes and pumping your leg up and down
- Hair twirling
- Hand wringing or other nervous hand movements
- Lip licking
- Finger or nail biting
- Touching the mouth or nose

Concentrate on eliminating such body language, not only because it sends negative signals to the interviewer, but because your own awareness of such movements—even on a less than fully conscious level—stokes the fires of your fear: "I'm pumping my leg and twirling my hair. I must be terrified!"

"But," you say, "I *feel* fear, and it's not just because my foot is tapping. If I weren't scared, I wouldn't tap!"

Chicken and egg time. Nervous body language is the product of fear even as it produces fear. Maybe knowing about this vicious cycle will help, maybe not. So what do you do?

Fake it. An interview is a performance. It's the theater. Act. Perform.

The Least You Need to Know

◆ Move Heaven and Earth to ensure that you are on time. If the employer is late, do not yield to anger; it won't help you when he finally does show up.

◆ Use waiting time effectively to practice subtle relaxation exercises, to do last-minute "reception room research," or both.

◆ Don't overlook the receptionist. Engage him or her as an ally. Be careful, however, not to patronize or flirt.

◆ Recognize that nervousness is part of interviewing. Try to harness your nervous energy. Don't let the physical symptoms of anxiety make the anxiety itself worse.

ary

3

17809769

s guide to the perfect

e Dance?

iges:
your entrance
ndshake
waiting
the interview by taking the lead

ie   eveloping, and maintaining rapport

interview about two (or more) people *talking?*

t, practically considered, an interview is about *com-*
mmunicating begins before a single word is spoken.
arch have shown that, in any act of communication,
message is conveyed nonverbally. Maybe even more.
an audience has formally and deliberately assembled
udy after study, audience members are shown to
...ongly to the speaker's facial expressions, posture, and hand
gestures than to her words.

7/26/18

This chapter shows you how to think of the interview as a dance—a meeting of would-be partners who move and maneuver about one another, communicating in a language of words and nonwords. It suggests strategies for avoiding bruised toes and making the experience seem effortless.

I'm Here!

"He (or she) really knows how to make an entrance!"

How many times have you heard this or something like it? Doubtless often enough so that it's become a cliché, and you don't think much about what it means. Well, think about it, because how you enter a room makes a powerful statement about who you are and who you think you are. Difficult—or unnatural—as it may seem to make a positive "first impression," it's a lot easier to do than to try to undo a faulty first impression. In fact, you may well not have the opportunity even to try.

Walk Tall

Just as deeper voices tend to convey greater authority than high-pitched voices, tall folks tend to command greater authority than short people. This isn't fair, and it's awfully superficial, but it's the way things are. Now, of course, this doesn't mean that short people with high voices can't become top-flight executives and high-flying political figures (behold Michael Bloomberg at five-foot-six), but, *on first impression*, height makes an unmistakable impact.

Does this mean you should wear lifts in your shoes?

Not necessarily. However, women of short or medium stature might consider wearing higher heels, and short men can do likewise, but neither women nor men should go overboard in this direction. By far the more effective way to add height is to walk tall. Don't enter cringing, stooped, or slouching. Concentrate on maintaining an erect posture as you enter the room forthrightly and without hesitation. The message you want to deliver is nonverbal, but it *can* be put into words: *I know how to carry myself.*

Don't Call Us ...

While a grim visage or an outright scowl is the worst interview look, avoid going to the extreme of a forced, plastic smile. Try to think of something pleasant—a quiet natural scene, perhaps, or a strain of your favorite music—and walk into the interview with *that* smile. Easy does it.

Smile When You Say That

Walking tall doesn't mean coming on like John Wayne, tight-lipped and impassive. Walk in smiling. The greetings that begin the meeting should also be delivered with a smile.

Eyeball 'Em

As soon as you walk into the room, target the principal interviewer and look him or her in the eyes. This communicates instant energy. You've probably heard people talk about the "sparkle" in someone's eye. Actually, we *all* have a sparkle in our eyes; it's just rarely noticed because most people don't make full eye contact when they meet or speak. *You*, too, have the sparkle. Exploit it. Come across as a live wire from the very beginning.

Put Your Heart in a Handshake

In the old days (at least as I remember them) fathers spent time with their sons (not their daughters, back then) explaining the vital importance of a good, solid handshake. "Son, this is important!"

Quaint, you say?

We like to think of ourselves as "civilized" and "sophisticated," which translates into "intellectual" and "verbal." But physical touch and physical warmth continue to make a powerful *human* impression, and I'll bet that most of us remember the handshake of some individual we have met—because it was exceptionally warm and powerful, or perhaps, colder and deader than any cold, dead fish. Either way, it made a memorable impression.

 Don't Call Us ...

Gentlemen, avoid shaking hands extra gently with women. Use the same *moderately* firm grip you deliver to another man. In a business context, an excessively soft handshake is likely to be perceived as patronizing or chauvinistic.

There is no mystery about delivering a hearty handshake:

1. Try to go in with dry palms. It's a good idea to carry a handkerchief with you and use it to wipe your hands before you enter the interview room.

2. Deliver a full, *moderately* tight grip.

3. Hold the other person's hand a few fractions of a second longer than you are naturally inclined to do.

4. While holding the other person's hand, look him or her in the eyes.

5. Start talking before you let go: "It's great to meet you" or "Glad to be here."

Please Wait to Be Seated

Avoid the embarrassing slapstick of an impromptu game of musical chairs by restraining yourself from rushing to find a seat after you enter the room.

Wait. Smile.

Not only is it more polite to be the last one seated, but it also gives you a few seconds to be looked up to—literally. Standing in a room in which the others are seated gives you an air of authority, however temporary.

When you do sit, try to avoid sofas or overly soft chairs. You want a chair that keeps you upright and that allows you to maintain erect posture. You don't want to be seen sinking or slumping or getting swallowed up in an overstuffed piece of furniture.

Let Your Partner Lead (If He Can)

The interview is a performance, and while the entrance is an important part of the show, the play's opening speech should not be yours. Let the interviewer(s) speak first.

And *listen*. That's not as easy—or, at least, as passive a matter as it sounds. In fact, effective listening is a *skilled activity* that is complex enough to warrant its own chapter, which comes right after this one.

Enduring the Silence

But what happens if the interview *remains* nonverbal? After all, there is no guarantee that the interviewer will be a self-starter—or will even be prepared. Many an interview has begun with a "How are you today?" only to peter out instantly into silence. A few minutes of silence will seem to you an eternity, and you will have difficulty resisting the impulse to fill the silence—with anything and everything that floats into your mind. Before you rush in, try to determine whether the interviewer's silence is a form of evaluation or a plea for help. If the interviewer looks down, aside, or slightly away from you, or if she seems to be looking over some papers (your resumé, perhaps), endure the silence. Here's how:

◆ Don't get nervous. You might become self-conscious, and start feeling that the interviewer is zeroing in on some flaw in your appearance or demeanor. Banish these thoughts. Your self-consciousness will start you fidgeting, adjusting clothing, clearing your throat, and generally *looking* nervous, perhaps even scared.

◆ Try to keep your eyes focused on the interviewer. Don't glare, but do look on with a calm, yet anticipatory gaze.

◆ Maintain your calm by silently counting the seconds that elapse during the silence: one elephant, two elephant, three elephant …

> **Clincher**
>
> Always frame your leading questions in a gentle, helpful tone of voice. The last thing you want is to convey the impression that you are trying to put the *interviewer* on the spot.

Filling the Silence

It is time to fill the silence when you see that the interviewer is asking for your help. Does the interviewer seem shy? Is *he* looking at you with anticipation—looking *at* you, not down, not aside, not at papers on his desk; eyes wide open, eyebrows arched, lips slightly parted (not tightly shut), as if he is about to speak or, more precisely, to respond to something you say. These are signals of expectation. It is time to take the lead.

Taking the Lead

Offer help—take the lead—by focusing on the interviewer's needs rather than on your own. This is *not* the time to start trotting out your credentials and qualifications, but to ask *leading* questions. You'll find a lot of excellent interview questions to ask in Part 3, but, for now, just be prepared to ask a variation on the salesperson's familiar opening gambit: "How may I help you?"

Actually, most salespeople make the mistake of approaching a silent customer with "May I help you?" Starting out instead with "*How* may I help you?" is more effective because it subtly compels the customer to focus his response, to tell the salesperson more or less precisely *how* she can help. Try asking the silent but expectant interviewer, "How would you like to see me fit into your organization?" Or: "How would you like me to function to increase sales (or cut downtime, or reduce costs, or accelerate response time, or whatever else you believe speaks most directly to the interviewer's needs)?" Then build on the interviewer's response.

Rapport Builders

Rapport is a relationship of mutual trust or emotional affinity. Typically, rapport develops over a long association between friends, between spouses, between business partners, between teachers and students. But, in the course of an interview, you don't have much time to develop rapport, though it's crucially important that you do.

The Magic Words: "We," "Us," and "Our"

Perhaps the fastest way of creating rapport is to *will* it into being through a few magic words. You *need* magic, because rapport is nothing less than a magical transformation of an *I* and a *you* into a *we*.

How do you do this? What are the magic words? They are *we, us,* and *our* instead of *I, me,* and *you.*

Here's how the magic works:

> **You:** What do you see as your greatest need in the such-and-such area?
>
> **Interviewer:** Definitely fulfillment—getting the orders out on time.
>
> **You:** I understand. Working together, *we* could solve that problem. I accomplished X, Y, and Z at Acme Widget, and I believe *we* could apply some of those solutions here.

Talk in Terms of the Team

Over the past two decades, the management model most businesses follow has "flattened." That is, traditional rigid management and supervisory hierarchies have increasingly yielded to structures in which personnel at all levels are expected to take greater initiative, exercise more authority and autonomy, and play roles of heightened creativity. Typically, this new orientation has entailed an emphasis on teams and teamwork. Some team structures are more or less permanent, whereas others are strictly ad hoc, with teams created as needed for particular projects.

You cannot go far wrong in any interview by revealing yourself as an able and willing team player. "Team player" does not mean being a yes-person, someone who relinquishes initiative and ambition to the group. No employer wants a staff of one-dimensional followers. No business can survive on "groupthink." As legendary World War II general George S. Patton Jr. was fond of telling his officers and men, "If everyone thinks alike, no one is thinking."

Being a team player means taking the initiative when it is appropriate to do so, but also yielding the initiative to other team members when doing so will advance a particular project or the enterprise as a whole. Team players are collaborative in attitude and orientation. They exhibit creativity, but they also possess a willingness and ability to promote the creativity of others.

Demonstrate awareness of teamwork and collaborative values. Come to the interview prepared to cite examples of your teamsmanship. Make liberal use of the words "team," "cooperative," "collaborative," and "cooperation." Speak both of "leading" teams and "working in a team setting."

More Words and Phrases to Use

We, us, and *our* are words of inclusion, cooperation, coordination, and alliance—the very essence of rapport. Other words that contribute to these values and feelings are …

brainstorm	offer
collaborate	open mind
collaborative	synergy
confer	team
cooperate	team player
cooperative	team up
good listener	together
huddle	work together

Try to use these words early in the interview. You can develop rapport further by choosing additional phrases from these five categories:

1. **Phrases that convey urgent energy:**

   "We could address that immediately …"

   "That is something I'd get right on …"

"It could be accomplished in [time frame] …"

"Don't worry. Together, we can handle this …"

"I can see how important this is to you …"

2. **Phrases to convey understanding:**

"I appreciate your position …"

"I understand the situation we will be in …"

"Let me make certain that I understand you …"

"We understand one another …"

"We speak the same language …"

3. **Phrases that promote a calm, controlled atmosphere:**

"Let's talk this over so that we …"

"Perhaps we could agree …"

"It was my impression that …"

4. **Phrases to head off confrontation:**

"Let me explain my thinking …

"We could look into alternatives …"

"I believe we could come to an understanding …"

"We should be able to agree …"

5. **Phrases for self-defense:**

"Here is the way I saw it …"

"It was a mistake, but, under the circumstances …"

"It was my feeling at the time …"

"I wish I had had the benefit of my present hindsight …"

"Here is how I thought it should be done …"

"Let me explain my reasons …"

Rapport Busters

Magic? Well, if rapport is magic, it's also a spell that's all too easily broken. Rapport requires concentration on the part of the interviewer and the interviewee, and that's not always possible. The fact is that you may be far more interested in the interview than the interviewer is. Even though he knows he needs to hire someone, the interviewer may well consider interviewing a burdensome chore and, what is more, an unwelcome interruption of the "real business" of his day. As a result, he may get distracted. Your task is to keep him on track by constantly and continually appealing to his self-interest.

Interruptions and Distractions

An interview punctuated by phone calls and by people sticking their heads in the door with this or that request can be infuriating, frustrating, demoralizing, and even heart-breaking. Or you can use this formidable rapport buster to your advantage.

Let's say you're saddled with a rude interviewer who takes calls every few minutes, maybe even *makes* a call or two, allows others to walk in to deliver or pick up papers, and so on. Your blood begins to boil. You feel like saying to her: "Look, I don't need this. If I wanted to be treated rudely, I'd stand in line at the DMV. Good day to you, ma'am!"

But, of course, you say nothing of the kind. Instead, you offer rapport-creating sympathy: "Wow! You really *are* busy. It certainly looks like you need some help here."

Chances are, she'll put down that phone, *really* look at you for the first time, shake her head, and say, "I'm up to my eyeballs. Yes. I *do* need help. Let's see if I can get someone to take these calls for now...."

Self-Absorption

Consider the following statement: *The employment interview is all about you.* At first glance, the sentence appears to be a tautology, a statement of a self-evident fact. After all, what else would an interview be, except "all about you"?

It pays to think beyond the first glance.

From your point of view, the interview is very definitely all about you. You want, you crave, you *need* this job. So, obviously, you are the central issue here. Right?

Wrong.

Nice Save!

If you are interrupted and the interviewer is obviously distracted, the loss of contact with her may deflate you, de-energize you, or take the wind out of your sails. Loss of drive and focus is a serious interview crisis, but don't give up. You need to act decisively to recover. Keep the following in mind:

- Don't take the interviewer's distraction personally. She didn't plan to ignore you.
- Try to engage the interviewer within whatever is distracting her. If she's getting one call after another, empathize with the pressure she's under: "You really *are* busy around here, aren't you? It looks like you can use all the able help you can get."
- Give her the time and space she needs: "Please, go ahead and attend to that call. I've blocked out ample time for this meeting."
- Do not apologize. *You're* not intruding.
- Don't suggest rescheduling. It's best for you to ride out the distractions. If the interviewer suggests rescheduling, however, cooperate fully (taking care not to make any appointment that may conflict with your other commitments).

An interview is, at bottom, a sales scenario in which you happen to be both the merchandise and the salesperson. No one ever sold anybody anything by appealing to his own self-interest.

"Mister, you have to buy this car, because I need the commission to pay this month's rent." This pitch, entirely based on the salesperson's self-interest, is hardly likely to result in a sale. Any successful sales professional knows that, whatever your motives, you make a sale by appealing to the self-interest of your customer.

"My friend, this car gives you better mileage than anything else in its class, it has more standard features, and it is priced below the competition." This salesperson may be desperate for a commission. Perhaps he really needs this sale. Despite this, his pitch contains not one word about what *he* wants or needs. Instead, it is focused on what the *customer* wants and needs.

Nothing kills rapport in a sales scenario—including a job interview—more thoroughly than self-absorption. *The employment interview is all about the employer—your customer.*

Sore Spots

Dentists suffer from an unusually high rate of depression, even suicidal behavior. Maybe that's because it's awfully hard to create rapport when you are probing a person's mouth with a pointy instrument, trying to find the tooth that *really* hurts.

When an interviewer hits a sore spot, rapport can crumble. If something bewildering or unpleasant is thrown your way, respond with a calm "I'm not sure I understand what you mean by that" rather than something harsher. Or just let it pass.

If an interviewer attacks you at a weak point—a past failure, for example—do whatever you can to preserve rapport by turning the attack to your advantage. Chapters 10, 11, and 20 suggest strategies for doing just this. In general, when a failure or other sore spot is probed, don't panic, don't shy away, don't offer excuses. Instead, *explain* your failure and *describe what you learned* from it.

Words and Phrases to Avoid

Don't risk torpedoing rapport with ill-chosen words and phrases. Avoid the following:

1. **Language that is abrasive:**

   "You don't understand ..."

   "I'm right ..."

   "What exactly are you driving at ...?"

   "You're wrong ..."

   "You're mistaken ..."

   "What kind of suggestion is that ...?"

   "I resent ..."

2. **Language that dodges responsibility:**

   "It wasn't my fault ..."

   "That wasn't my responsibility ..."

   "I knew nothing about that ..."

   "It wasn't my business ..."

   "So-and-so should have done such-and-such ..."

3. **Pointless or superfluous language:**

   "Sort of ..."

   "More or less ..."

   "Kind of ..."

"I guess ..."

"If you know what I mean ..."

"What I'm really trying to say is ..."

"You know" (as in, "I was considered a team player, you know.")

"Right?" (as in, "You can't expect success that way, right?")

"You understand?" (as in, "That was the only way to accomplish the task, you understand?")

"Like" (as in, "I will do that, like, immediately.")

Body Language: Eloquence Without Words

We began with the body language of your entrance and first impression. Don't neglect this key aspect of your performance as the interview progresses.

Charge Up the Interview with "Relaxed Energy"

We've all heard the term "nervous energy." That is absolutely not what you want to convey in an interview: foot tapping, eyes darting, fingers drumming. Instead, you want to create an impression of relaxed energy, a combination of enthusiasm and confidence—what might be summed up in the word *poise*. The following will help you achieve the relaxed energy of poise.

Learn to Breathe

We all have breathing patterns that are natural and comfortable for us. When we become upset or nervous, breathing typically becomes shallower, shorter, and faster, and may be punctuated by sighing—deep intakes of breath. This is noticeable not only to you, but, most likely, to any astute interviewer. Fortunately, you can train yourself to breathe slowly and normally, even when you are nervous. It takes some thought, but it can be done, and doing so will benefit you in two ways: (1) It will keep your nervousness from being broadcast, and in turn, (2) It will also make you feel less nervous. Remember William James in Chapter 7: We are afraid *because* we run.

If you feel yourself getting panicky, try taking a *short* breath, then exhaling a *long* breath. Repeat this, deliberately, until you feel calmer. Concentrate on it.

Never Hand 'Em Your Head

For better or worse, your head and face "speak" body language with great eloquence. Here's the basic vocabulary:

◆ Tilting your head to one side indicates interest and close listening.

◆ Scratching your head indicates confusion or disbelief.

◆ Lip biting signals anxiety.

◆ A slightly out-thrust chin conveys confidence; a boldly out-thrust chin will probably be interpreted as arrogance.

◆ A lowered chin conveys defensiveness or insecurity.

◆ Sighing is interpreted as a sign of either distress or boredom.

◆ Narrowing your eyes communicates disagreement, resentment, anger, or disapproval. Marked narrowing may suggest puzzlement.

◆ Avoidance of eye contact conveys insincerity, fear, evasiveness, or, at the very least, lack of interest.

◆ A steady stare suggests at the very least an arrogant need to control; at worst, vacant staring just seems weird.

◆ Raising your eyebrows indicates surprise—or disbelief.

◆ Peering over the top of your glasses suggests doubt and disbelief.

 Clincher

Taking notes can be an interview asset, but always ask the interviewer's permission first (some find note-taking distracting). Don't become so absorbed in taking notes that you break off contact with the interviewer; *use* the notes as a means of organizing your thoughts and questions so that you can provide intelligent feedback to the interviewer.

Some Handy Advice

Next to the head and face, the hands are the most fluent conveyors of body language. You can use them consciously to help harness nervous energy into more positive calm energy. For example, you may want to take notes during the interview. You may also want to gesture with your hand to drive home various verbal points.

It is important, however, that you don't let your hands and arms get out of control, gesture too broadly, or fidget. Be aware of the following signs and signals:

◆ Open hands, palms up, suggest honesty and openness.

◆ Crossing your arms in front of your chest communicates defiance, defensiveness, resistance, aggressiveness, or a closed mind.

◆ Rubbing the back of your head or neck suggests frustration or impatience.

◆ Rubbing your eyes, ears, or the side of your nose indicates doubt.

◆ Hand wringing is a strong sign of anxiety.

◆ Rubbing your hands together communicates positive expectancy.

◆ Holding the fingers of the hand steeple-fashion conveys confidence.

As with head movements, head position, and facial expression, do not hold or repeat any single gesture for a significant length of time. Whatever subtleties of body language you aim to convey, your main object, before all else, is to look alive!

The Least You Need to Know

◆ A great deal of your message—at least 65 to 85 percent—is communicated nonverbally, through body language, and this communication begins with your entrance into the room.

◆ Avoid appearing overanxious: Don't scramble for your seat, and don't rush to fill awkward silences. Know when to endure silence and when to take the lead.

◆ Difficult as it may be, shift your attention from yourself to the interviewer. Focus on her needs, not yours.

◆ Building rapport—a feeling of trust and mutual interest—with the interviewer is vital; it is established through verbal and nonverbal means. Pay attention to the words you use as well as your body language.

Chapter 9

Listen Up!

In This Chapter

- ◆ Don't just perform—interact
- ◆ When to be silent and when to speak
- ◆ How to be an active listener
- ◆ Forging a bond of common interest with the interviewer
- ◆ Focusing the interview on key themes
- ◆ Interpreting the interviewer's body language

Thinking about the interview as a *performance* is mostly a good thing. It gives you a feeling of greater control. More important, it encourages you to prepare, to rehearse, to set specific goals concerning just what it is that you wish to communicate. Thinking this way, however, does have a serious shortcoming if it causes you to neglect the interactive aspect of interviewing, the give-and-take between you and the interviewer. The truth is that star performers on stage do not simply "broadcast" to their audiences, but learn to "read the house," to pick up on the signals the audience sends their way. They respond, in give-and-take fashion, to the needs of the audience. On stage at the interview, you need to develop a similar skill. It's called *listening*, and this chapter suggests techniques for persuading with your ears.

Persuade with Your Ears

An employment interview is a highly interesting situation. Although it's all too true that *you* are on the spot, your task is to keep your own focus not on yourself, but on the needs of those interviewing you. Even as you concentrate on presenting yourself, answering questions, asking questions, and reviewing your qualifications and accomplishments, you need to give each interviewer plenty of room to speak, to respond, to comment, to interact with you, and to let his needs be known.

> ### The Skinny
> The mere presence of a listener helps the speaker direct his or her communication toward a goal.

Interviewing is a lively art. If it required nothing more than a performance, in the strictest sense of the word, you could just e-mail a video of your spiel and rise or fall by that. But interviewing presupposes at least two living, breathing human beings exchanging thoughts, proposing and reacting, offering and taking.

Practice Lively Restraint

Every grade-school class has at least one superstudent, a little boy or girl who cannot resist raising a hand to answer each and every question or to comment whenever the teacher pauses for so much as a breath. Well, just wait till you find yourself on the interview hot seat. In your eagerness to keep the conversation going, to parade your knowledge before the inquisitors, to answer questions before their mouths have even closed, you will discover sudden kinship with the overanxious hand raiser back in the fourth grade.

Don't get me wrong. If you sit in an interview as dumb as a log, you won't get the job. But it's also a great mistake to launch into a stiff, overly rehearsed presentation. Even if what you spew out is mighty impressive, the interviewer will probably see you as inflexible—and then, you're dead in the water. To an employer, *inflexible* is synonymous with *bad fit*.

The little lad in grade four couldn't help himself. He was a child, after all, anxious to please the grownups. But you are an adult, and you should be able to control yourself—to adjust to a regular rhythm of giving and taking, of talking and listening.

This does not mean that you should bite your tongue and sit on your hands. Make a conscious effort to appear as if you are enjoying the conversation—that you are intensely interested in what the interviewer is saying to you. Keep your self-restraint lively. Smile. Nod when appropriate. React.

Make Yourself a Mirror

React.

Stand-up comics express failure in the most dire terms. If his routine fails to elicit the requisite yuks, the comic will moan over his after-show martini: "I *died* up there tonight. I just *died.*"

And so you know what it feels like to say something in the anticipation of a certain response, only to receive nothing but stone-faced silence. Know this, too: the interviewer will be disappointed, even pained and embarrassed, if you fail to react appropriately to what she says. Like you, the interviewer feels as if she is performing. She does not want to "die up there" any more than you do, and it is definitely not in your best interest to let her come away from your interview with *any* negative feelings. Don't *let* her die.

This does not mean that you must synthesize obviously phony responses to each and every thing the interviewer says, but it does require that you bear in mind this basic principle: *demonstrate that you are listening—really listening—by mirroring the speaker's message.*

If the speaker is excited about something, get excited, too. If he expresses delight, smile in return. If he raises an issue that is clearly of critical importance to him, focus your gaze, bring your hand thoughtfully to your chin—*show* that the subject is of critical importance to you, too. And remember, mirroring is as important in an online interview (via webcam) as it is in a person-to-person interview.

Clincher _____

Show, don't tell. It's more important to demonstrate that you hear and understand what the interviewer expresses to you than to tell him absolutely everything you believe he should know about you. Your object is to give the interviewer the feeling that you are *worth* talking to. Some people enjoy talking, period—dialogue, monologue, it's all the same to them. But most folks would rather engage in conversation with a person who enjoys and responds to their words.

Stoke the Fire and Stroke the Speaker

You need not limit your "mirroring" to nonverbal cues. Lively restraint does not mean keeping silent. Respond to important points in the interviewer's conversation with words and phrases that add fuel to the dialogue.

Words and phrases that keep the dialogue going include:

accurate	evaluate
additional	extraordinary
consider	fertile
correct	further
opportunity	positive
right	productive
"Can we discuss that further?"	"Can you explain that further?"
"I agree"	"Take into account …"
"I appreciate that"	"Tell me more"
"I hadn't thought about it that way"	"That's a concern of mine, too"
"I see"	"That's interesting"
"I understand"	"We should discuss …"
"It's an issue we face"	"Yes"
"Can we pursue that further?"	

Punctuate your listening with such language, but avoid bringing the conversation to a halt with such negative expressions as:

"Absolutely not"	"That's not the way I do it"
"Couldn't possibly"	"That's settled"
"No" or "No way"	"You're mistaken"
"That can't be done"	"You're wrong"

His Interest in You = Your Interest in Him

Does lively restraint and active listening require that you always agree with the interviewer and his point of view?

Of course it doesn't.

It's a bad mistake to check your opinions and ideas at the interviewer's door, but you should consider *suspending* them long enough to hear the interviewer out, to learn what interests him, what concerns him, what he needs, what he wants. Then, introduce your opinions and ideas, whenever possible, from a foundation of common interest. Here's how to do it.

You walk into an interview believing that Task A is important and that the best approach to Task A is through Method 1 and Method 2. The conversation turns to Task A, which, like you, the interviewer thinks is important, but he believes that the best approach is through Methods 2 and 3. Now you can choose not to express your opinion, and just agree with the interviewer; you can choose to disagree; or you can choose to agree as much as possible, and then, taking off from this common ground, explain how and where your opinions differ:

> **Interviewer:** Task A is crucial to our operation. The approach I favor is Method 2 and Method 3.
>
> **You:** I certainly agree with you that Task A is extremely important to achieving our goals. I also favor Method 2, but have you considered using Method 1 instead of Method 3?
>
> **Interviewer:** Why should I?
>
> **You:** Well, these are the benefits I've found …

Focus on the *Interviewer's* Needs, Not Your Own

Your goal is not to come across as a mindless "yes person," but always to express yourself in a way that exhibits your interest in the interviewer—*his* needs, *his* concerns— even when you are discussing your own point of view. To whatever degree possible, take your cues from the interviewer.

Be certain that the ideas and opinions you express are relevant to the needs and concerns the interviewer expresses. This begins with an understanding of who the interviewer is. Let's say you're a well-qualified accountant with experience in using management and accounting software. If you know that the interviewer is primarily concerned with management issues, don't show off your expertise in software. Focus on management. Demonstrate a good fit from the start.

Stalk the Main Thought

Do you remember how your high-school English teacher struggled to get you to focus the essays you wrote? "State your theme! Begin each paragraph with a topic sentence! And make sure your paragraphs support your theme."

Clincher _____

Please pay careful attention to "Tune In and Turn On" later in this chapter. People send nonverbal signals when they talk about something important to them. Learn to recognize these body language accents to help you "read" the interviewer's needs and priorities.

That was good advice. Starting with a clear, strong statement of theme keeps your writing focused and makes your essay far more persuasive. Nobody enjoys reading a pointless, meandering essay. It's frustrating and a waste of time.

Frustrating and a waste of time. That's _not_ how you want your interviewer to feel about her exchange with you. Take a hint, then, from your high-school English teacher. Just as you developed a theme for your essays, identify and develop a main thought (or several) in the interview.

Pounce and Develop

The dynamics of an ordinary conversation can be fascinating. You're riding the commuter train to work. The fellow seated next to you strikes up a conversation. To be polite—although you'd just as soon keep reading your paper—you respond. And so it goes for the next two or three stops. Then, suddenly, he says something that strikes a chord—that _interests_ you—and the entire conversation takes on direction and purpose. It has acquired a theme, a main thought. You're almost sorry when the train pulls into Grand Central.

It's even more exciting, of course, when interviews click like this. You can increase the chances of striking such sparks by consciously looking for a main thought to kindle and fuel the interview. Ideally, the main thought should come from the interviewer. It should be an idea, a concern, a need, or a problem he expresses and that you jump on:

Interviewer: Cash flow is always a _very_ big problem for us.

You: I understand completely. I contend with cash flow problems daily in my current position, and the issue really interests me. Exactly what kind of problems are you struggling with?

Don't count on this ideal situation coming to pass, however. You can't rely on your interviewer to say anything worth building a conversation on, anymore than you can count on your commuter-train buddy to come up with the kernel of a great conversation. Go to your interview armed with a few strong main thoughts on which to build a unified interview.

What You Can Afford to Forget

It's easy to feel overwhelmed when you're preparing for an interview. There is *so* much to remember!

Or is there?

Let's return to the subject of conversation. If you felt that you had to pack everything you know into every conversation you had, you would quickly be too swamped ever to utter a word. Well, an interview is a conversation—a *very* important conversation, to be sure, but a conversation nonetheless, and you are not responsible for packing your entire life experience into it.

But how do you decide just what you can afford to forget?

Prepare for the interview by formulating some main thoughts: the themes, ideas, and issues that you believe are absolutely necessary to orchestrate an interview with a point.

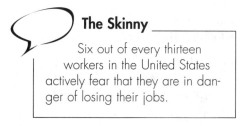

The Skinny

Six out of every thirteen workers in the United States actively fear that they are in danger of losing their jobs.

Secrets of Dynamic Listening

Here are two interviewing *don'ts:*

1. Don't turn the interview into a monologue resembling a rehearsed presentation.

2. Don't restrain yourself so much that you appear to be a passive listener, without ideas and opinions.

How do you avoid these two extremes? Practice *dynamic listening,* which is neither monologue nor passive reception and reaction. Dynamic listening is listening with your mind and imagination, not just with your ears. It is based on identifying the interests you have in common with the speaker and responding to the speaker's themes so that the conversation is energized by active give and take.

Find Your Motivation

So far, I've pleaded with you for almost superhuman selflessness: *focus on the* interviewer's *needs, not your own.* Although the interviewer does care about his needs above all else, your focusing on his needs and interests does *not* require you to abandon your own. On the contrary, in many respects, your self-interest will most likely coincide with the interviewer's. If this weren't the case, your resumé or cold call or query letter probably wouldn't even have produced an interview.

Assume you've got something in common, and use this assumption to explore the interviewer's self-interest.

Connect with Your Own Interests

Let's go back to that remark about cash flow, which you pounced on as the kernel of a main thought:

> **Interviewer:** Cash flow is always a *very* big problem for us.

I'll bet that cash flow is a problem for you, too. Think about it. What does a cash flow problem *feel* like? Connect with the urgency of this issue. You have strong feelings about it. The interviewer has strong feelings about it. Strong feelings are the basis of not just a conversation, but a relationship. Connect with those feelings and let them drive your remarks. I'm *not* saying that you should complain to the interviewer about how you're always broke! All I'm saying is that you should harness your personal feelings and passion to energize your business-focused remarks:

> **You:** I agree. Cash flow is an urgent issue and one that I am eager to tackle. We need to formulate creative strategies for turning receivables into cash, and we need to be relentless about it.

Tune In and Turn On

In the preceding chapter, we considered issues of body language—*your* body language. But nonverbal communication works both ways, and knowing how to pick up on and respond to the interviewer's nonverbal cues is a valuable listening skill.

Body Language Works Both Ways

The very signals that you may or may not nonverbally broadcast *to* the interviewer are the same ones to watch for *from* the interviewer:

- If the interviewer tilts her head to one side, you can assume that she is listening intently to what you are saying and is interested. This is a *buy signal* and suggests that you should continue in the current vein.

- Head scratching indicates confusion or disbelief. Don't panic. Instead, pause and ask a question: "Am I making myself clear enough here?" Or: "I'm not sure I'm making myself clear. Let me put it another way …"

def•i•ni•tion

A **buy signal** is a term salespeople will be familiar with. It is a verbal or nonverbal cue that suggests your "prospect" is responding positively to what you are saying—or selling.

- Lip biting is an indication of anxiety. This may suggest that an issue you've brought up has touched a nerve. It may also signal concern about something that has come up in the conversation. If you are aware that an area is sensitive, you will have to exercise judgment as to whether to move on quickly to another topic or express your understanding of the sensitive nature of the issue: "I realize that this is an area that causes anxiety, but I think it's an important issue to explore."

- Look out for an interviewer who rubs the back of his head or neck. This gesture signals frustration and impatience. Probably the best thing to do is move on to another topic as gracefully as possible: "But, of course, that's not nearly as important as XYZ." Alternatively, you can pause and ask the interviewer where *he* wants to go: "If you like, I can share more about my qualifications as XYZ, or we can move on to ABC."

- An interviewer who lowers his chin markedly is broadcasting feelings of defensiveness. It is possible that something you've said has been interpreted as a criticism. Make a soothing remark: "Of course, I recognize that each department has its own management style. I am prepared to be flexible."

- When an interviewer nods up and down, take it as a buy signal. Keep the conversation going in the current direction.

◆ If something you say elicits a head shake from side to side, be aware that what you have said is being rejected. This is an obvious enough signal for you to respond to directly. "I take it that you don't agree with me on this point. What part of my position gives you trouble?" A question like this will keep the conversation from grinding to a halt, and it will also demonstrate your acute powers of perception.

◆ Interpret a narrowing of the eyes as you would a side-to-side head shake. Again, it is possible to respond directly: "I sense that we're not in agreement on this point. Can you tell me what disturbs you about what I've said?"

◆ A severe narrowing of the eyes suggests puzzlement rather than disagreement. Pause. Then offer: "I'd like to be very clear on this point. Let me put what I've said another way."

◆ Raised eyebrows indicate surprise—or out-and-out disbelief. Meet this head on: "I know this is hard to believe, but …." An interviewer who peers over the top of her glasses is also signaling doubt and disbelief.

◆ Avoidance of eye contact can be difficult to interpret. If eye contact has been tenuous or nonexistent from the start of the interview, the interviewer is probably shy and uncomfortable. The best response is for you to be friendly and to take the lead. However, if eye contact drops off noticeably during the interview, you are losing the interviewer's interest. Take quick action: "I can say more about ABC, but perhaps I should move on to XYZ. Shall I?"

◆ An interviewer who stares intently at you is probably trying to be intimidating, to see how you'll react to pressure. Do your best to ignore this tactic.

Watch Him Breathe

It may sound crazy, but you can actually learn something by observing the interviewer's breathing pattern. Look for signs of breathlessness—the shallow, rapid breathing patterns typical of anxiety. Respond with reassurance: "Of course, that's a problem we can solve." Look for the caught breath, a sudden intake of air that indicates the interviewer's eagerness to say something. Pause—and let him speak.

The most serious breathing signal to watch for is the sigh. This suggests frustration or boredom. It is a signal that you should move on to another topic.

You Have More Time Than the Speaker—Use It

All good conversation has a rhythm to it, and a successful interview, as good conversation, is no exception. If good conversation is about give and take, then someone is always giving while the other is taking. Right? One great advantage to being the taker, or listener, rather than the speaker is that you can be thinking—faster than the other person is speaking. The listener always has more time than the speaker. Use that time to prepare thoughtful responses and thoughtful questions—questions that will lead the interview into new territory.

Ending It Without Ending It

In general, you should constantly try to fuel the conversation and keep it going, but, as the old saw goes, all good things must come to an end. So, be aware of the verbal and nonverbal signs that the meeting is coming to a close. These include …

- Phrases beginning with "Well, it's been …" Or: "I want to thank you …" Or: "Is there anything else you'd like me to know about …"

- The interviewer rising from his chair.

- The interviewer eyeing the door.

- The interviewer looking at his watch.

Of course, the interviewer may simply tell you outright that "We've come to the end of our time," or something like that.

Whatever the signal, now is the time to ask those "Questions That Close the Sale," described in Chapter 14. Do not seek to prolong the interview beyond this. A big part of making a successful impression is knowing *when* the impression has been made. As old-time sales folk are fond of saying, "Once you've made the sale, it's time to shut your mouth."

The Least You Need to Know

- Come to the interview well prepared, but don't rehearse to the point that you deliver a formal presentation. The interview is, in part, a performance, but it is also a live, interactive exchange.

- Practice dynamic listening so that you can identify the interviewer's concerns and issues as well as the concerns and issues you have in common.

◆ Be attentive to the nonverbal as well as the verbal cues the interviewer gives. Read his body language and respond accordingly.

◆ Be sensitive to the signs that signal the end of the interview. Prepare to stop selling and start closing the sale.

Chapter 10

How to Answer the Questions Everybody Asks

In This Chapter

◆ How to speak the language of business

◆ Keeping answers upbeat and positive

◆ The three major kinds of questions interviewers always ask

◆ Translating experience into skills

◆ Why (and how) to evade the salary issue

Picture, if you will, the store shelf or online catalog from which you picked this book. Undoubtedly, you'll remember a host of books on interviewing, and, of those, a sizable number promising you the "best answers," the "surefire answers," or just "*the* answers" to the most frequently asked interview questions.

But are you really going to pore over hundreds of questions and answers, commit them to memory, then spout them at the interview?

No. The best plan of attack is to use the questions and answers that follow neither as holy writ nor as a cheat sheet, but as a starting point to inspire and provoke your own thoughts.

First, Speak the Language of Business

Do you want to know how to make yourself heard in the world of business? Here's the answer in a single sentence: *Speak the language of business.*

Regardless of where the particular business is located or what the particular business does, business speaks in but a single tongue: the language of money. To the degree that you can, frame all your answers to interview questions in terms of money: money you'll make for the prospective employer, money you'll save him, money you have made for other employers, money you've saved them, and so on.

The Answers You Should Always Give

Of course, it is not possible to quantify each and every answer, but it is possible to quantify more of them than you might think, and even those that don't lend themselves to direct dollars-and-cents answers usually allow *indirect* money responses:

> **Interviewer:** How many projects can you take on at one time?
>
> **You:** Of course, that depends on the nature and scope of the projects, but, in general, I'm a great believer in parallel processing and efficiently getting more than one thing accomplished at a time.

You could stop here, but you should not.

> … I'm a great believer in parallel processing and efficiently getting more than one thing accomplished at a time. This has a significant positive impact on the bottom line.

That's translating the answer into the language of business—money—at least indirectly. If you have some figures at your command, you're in even better shape. Continue:

> … This has a significant positive impact on the bottom line. In my current position, I'd estimate that parallel processing cuts turnaround times by at least 30 percent, and time, of course, is money.

You haven't given a literal dollars-and-cents response, but you've provided the context in which the interviewer can draw his own conclusions.

> **The Skinny**
>
> Never overlook small businesses in your job search. Eighty percent of all private businesses employ 50 people or fewer. It is this 80 percent that generates two thirds of all new jobs.

Beyond speaking the language of business—answering directly or indirectly in terms of dollars and cents—keep your answers upbeat. This does not mean spouting empty boasts or painting inanely rosy pictures, but, rather, always casting your responses in the best possible light.

> **Interviewer:** Cash flow is critical with us, but we're plagued by slow-paying customers. What has your experience been with this problem?

Here's one response:

> **You:** I hear you! It's a really tough problem for us, too. Well, what can you do? That's the way things are.

And it's a bad one. Instead, empathize. It's also helpful to be honest about facing problems, but it's fatal in an interview to *leave* the conversation at that. In your answers, never run away from a problem or difficult issue, but embrace it as an opportunity:

> **You:** I hear you! It's a really tough problem for us, too. But I look at it not only as a problem, but as an opportunity to actually build closer relationships with customers. My approach to slow payment is to find ways to help that customer pay. You see, my assumption is that he really does want to pay, and so far as cash-flow management goes, I see my job as working with the customer to help him do what he really wants to do. Ideally, I'd like to make the collection process part and parcel of satisfying the customer.

The Answers You Should Never Give

It's a fact of life: there are more wrong answers to any particular question than right ones. Obviously, listing a bunch of wrong answers is an instructional approach doomed to futility, so I won't do that. But here are more general guidelines about what to *avoid* in answering questions:

◆ **Avoid one-word or one-sentence answers.** Indeed, avoid any answers that end conversation. Effective salespeople know that the best way to pitch their goods is to ask the prospect questions, a tactic that keeps the conversation going and the prospect engaged. The more time the prospect

 Clincher

The interviewer will judge your answers to her questions, but what she'll remember on an emotional level is the conversation as a whole. Was it stimulating? Did it have energy? Was it consistently interesting?

invests in considering the proposition, the greater the chance of making the sale. Take your cue from the effective salesperson, and give answers that spark rather than conclude conversation.

◆ **Avoid negative answers.** In the misguided belief that admitting errors and discussing shortcomings is a demonstration of admirable self-critical honesty, many job candidates actually dwell on problems and disasters. If you cannot cast a problem into a positive, productive light, avoid discussing it altogether.

◆ **Avoid transparently glib answers.** Answers like "Sure, I can do that. No problem!" never ring true. Make your responses as positive as basic honesty will allow.

◆ **Avoid answers that criticize your present employer, colleagues, or supervisor.** Some interviewers may actually bait you into such responses. Don't take the bait.

◆ **Avoid wrong answers.** Does this seem self-evident? What I mean is, don't fake it. We all know people who have an opinion on everything and never hesitate to give an answer, even if it is the wrong answer. If you are asked a question that calls for a factual response—"What is the capital of Ethiopia?"—and you don't know the answer, don't make one up. Look the interviewer in the eye and respond, "I don't know the answer to that one."

Questions of Ability and Suitability

Most interview questions, however, are not factual. They are usually qualitative probes, efforts to gauge your "fit" with the job in three areas:

1. Ability and suitability

2. Employability

3. Affordability

Of these, the first is usually of greatest concern to the potential employer.

Sell Achievement, Not Experience

The most common opening question is also the worst possible question anyone can ask you.

What can you tell me about yourself?

The danger of a question this broad is that it is overwhelming, instantly burying your consciousness in a vast white blank. Yet it is one question you can almost count on getting asked, so you'd better be prepared for it. Answer in two parts. The first is a simple five-item list:

1. "My name is _____."

2. "I've worked for x years as a [job title]."

3. "Currently, I'm a [job title] at [company]."

4. "Before that, I was [job title] at [company]."

5. "I love the challenge of my work, especially the major strengths I offer, which include [A, B, and C]."

With this out of the way, swing into the second part, which is a question *you* ask: "But what would you like to know about me that would be most relevant to you and to what your company needs?" This will help focus the obviously unfocused (that is, typical) interviewer and should keep the conversation from grinding to a halt.

Clincher _____

Emphasize your portable (transferable) skills—the skills that you carry with you rather than the skills affixed to a certain job.

You can also count on being asked questions that attempt to zero in on your experience and qualifications:

◆ "Give me an idea of your experience."

◆ "List a few of your most important qualifications."

◆ "What are your strong points?"

◆ "So what, exactly, do you do at [current company]?"

◆ "What makes you think you're qualified for this job?"

All of these questions and others like them can be answered in a similar way. Translate them from the passive terms of mere experience—how you passed time the last few years—into the dynamic terms of achievement. That is, frame your answers not in terms of what functions you have performed, but what you have achieved. This suggests to the prospective employer what you will *achieve* for him. Don't evade the stated question, but translate it in order to get at the more important underlying question, which has to do with your achievements.

My management of A, B, and C for XYZ Company not only brought in X dollars last quarter, but has allowed me to develop skills in D, E, F, and G. These are what I bring to the table.

To frame this as a response to "So what, exactly, do you do at [current company]?" for example, begin by stating your current job title, then continue with "My management of A, B, and C ...."

Offer Mastery

Your answers to questions concerning experience or qualifications should cover at least two dimensions—achievement, which we've just discussed, and mastery. Achievement is the supporting evidence needed to build a case for your mastery of the knowledge and skills necessary to do the job the employer wants you to do. The response we just discussed emphasizes achievement to back up a claim to mastery: "My management of A, B, and C for XYZ Company not only brought in x dollars last quarter ...." The revenue generated is the achievement that demonstrates mastery.

Mastery should not be defined in personal terms—"My sales record gave me a deep sense of satisfaction"—but in terms of benefit to the employer. To the extent that it is possible to do so, express this in dollars and cents:

As a manager for XYZ Company, I developed innovations in A, B, and C, which the company has adopted organization-wide. We estimate that the innovations I introduced save the company x percent in costs for fulfilling each order.

Thus far, we have emphasized translating vague questions into specific responses that highlight your achievements and mastery. It's possible, however, that the interviewer will be more specific. Be prepared for this—and be thankful for it. After all, a good question makes it that much easier to give a good answer, an answer that exhibits you at your best:

What have been your three most significant accomplishments in your current position?

Make certain that you walk into the interview armed with specifics. This question is a strong cue to prompt you to offer your interview kit (see Chapter 4) and launch into a major discussion of achievements:

I've brought some material with me that speaks directly to that. I've had many opportunities at XYZ Company, but I think my most enduring contributions to the company have been ...

Play it by ear. If the interviewer is buying what you are selling, don't limit yourself to the arbitrary three-achievement limit she has set. Ask permission to continue: "Would you like me to go on?"

Make Your Way Through the Minefield

The flip side of questions about your experience, qualifications, skills, and achievements are questions about the experience you don't have, about what you don't know, what you've failed to achieve, what mistakes you've made, and what your weak points are. Don't evade these, but don't let them dominate the meeting, either. Use them as springboards to demonstrate your strength of character and your resourcefulness.

Most interviewers are naturally polite. They will not come out and ask you to describe your "five weakest points," but they will probably say something like "Are there any areas in which you feel you could use improvement?" Or: "Is there any aspect of the field you wish you had more experience in?" Be careful that such disarming questions don't press your insecurity button, unleashing a stream of self-doubt: "You know, now that you mention it, I've never really understood how such-and-such works. The procedure is just something I usually guess at and hope for the best. So far, so good." Face the question, but frame it in as many positives as possible:

> I've developed considerable proficiency with Y and have reduced typical turn-around time by x percent, but I've also reached the conclusion that, if I had more experience in Z, I could cut the time even closer to the bone. I am working on this now.

Notice that this response begins with a positive (proficiency) and ends with a positive (self-improvement), thereby framing the negative element and putting into a subordinate perspective. Nevertheless, it is possible that an interviewer will seize on whatever negative you offer: "So you're telling me that you're weak in Z?" Don't deny it, but don't agree, either. Keep framing your response in positives:

> No, what I'm saying is that I've brought Y to new levels of efficiency for our firm, but I've come to believe that we could go even farther. In order to do that, I'm aware that I've got to learn more about the complexities of Z. It's an area of growth I've defined for myself.

Clincher _____

In answering why-did-you-leave or why-do-you-want-to-leave questions, it's extremely important that you convey straightforward, open honesty with your body language. Maintain eye contact throughout your response. Avoid bringing your hands any where near your face or neck. Don't fidget. You're under suspicion until you deliver a good, positive reason for changing jobs.

Questions of Employability

I've written enough to have come to a few conclusions about what publishers want and don't want. Actually, I believe I can express what they want in a single sentence: *they want to publish something entirely new that's worked well before.*

Employers are a lot like book publishers. They, too, want "new blood"—fresh ideas, fresh perspectives, fresh ambition—provided the "fresh" candidate can prove that she's worked well in the past. Employers want some assurance that they are buying a pack of solutions, not a peck of problems. This can lead you into a nasty Catch-22 situation:

1. You are available for hire. (Yippee!)

2. This means you either left or intend to leave your present job. (Uh-oh.)

3. If you were happy with your current employer (or, more to the point, if he were happy with you), you wouldn't be talking to me. (A-ha!)

So the interviewer is at best wary, at worst suspicious. He will ask questions that are variations on "Why did you leave (or why do you want to leave) your present job?"

I Want to Grow

The classic response to the why-did-you-leave question is some version of "I want to grow." This is not a bad response, as far as it goes. To be sure, it is better than *any* negative reason, such as …

◆ "My boss is a jerk."

◆ "My supervisor is uncreative. I just can't stand it."

◆ "I'm bored stiff."

◆ "I don't make enough money to put food on the table."

"I want to grow" is okay, as far as it goes. But it doesn't go far enough.

Here's what to do to make the answer go farther. Instead of allowing the interviewer's question to focus your response on why you want to leave or have left an employer, refocus your response on why you want to *move* to the prospective employer.

Let's say your current job bores you and has limited potential for growth. You could answer, honestly enough, "I just don't get enough challenges at ABC Company," but try instead to shift from the old company, which the prospective employer doesn't really care about, to the prospective employer's firm: "I am eager to take on more challenges, and that is what I believe I will find with your firm. I want an opportunity to apply my skills where I can really make a difference in the future of the company." Not only does this answer transform a gripe into a positive motive, it adds the dimension of what's-in-it-for-the-employer.

"Laid Off, You Say?"

If a voluntary move from one job to another is eyed with suspicion, how high will a *layoff* raise the interviewer's eyebrows?

Strictly speaking, getting laid off is not your fault; it is the loss of a job because of circumstances beyond your control. Nevertheless, some prospective employers will feel that, had you been sufficiently valuable to your former employer, the company wouldn't have dumped you. Fault or no fault, you've got some cumbersome baggage to deal with.

def•i•ni•tion

A **layoff** is the termination of an employee for reasons unrelated to his or her performance or behavior. Layoffs are usually the result of economic reversals, or mergers (in which certain departments or individuals become "superfluous").

Make certain that the circumstances "beyond your control" you cite as the cause of your layoff really were beyond your control. It's okay to say that you were laid off because sales dropped dramatically at your firm—as long as you weren't in the sales department.

Don't be the one to raise the issue; however, if it comes up, be certain to have an answer ready that takes the heat off of you:

◆ "As you may know, we merged with XYZ Company, and a 30 percent staff cut was ordered across the board. Unfortunately, my position duplicated one at XYZ, held by a fellow with seniority over me. So, I became one of the 30 percent to go."

◆ "Sales were off by 25 percent at ABC Corporation and management tightened its belt. I became one of the 150 out of 600 staffers who were laid off."

The Stickiest Wicket: You Got Fired

Make no mistake, this is a hard one. Getting laid off may not be your fault, but—at least as far as your former employer was concerned—getting fired is.

As with getting laid off, don't volunteer the information that you were fired. Keep your resumé noncommittal, and if the interviewer asks you why you left your last job, you might explain that your approach differed from management's, and then go on to detail the positive aspects of "your approach." This may satisfy the interviewer, and it is one way to put your involuntary termination in a positive perspective.

There is also another way. People make mistakes, and, if it is clear that the mistake you made has resulted in learning and growth, employers are often willing to forgive and forget, provided that you explain events clearly and forthrightly and put them in the best possible light: "Mr. Smith, I have to say that my termination was my fault. I had personal problems at the time, which are now completely resolved. But at the time, I was frequently late. My supervisor—with whom I am still very much on cordial terms—was under orders to reduce the workforce in any case, and, quite honestly, my attendance record at the time gave him the reason he needed to let me go."

Don't wallow in remorse, and, if possible, conclude by putting your firing in a mitigating context. Try to find out how many others were fired, laid off, or even left voluntarily during the period in which you were dismissed. Close your answer with, "I'm 1 of 34 people who have left so far this year."

Nice Save!

This may be painful for you, but give it some thought. Contact the employer who fired you. Ask him what he intends to say about you now. "Mr. Harris, I'm in the process of looking for a new job, and I'd like to see how I stand with you. If you are asked as part of a pre- or post-employment reference check, how would you describe the circumstances of my leaving the company? Would you say that I was fired? Would you say that I was laid off? Would you say that I resigned? My problem is that, every time I tell a prospective employer about my termination, I blow another shot at a paycheck." This may persuade your former employer to use less pejorative terminology in describing your departure from his company. If he is willing to cooperate, you may be able to skirt the entire issue of having been fired.

Questions of Affordability

None of the potential employer's questions mean much of anything if he concludes that he can't afford to hire you. A cardinal rule of salary negotiation is that the first person to mention an actual figure is thereby thrust into the weaker position. So nerve-wracking as it may be, your objective in the interview is to avoid being the first to bring up a figure.

"How Much Are You Looking For?"

When asked how much "you're looking for," you are confronted with a dilemma. Giving a figure that's too high may take you out of the running. And if you pin yourself down to a bargain-basement figure and then get hired, you'll kick yourself each and every day you come to work.

First and foremost, never go into an interview without having researched the levels of compensation common in your field, particular position, and industry. Chapter 13 tells you how to scope out the salary situation before you walk into a negotiation.

So prepared as you are with research on prevailing, reasonable, and desirable salaries, avoid being the first party in the interview to state a figure. Try instead to prompt the other party to volunteer a number. Answer the salary question by itemizing the skills, talents, abilities, and responsibilities the target position entails: "If I understand the full scope of the position, my responsibilities would include so-and-so and such-and-such. Given this, what figure did you have in mind for a person with my qualifications in a key position like this one?"

Another useful reply to a question about compensation goes something like this: "I expect a salary appropriate to my qualifications and demonstrated abilities. What figure did you have in mind?" Or: "What salary range has been authorized for this position?"

If the interviewer presses—"Come, now. Don't try to evade the question"—propose as broad and as vague a salary range as possible, based on the topmost end of what your research reveals: "I'm looking for a starting salary in the upper thirties."

"How Much Are You Making Now?"

This question is even more difficult than the previous one to sidestep, reshape, or otherwise productively expand upon. You cannot avoid answering it, but you can frame your response so that it doesn't cage you in: "I'm earning $35,000, but I'm not certain that helps you evaluate what I'm worth, since the two jobs differ significantly in their responsibilities." Unless you are happy with your present salary, fashion a reply that provides the information requested, but that divorces your salary expectations from your current salary level. The interviewer is looking for a ceiling-setting precedent. Don't give him one.

On the surface, this is a factual question. You know what your salary is, after all. But don't be too hasty about responding. Be certain that the figure you furnish is the absolute maximum you can honestly report. Take into consideration all perks and benefits, including insurance, profit-sharing, bonuses, commissions, stock options, vacation, and so on.

Why not just make up a figure when you're asked about your salary? You know, *lie*. Well, aside from the fact that it's wrong to lie, you might also get caught. The target employer probably won't take positive steps to verify your salary, but she might make it a condition of employment to see your last payroll stub or your W2. What if this request comes *after* you've given notice to your current employer? You can't afford to get caught in a lie like this.

The Least You Need to Know

◆ Try to translate your interview answers into the "language of business": dollars and cents and things that either produce or save dollars and cents.

◆ Don't evade questions that probe negative issues, but always frame the answer in the most positive terms possible.

◆ Keep all your answers positive and upbeat.

◆ Find ways to answer questions about experience in terms of your achievements and mastery; shift the focus from what you have done to what you are capable of doing.

... And the Questions Almost Nobody Asks (But Just Might Ask *You*)

In This Chapter

- Answering problem-solving questions
- Answering behavior-centered questions
- Answering unrelated or unexpected questions
- Handling illegal, inappropriate, or offensive questions

If you stop reading right now, you'll come away from this book in danger of under-estimating what an interviewer can throw at you. Yes, it's true, an overwhelming majority of interviewers are poorly prepared and desperately in need of your guidance, but let's not overlook the significant minority who actually give serious thought to the interview process. Although these interviewers ask the tough questions, you're probably better off dealing with one of them than with any of those unfocused types who haven't devoted enough time or energy to sorting out what they want and need.

A challenging interview is an opportunity to excel, and this chapter gives you some suggestions for doing just that.

Problems, Problems, Problems

The previous chapter dealt mainly with informational questions, emphasizing the presentation of qualifications and skills, but you may also encounter hypothetical questions, questions that paint a quick problem scenario and ask, "What would you do?"

Expecting the Unexpected

You cannot know in advance exactly which *problem-solving questions* you will be asked—or even if you will be asked such questions—so you should try to prepare yourself for any possible circumstance. Take the following three initial steps:

def•i•ni•tion

A **problem-solving question** poses a hypothetical scenario or sets a hypothetical task and asks the candidate to formulate solutions and procedures.

1. Decide whether it is likely that you *will* be asked problem-solving questions. If the job calls for creativity, for thinking on your feet, for resourcefulness, in short, for problem solving, expect that you will be put to the test.

2. Once you decide that problem-solving questions are likely, review what you know about the prospective employer in order to anticipate probable areas of questioning.

Let's pause a moment before going on to point number 3. It isn't as difficult as it may at first seem to guess what kinds of problem-solving questions you're likely to encounter. For example, if you are interviewing for a position primarily in sales, expect to be asked to *sell* something:

Interviewer: Do you like my fountain pen?

You: Yes …

Interviewer: Good. Sell me this pen.

If you are interviewing for a supervisory or management position, expect to be asked some hard-hitting personnel questions:

Interviewer: I am your administrative assistant. I consistently fail to complete assignments on time. Fire me.

Clincher _____

Popular Internet search engines such as Google, Yahoo!, and the omnibus search engine Dogpile allow you to search specifically for news. Prepare for the interview by using this feature to look for recent news articles on your target company or your target industry. You may well turn up topics and issues of current concern to the target employer.

Management candidates may also be asked very direct problem-solving questions:

> **Interviewer:** We have an ongoing problem with _____. Solve it.

Any interviewer may ask this one:

> **Interviewer:** If you were sitting in my seat, and I were in yours, what would you ask me?

So stretch your mind muscle *before* the interview and think of some likely problem-solving questions. Then proceed to step 3:

3. Formulate a strategy for dealing with problem-solving questions.

Strategies for Answering Problem-Solving Questions

The strategy for answering informational questions is simple: do everything you can to give the right answer. With problem-solving questions, however, you must shift your strategy from the end (a "right" answer) to the means (how you come up with the answer). Problem-solving questions are less about answers than they are about processes, methods, approaches, and attitudes. Accordingly, you should do all you can to impress the interviewer with your problem-solving ability.

You first need to listen carefully to what is being asked. Having done this, you are not completely on your own. Be certain next to *ask* questions in order to define and clarify what the interviewer is looking for.

Clincher _____

In posing a problem-solving question, the interviewer is not looking for the "right" answer, but rather, wants to see how you handle the question, how you respond, and how you approach the problem. Don't second-guess yourself. Take the problem and work with it as best you can, fully exposing the *process* by which you reach your conclusions.

From here, a prudent next step is to tell the interviewer that your first problem-solving action would be to gather all the necessary information: data. Then proceed to a description of how you would use the data to formulate possible solutions to the problem. Finally, pull your answer together by listing the available options and then choosing among them. Explain the basis of your choice in terms of …

◆ The nature and objectives of the position for which you are applying.

◆ The nature and objectives of the prospective employer's company or department.

How to Have Fun with It

If this looks like hard work, it is. But it is also creative work, with a strong element of make-believe. Try to run with the problem. *Show enthusiasm* for the task of solving the problem. Telling the interviewer at the outset that you would begin by gathering data is ample demonstration of your care and prudence. Having established this, it is best to cast aside timidity and move as boldly toward an answer as possible, explaining your actions every step of the way. At the very least, pretend you are having fun with the process.

Let's try this strategy on the sales question:

Interviewer: Do you like my fountain pen?

You: Yes …

Interviewer: Good. Sell me this pen.

Now you could just try to be charming and persuasive, extolling the qualities, value, and benefits of the pen and why the "customer" would want to own it. While such a performance might display some fine qualities, it's not really what the interviewer is looking for. He doesn't *really* want to buy his own pen. He wants to *see* how you go about selling it. So, *show* him. Here's how:

◆ Ask questions. "What's the intended market for this pen?" Then follow up with your own answer. Let's say it's one of those fancy "writing instruments" named after a mountain in Switzerland. What does this tell you about the market? Having assessed the market, secure the interviewer's agreement with your assessment.

◆ Explore the features of the pen. Define its benefits—the "good things" it does for the owner. Define its value—price versus beauty, durability, writing quality, and so on. Ask the interviewer whether he feels that you should include any other features and benefits.

◆ Explain how you would obtain full data concerning market, features, benefits, and value. Options include focus groups, questionnaires, direct-mail surveys, and so on.

◆ Explain briefly how you would use the data to formulate marketing-plan options.

◆ Paint a quick but vivid picture of just who the prospective customer is, and, based on this, choose one of the options you have named.

"Tell Me About a Time When You ..."

Related to questions that attempt to assess your problem-solving skills are those that try to plumb your character. *Behavior-centered questions* usually begin with "Tell me about a time when you ..." or some variation on this opening. These questions are aimed at assessing a candidate's character, attitude, and personality traits by asking for an account of how the candidate handled certain challenging situations.

Strategies for Answering Behavior-Related Questions

Common sense, more than anything else, should help you anticipate what traits of character, habits of conduct, and attitudes will be most appealing and most important to a prospective employer. Modify common sense with what you know about the issues of concern to the employer and the industry. For example, if you are applying for a position as credit manager for a firm, it's a safe bet that the prospective employer will be looking for evidence of prudence combined with flexibility. If you are going after a sales job, the sales manager will want to see evidence of a positive, persuasive personality. If the prospective position involves a lot of customer service, you'll probably be asked about "the time you had to deal with an irate customer." And so on.

Here's the basic strategy:

1. Anticipate and define your desirable traits of character and habits of conduct, both in general and as specifically relevant to the needs of the industry or prospective employer.

The Skinny

Ideally, the exemplary stories you tell at an interview should be directly job-related; however, you might also talk about relevant experiences outside the job—how you formulated an innovative fund-raising project for your local parent-teacher organization, for example.

2. Come prepared with a repertoire of stories about your experience that demonstrates a range of desirable traits and habits of conduct.

3. Listen carefully to the question.

4. Don't feel compelled to jump right into your answer. Ask clarifying questions first.

5. Tell a story. (See step 2.)

6. Conclude by explaining what you intended your story to illustrate. Don't rely on the imagination and perception of the interviewer. Drive the point home—firmly.

7. Ask for feedback: "Does this tell you what you need to know?"

Clincher _____

Many apparently behavior-related questions are really little more than ordinary informational questions phrased in a slightly different way. Asking a clarifying question will help ensure that you give the kind of answer the interviewer wants. To the question "Tell me about a time when you faced a major problem at work," you might respond: "Do you want me to discuss the major problems I deal with in my current position?"

Stirring Memories

Let's return to step 2 for a moment. Nothing is more frustrating—or more common—than the experience of going through an interview, riding the elevator down to the lobby floor, and, as each floor goes *ding*, thinking of some story or anecdote you *should* have mentioned. Look, you're only human, and it's difficult to dredge up your entire professional life within the space of the few seconds between the asking of the question and the anticipation of the answer. The solution to this problem, as step 2 suggests, is to do your dredging at home, before you come to the interview. It's wise to prepare professional "war stories" that answer and illustrate as many of the following questions as possible. They all begin with, *Tell me about the time you …*

◆ Coped with a difficult personnel situation.

◆ Creatively solved a problem.

◆ Made a big mistake.

◆ Made a difficult decision.

- Had to deal with an irate customer.

- Persuaded key personnel to your point of view.

- Made a great sale.

- Blew a great sale.

- Conquered a major obstacle.

- Had to take a calculated risk.

- Had to make a decision based on limited information.

- Had to fire a good friend.

While you shouldn't dodge a negative question—"Tell me about the time you blew a great sale"—don't get bogged down in it. If you relate a negative anecdote about yourself, be sure to conclude by talking about what you learned from the experience and how it strengthened you. For example, conclude by discussing how blowing that sale has made you a much better salesperson: "It taught me some hard lessons about what *not* to do and, more important, what to do *next time*."

The Truth of Fiction

What do you do if you can't come up with a true-life anecdote to cover each of the likely questions? You could make something up—and hope that you aren't caught in your lie—but a better strategy is to offer a hypothetical example:

> **Interviewer:** Tell me about the time you had to fire a good friend.

> **You:** Fortunately, that situation has never come up. But I could tell you how I *would* handle such a situation, if it ever did arise.

Secure the interviewer's permission and proceed to weave your fiction.

Dealing With the "Desert Island" Scenario and Other Bizarre Questions

At least 50 percent of the reason for asking a question from out of left field is to see how you will react. If the wacky question stuns you into silence, you lose big points. If, on the other hand, you take the question in your stride—even if you can't come up with an immediate answer—you'll get at least half credit for it.

> **The Skinny** _____
>
> Most left-field questions are attempts to probe character and self-image. Some are intended to see how your mind works, while others are attempts to guess how you'll fit into the prevailing workplace environment. The key to answering bizarre questions is to be prepared to give *reasons* for your answers. The interviewer is probably interested more in process and rationale than result. A sense of humor is almost always welcome.

The subjects of bizarre questions range from deceptively obvious ethical issues to riddles: "Why are manhole covers round?" Answer: "No matter what you do, two equally sized circles won't fit through each other; if the manhole were any other shape, its cover could possibly fall through it." Think about it.

Alternative answers to the Manhole Cover Question include:

1. Because most of the people who go through manholes are round.

2. Because it's cheaper to make round covers than rectangular, triangular, square, pentagonal, hexagonal, or octagonal covers.

The following is an ethical question bounced off the wall, which Arlene S. Hirsch discusses in her book *Interviewing, Third Edition* (Wiley, 1999). The manager of a new and aggressive high-tech company paints this scenario for a candidate: "We are sending you on assignment to Carmel, California. You have an unlimited expense account. What kind of car are you going to rent?"

The knee-jerk response is to be prudent, conservative, modest, and "save the company money" with a no-frills compact. But if the prospective employer wants somebody who responds reflexively, she could hire an earthworm. Hirsch points out that the three most "successful" answers were Porsche, Ferrari, and Jaguar. The candidate who suggested a sensible Honda Accord lost, as did the one who opted for an expensive (but too conservative) Mercedes-Benz sedan. *Think.* You are representing a young, aggressive company in a highly competitive field. You are not driving to Podunk, but to Carmel, a Pacific Coast town of unconventional multimillionaires whose former mayor was Clint Eastwood. The best answer reflects an awareness of image and situational context, not a one-dimensional grasp of simple corporate ethics.

A favorite off-the-wall question is the desert-island scenario "If you could take only three things with you on a desert island, what would they be?" Some interviewers might make an effort to update this classic: "Recently, scientists have found evidence of life on Europa, a moon of Jupiter. What three things would you take on a trip to Europa?" But, of course, the question is really the same.

How you answer the desert-island question says as much about you as it does about your understanding of the prospective position. If the position calls for a great deal of creative imagination, your take-along list might include a copy of *Moby Dick*, your sketch pad, and a boat (or spaceship) to get you home when you were ready to leave. If the position calls for nothing but feet-on-the-ground practicality, specify a supply of water (or oxygen), an expert on desert (or extraterrestrial) life, and that reliable boat (or spaceship).

Don't Call Us ...

Don't allow small talk to lead you blindly into controversial topics, and don't let it lead you into unwise revelations:

Interviewer: Is it still raining outside?

You: Yes, thank goodness. I hope the rain washes out some of that pollen. My allergies are killing me.

Maybe the interviewer is a fellow sufferer and will commiserate with you. On the other hand, maybe she sees a string of sick days in your future, as your work piles up and languishes on your desk.

Questions You Don't Have to Answer (and How Not to Answer Them)

Employers are forbidden by law to make hiring decisions based in any way on marital status, sexual orientation, age, ethnic background or national origin, race, religious beliefs, gender, or disabilities. There are exceptions, in cases where a *bona fide occupational qualification* (*BFOQ*) can be demonstrated, but, in general, these personal characteristics and attributes are protected by law. So it follows that most questions concerning your marital status, sexual orientation, age, or ethnic or national origins are either blatantly illegal or tread on very shaky ground.

def•i•ni•tion

A **bona fide occupational qualification (BFOQ)** is an employment criterion that permits discrimination based on personal attributes in certain cases; for example, a women's bathing-suit manufacturer needs to hire models for its catalog. No men need apply. A delivery company needs drivers capable of lifting 80 pounds. The applicant who is disabled by a chronically bad back and is therefore incapable of repeated heavy lifting may legally be rejected.

So, what are you going to do if one of these taboo questions is asked? Take offense? Invoke the law? With justification, you could do either. However, you'll probably end up alienating the interviewer and losing the job. Could you subsequently sue on the grounds of discrimination? Probably. But it's expensive, difficult, and extremely time-consuming to litigate issues of discrimination. That the papers and TV occasionally report million-dollar discrimination-in-hiring settlements should tip you off as to just how rare such judgments are. If they were common, they wouldn't be news. No, such profitable legal victories are the exceptions—and besides, do you want to sit in court, or do you want to get a job?

In general, if you feel comfortable answering a question—even a possibly illegal or certainly inappropriate question—answer it. But if you find that you cannot answer, respond with a few *ifs*. For example, to the question "Are you married?" you might reply, "I'm not sure what you wish to learn from that question. If you're concerned about how much time I can afford to spend on the job, you should know that I am a professional, and I keep my professional life separate from my private life. I intend to devote as much time as necessary to be successful at my job."

Marital Status and Family Plans

You might not be asked the marital status question so directly. Some employers troll for this information with such innocent-sounding inquiries as "Where does your husband (or wife) work?" or "What next-of-kin do we contact in case of an emergency?" The best strategy is simply to answer these questions (although you *could* finesse the second question by replying that you will "supply that information after you are on board"; it is, in fact, illegal to ask for next-of-kin information before hiring).

"Do you plan to have children?" This question is almost exclusively directed at women. You might ask the interviewer to "Explain what bearing this has on the position. I'm not sure I understand the relevance of the question." If it seems to you that a *yes* will jeopardize your shot at the job, you might also simply answer *no*. It's only a word, and it does not legally bind you to remain childless. If you really do want children and feel you must be up-front about it, answer positively: "Yes, eventually, I want a family. However, those plans are directly dependent on the success of my career."

Sexual Orientation

It is not likely that you will be asked point-blank "What is your sexual orientation?" However, you might be asked about your marital status in a way that is designed to ascertain this information: "So you've *never* been married?"

There's no graceful way to respond to questions such as these. Either reply to indirect questions as neutrally—and calmly—as possible, or quietly offer: "I don't think that question is appropriate."

Age

"How old are you?" is a patently illegal question. It may also be asked in some less direct ways: "You've had a very long career, Mr. Smith. Are you sure you're up on the new technologies?" The best way to respond is to turn your age to your advantage. Translate *time* into experience, skill, expertise, and seasoned judgment: "Now that I'm in my fifties, I've had more than three decades of experience in the widget industry."

Ethnic Background or National Origin

An employer may simply ask "Where were you born?" Or the question may be couched as polite or ignorant curiosity: "So many consonants in your name! What is it? Polish? Czech?"

Answer directly, but, in so doing, politely flush the interviewer out of hiding: "It's Czech. Are you concerned that where I was born will have some bearing on how well I can do this job? I'd like to put any possible doubts to rest."

Race

Your race is probably evident in your appearance; however, you may be asked something like "Do you think you'll have a problem working for a black woman?" Or "Many of the staff here are Latino. Can you handle that?"

Questions like these are insensitive, crude, and provocative, but deliver your answer calmly and without skipping a beat: "Of course, I have no problem with that. I am a team player who enjoys working with people, period. I have no problems with any race—people are people."

Religion

You may be asked directly whether you believe in God, or, less sweepingly, "What church do you attend?" If you *want* to answer, keep your response general: "I worship regularly, but I make it a practice not to involve any of my personal beliefs in my work." If you prefer, respond calmly and evenly: "My personal spiritual beliefs are very important to me, and while I am guided by them, I don't put them on display in my professional life." This is an especially good response if you have no religious beliefs or beliefs that some may think unconventional.

If religion is important to you, you may want to make it clear that your spiritual beliefs inspire you and inform your ethics, including your business ethics; however, it is best to avoid references to a specific religion or denomination.

Disability

"Are you disabled?" The question is illegal, but answer it honestly—with a positive spin: "No, I am not disabled. I *am* in a wheelchair, but that does not disable me in any way from managing a customer service department."

The Least You Need to Know

◆ Unexpected and challenging questions often relate to problem solving, behavior and attitude, issues apparently unrelated to the job, and personal attributes and beliefs.

◆ In answering problem-solving and behavior-related questions, focus on the process rather than on the final answer. The interviewer is most interested in how you think.

◆ Don't evade answering negative questions (for example, those concerning mistakes you made), but conclude your answer on the most positive note possible.

◆ Even if a question is inappropriate or downright illegal, look for a positive way to answer it. Keep your options open.

Chapter 12

Take Control and Start Selling Yourself

In This Chapter

- ◆ Viewing the interview as a sales situation
- ◆ Taking the initiative
- ◆ Identifying what the prospective employer "must have"
- ◆ Prompting a positive response
- ◆ Learning how to "read" an interviewer
- ◆ Putting yourself across as a problem solver and a force multiplier

As you already know, you *will* be asked questions at an interview. You'll also probably find yourself in an office on the visitor's side of the desk. The interviewer, of course, will be seated behind the desk, in the position of possession and authority. None of these circumstances should discourage you from trying to take control of the interview.

This is the most effective way of presenting yourself: taking control of the interview without *seeming* to. This is also how a successful salesperson manages a sale: she listens to the customer and makes it clear that the customer's concerns are all-important and that what she is selling will address those concerns, but then she guides the customer, carefully shaping his actions toward the decision to buy. In this chapter, I'll suggest ways you can apply such selling techniques to the employment interview.

Get Out of the Backseat and Take the Wheel

So far, we have looked at two dimensions of the interview: as performance and as an interaction.

Now for the third dimension: The interview as a sale, in which you subtly take control in order to guide the interviewer into making the decision to offer you a position.

Your best chance for success is to understand and use all three dimensions of the interview to your advantage. Climb out of the backseat, take the wheel, and *steer.*

Follow That Lead

Steering, however, means nothing unless you have a destination. Go from being a stranger to the interviewer to becoming somebody the interviewer's organization has "gotta have."

Clincher _____

The beauty of taking the initiative is that you don't *have* to be right. Merely raising intelligent issues and demonstrating knowledge of the company and its concerns will help to begin the "sale."

First, find the road. Forgive me, but at this point the analogy falters. Were you behind the wheel of a real vehicle, you'd rely mainly on your eyes; in the interview, you'll find the road with your ears. Listen to what the interviewer says about his or her company, its needs, its goals, its problems. Listen to what the interviewer says he or she needs. Then respond to what you hear. Now you have begun the transformation from a stranger looking for a job to a potential partner willing to pitch in and solve problems.

Don't Call Us ... _____

Maybe you're not so sure you've got what the target employer is looking for, but this is neither the time nor the place to give voice to your doubts. Go ahead and assume that what you bring to the table is *exactly* what the interviewer wants. You can deal with any lingering doubts after you get an offer and before you accept the job.

Strike Some Sparks

Your success in getting the interviewer's attention through active listening depends, in large part, on how forthcoming the interviewer is about expressing what she needs and wants from you. If she fails to express this, you must take the initiative. In Chapter 9 I discussed the techniques of active listening. Use them here, and be prepared to augment them with the following moves:

◆ Demonstrate that you are listening, ensure that you are understanding, and keep the conversation going by frequently underscoring the interviewer's most important points. Do this by repeating and rephrasing them: "What I hear you saying is …" or "If I'm understanding you correctly …"

◆ If the interviewer is still not forthcoming with the information you need in order to build the conversation, take an even more direct approach: "Ms. Thomas, may I ask you a question?" Ms. Thomas will answer, "Of course!" Then you must draw on your research and preparation: "It seems to me that the company's operations have been wholly dependent on X, Y, and Z. Has any consideration been given to adding A and B to the mix?" This will not only impress Ms. Thomas, but it will relieve her of the burden of carrying the entire interview. Even more, it will demonstrate your knowledge of the company and the industry.

Fan Those Flames

Make an effort to turn everything you say into an expression of accomplishment, achievement, or qualification. Keep the conversation as specific as possible. "I'm a super salesman" will get you nowhere, but the following is highly persuasive: "As a salesman, I make it my business to discover and understand what each of my customers wants and needs. For this reason, I was responsible for x dollars in widget sales last quarter."

Transform Interest into Involvement

Persuasion is not the same as simply hammering away at the interviewer. It is an interactive process. Monitor the interviewer's responses to what you are saying. Watch his body language (see the "Tune In and Turn On" section in Chapter 9) and listen for "buy signals," indications that the interviewer's interest in you is high or increasing. These include some obvious ones:

- "That interests me."
- "I like that."
- "Great!"
- "Terrific!"
- "Sounds good to me."

But it's the rare interview that produces anything so direct. Usually, buy signals emerge more neutrally, as requests for additional information:

- "Tell me more about …"
- "Can you be more specific about …"
- "Please explain …"

- "I'd like to hear more …"
- "Can we return to …?"
- "Let's not leave that point yet …"

Clincher

For many of us, an interview is an uncomfortable experience, even when it's going well. It's natural to want to get it over with. You may even dread being asked for additional information. But the fact is that *any* request for more information is an expression of interest and, therefore, a buy signal. Treasure it. Capitalize on it.

However the buy signal is expressed, it indicates that you've pressed the right button. Once you elicit a buy signal, swoop down on whatever it was that produced the positive response.

Let's say you're interviewing for a position as an executive assistant. You've just said, "I specialize in handling details and anticipating needs, so that you can be more efficient." Wow! It was just the right thing to say, because the interviewer responds with a buy signal: "Can you tell me more about that?"

It's time to get specific. Don't *praise* yourself any further, *list* some of the great things you do:

I approach the task actively. For example, I maintain active "hot files" in which I track the issues of most immediate importance and ensure that the relevant documents are instantly accessible. On day one, I would want to work with you to develop a list of hot topics and hot contacts—the issues and the people who must be given your immediate attention.

But don't leave it at this. Listing skills or achievements is certainly useful. It's like the list of *product features* in a merchandise ad. To move the sale toward a successful conclusion, however, you must translate the product features into *product benefits*—what your skills will do for the employer:

> Really, I see the most important aspect of my position as a kind of contact manager. The most important benefit I provide is giving you more *useful* time. My goal is to give you the time you need.

def•i•ni•tion

As marketing people define it, a **product feature** is an attribute of the product; for example, a high-speed microprocessor that makes one PC faster than another. A **product benefit** is something good a product or its features do (or is perceived to do) for the buyer; for example, the high-speed processor on that new PC makes you feel more productive. The benefit of the processor—a perceived increase in productivity—may justify the buyer spending more money for it.

Notice that the example I've chosen here is a candidate for an entry-level or near-entry-level position, an executive assistant. The point is that even an entry-level position can be defined in terms of benefits for the employer. If you have more experience, however, and are moving from one position up to another, devote more discussion to your actual track record, your accomplishments. But even when you do this, point out the benefits you offer:

> I brought in revenues of x dollars, and I learned how to increase the number of closed sales—consistently and dependably. I want to use what I've learned to increase the productivity of your sales force.

Get Action Now

Most job candidates take a fatalistic view of the interview, which, on the surface, seems realistic as well as emotionally sound: *I've done my best, presented my skills. Now it's in the hands of the interviewer.*

But no successful salesperson would think this way; and, remember, the third leg of the stool on which the interview will either stand or fall is *selling*. A salesperson does not invest time and effort making a pitch only to walk out the door as soon as he's finished. Instead, he lingers long enough to try to *close* the sale by prompting the prospect to action.

An effective salesperson asks plenty of questions, but tries to limit them to those that prompt a *yes*. You might direct the interviewer toward a positive conclusion by asking something like this:

> Based on what I've told you, don't you think I could give you all that you need in this position?

Sure, a *no* is still possible, but, by defining a set of conditions—"what I've told you" and "all that you need"—you've at least directed the interviewer toward a *yes*.

But trust your instincts and how you sense the interview has gone. If you don't feel that you've adequately connected with the interviewer, direct him differently:

> Mr. Smith, this has been a pleasure, and I believe I have a great deal to give to this company. But, please, tell me, is there anything I haven't addressed to your satisfaction? What could I tell you that would prompt you to make an offer?

Many candidates find it difficult to "close the sale," not because they lack the skills the position requires, but because it is emotionally difficult to take responsibility for bringing the interview to some firm conclusion. But closure is the objective of the interview—a specific action, preferably an offer of employment.

This may actually happen. It may also come to pass that the interviewer tells you, right then and there, that "it just doesn't look like we're right for each other" or words to similar effect. More likely, however, the alternative either to an immediate hire or rejection is an announcement that the whole matter must now be reviewed by "The Committee" (or a similar body), or that the company still has several other candidates to meet before notifying those chosen for a second round of interviews. In this case, do not fail first to thank the interviewer and then to ask when you should expect to hear from him. This is at least some form of closure. A push toward action—even if it's nothing more than an estimated time span for a decision—conveys a degree of urgency without making you look overanxious, let alone desperate. It leaves the interviewer aware that you are important and valuable and that you are well aware of your own importance and value.

How to Read an Interviewer

It may or may not be possible to find out anything about the interviewer in advance. If you are interviewing with a small firm, it's likely that the owner or CEO will meet with you personally. Perhaps you can uncover some background on her through articles in industry newsletters or in informational/promotional material distributed by the company. If you're interviewing with a larger organization, you still may be able to find published material on the relevant department head, who could be the person responsible for interviewing you. Make use of your network. Maybe you know someone who knows someone who knows the interviewer, and can tell you what to expect.

If you can ascertain little or nothing about the interviewer beforehand, you'll have to do your best to size her up during the course of the interview itself. Next, I discuss some common interviewer types to look out for, and tips on dealing with them.

> **Don't Call Us ...**
>
> The "Tell me all about yourself" opener is basically an invitation to deliver a rambling autobiography. True, the interviewer asked for it—but he doesn't really want it. Focus his request in order to discover what he really wants; then deliver it.

Victor Vague

He is the interviewer you are most likely to encounter. Although I haven't mentioned him by name, I've been talking a good deal about him, because it's a safe bet that you'll meet one day.

Victor's interviews begin in one of two ways: with small talk that, if you let him, he'll continue churning out for the balance of your visit, or with the dreaded "Tell me all about yourself" opener.

What Victor Vague needs is focus, and *you* can give it to him. Terminate the small talk by asking permission to ask a question, then launch into something you know about his company: "I read in *Widget Weekly* that you believe the biggest problem facing this industry is _____. This is a subject area that is very interesting to me. Can you say something more about how it specifically affects your company?" Then respond to Victor's answer. Try to build the foundation of the interview on that.

The "Tell me all about yourself" opener can also be focused, as we've seen in Chapter 10, by delivering a few essentials and then asking the interviewer to zero in: "But what area of my background is most relevant to *your* needs? Perhaps I can be most helpful to you discussing that."

Harried Harriet

You're eager, excited, and you've concentrated all your energy for the past two weeks on preparing for this interview. Now that you're here, the interviewer barely looks you in the eye, keeps answering the ringing phone, pauses to address issues raised by people who poke their head into her office, and, in fact, does almost everything but pay attention to you.

Your first impulse is to give in to a mixture of heartbreak, frustration, and anger. All of these feelings are justified and understandable, but they will not help you rescue this interview. Is Harriet being deliberately impolite? Purposely cruel? Probably not. More likely, she's overworked, and the spectacle of Harried Harriet is living, breathing proof that she needs your help. When you can manage to get a word in, point this out: "You really *are* busy! It's obvious that I could be of great use to you in an environment like this."

With luck, this will get Harriet's attention. She'll put down the phone, close the door, and turn her attention to you.

Mike the Machine

Mike the Machine never connects with you on a person-to-person level. His approach is a monotone. He ticks off one question after another, barely giving you time to formulate an answer, never following up on your answers, never allowing your responses to blossom into real conversation. It's bang, bang, bang, then out the door.

How do you get through to this interviewer?

Your best hope for stopping the Machine is to throw in a few monkey wrenches. Mike the Machine is built to grind out questions. He does not expect questions in return. Try to identify an area of particular concern to Mike or his company, then *you* ask one or more questions concerning that area. But first you'll have to turn the question-answer tables on Mike:

> **Mike:** What experience do you have working with advertising copywriters?

> **You:** I can review that for you. But let me ask you first, what copywriting issues do you find most critical on a day-to-day basis?

It takes real guts to turn the tables like this, but if an interview is proceeding mechanically and unenthusiastically, you must assume that no issues of critical importance have yet been discovered, and you need both to discover them and to shake things up. And you need to do it *now*.

Ted the Techie

Ted is interested in assessing your knowledge of the nuts and bolts of the job for which you are interviewing. You cannot ignore this, of course, because the nuts and bolts are important—without them, everything just falls apart. So, satisfy his need to know by doing and saying everything you can to demonstrate your technical mastery. Be aware, however, that in spite of himself, this is not *all* Ted wants to know. Although he may fail to express it, he does want to see you as a whole being, bristling with skills beyond technical know-how. Whenever possible, expand your technically oriented responses to demonstrate such skills and traits as leadership, initiative, decisiveness, ability to work well with people, and so on. Leave Ted with *more* than he asked for.

Mary the Monopolizer

I've discussed the common mistake overanxious job candidates make, of trying to fill every minute of the interview with the sound of their voice. Unfortunately, some interviewers are capable of this as well. They call *you* in for an interview, to find out who *you* are and what *you* offer, then take up *your* time with *their* words!

Deal with Mary the Monopolizer first by learning whatever you can from all those nonstop words. Listen to what she says is important to her, and then use one of those points as a springboard into the conversation. Appeal directly to her self-interest and self-absorption. You may have to be slightly aggressive about it:

> **Mary:** … So, as I say, I really have to struggle to ensure adequate cash flow …

> **You:** Let me interrupt you just a moment—because what you are saying is really exciting. Cash-flow management is the chief area I've been trying to revise and streamline in my current position. I'd like to share one idea with you—and get your reaction to it. I think you'll find this quite interesting …

Be a Problem Solver and a Force Multiplier

This point has been made before, but, after our rapid review of interviewer types, it's worth repeating. There is one thing all interviewers look for: *someone who'll solve their problems and be a force multiplier, a person who brings to the enterprise even more than he came with.* Enter the interview focused on what you can do for the interviewer, the employer, not what he can do for you. Of course, you're a job seeker. Why else would you be taking the time and trouble to show up at the interview? But just because you are a job seeker doesn't mean you have to come across as one. Instead, present yourself as a resource, somebody with skills, expertise, and accomplishments to offer.

Nice Save!
Even if you are less than adequately prepared for the interview (for example, you haven't made an effort to discover the problems and issues that especially concern this particular company), don't give up. You can still put yourself across as a problem solver by imagining what a *problem employee* does—is frequently absent or late, needs constant supervision and correction, doesn't meet deadlines, and so forth—and then presenting yourself as exactly the opposite.

The Least You Need to Know

- The interview is essentially a sales situation, with you as the salesperson *and* the "merchandise."

- If you sense that the interview is drifting, it's critical that you take the initiative. Work to focus the interviewer.

- Learn to "read" the interviewer so that you can ask questions that prompt a positive response and present yourself as the answer to the employer's needs and a solution to his problems.

- The objective of the interview is action on the part of the interviewer—ideally, a job offer—and you should direct everything you say and do toward that objective.

Chapter 13

Money Talk

In This Chapter

- ◆ Why you don't like negotiating salary
- ◆ Calculating a target salary range
- ◆ Getting the interviewer to name a figure
- ◆ Responding to the offer
- ◆ What is—and isn't—negotiable
- ◆ Overcoming employer salary objections

Salary: You're afraid to ask for too little or too much—*either* of which can take you out of the running—and, like many folks, you're uneasy with the notion of putting a price on your own head. But, most of all, both you and the interviewer are aware that the first one to mention a salary figure puts himself in the weaker negotiating position. So the issue hangs there, staring you in the eye.

This chapter will help you do something about the salary monster.

First, Some Homework

Just because you should avoid being the first to mention a salary figure doesn't mean you should wait until you are sitting in the interviewer's office to start thinking about salary. Part of your pre-interview homework should be determining a workable and reasonable salary range.

Create a Cash-Need Worksheet

Let's think about those two terms: *workable* and *reasonable*. You can go about defining *workable* by determining your own minimum cash requirements. This does *not* mean the bare minimum needed for subsistence, but the least you need to feel secure and comfortable. Ultimately, only you can determine what "secure and comfortable" means, but a good rule of thumb is to figure what you need to meet all of your monthly obligations, *and* be able to put away and save at least 3 percent of your monthly income, *and* have another 10 percent (on average) that you can count on for that proverbial rainy day. Use the worksheet on the following page to figure out your monthly expenses and a workable salary.

Take two swings through this list. First, pencil in the minimum figures—what you absolutely need to earn to meet your expenses and achieve some level of comfort and security. In your second pass, fill in the amounts you would ideally like to earn.

Minimum Monthly Cash Needs Worksheet

Housing	
Rent or mortgage payments	$_____
Electricity/gas	$_____
Water	$_____
Telephone	$_____
Cable TV	$_____
Internet	$_____
Garbage removal	$_____
Cleaning, maintenance, repairs	$_____

Food	
Groceries	$_____
Eating out	$_____

Clothing

Purchase	$_____
Dry-cleaning, laundry	$_____

Automobile/Transportation

Car payments	$_____
Gas	$_____
Repairs	$_____
Public transportation (bus, train, plane)	$_____

Insurance

Auto	$_____
Medical	$_____
House and personal possessions	$_____
Life	$_____

Medical Expenses

Doctors' visits	$_____
Prescriptions	$_____
Fitness costs	$_____

Support for Other Family Members

Child care costs	$_____
Child support	$_____
Support for your parents	$_____

Charity	**$_____**

Education	**$_____**

Pet Care	**$_____**

Bills and Debts (Monthly Payments)

Credit cards	$_____
Local stores	$_____
Other	$_____

Taxes

Federal	$_____
State	$_____
Local/property	$_____

continues

Minimum Monthly Cash Needs Worksheet (continued)

Bills and Debts (Monthly Payments)

Amusement

Movies, video rentals, and so on	$_____
Other entertainment	$_____
Newspapers, magazines, books	$_____
Gifts	$_____
Savings/Investments	$_____
Contingency Fund	$_____
TOTAL MONTHLY AMOUNT NEEDED	$_____

Compare your workable figure with your reasonable figure. If what's workable significantly exceeds what's reasonable, you'll have to rethink your needs or your career goals or both. If, however, the two numbers are fairly close, use them to formulate your desired—workable and reasonable—salary range.

Scope Out the Market

The *reasonable* part of your homework assignment requires that you determine your "market value"—that is, the going price—in a particular industry, for someone with your qualifications and skills.

Consult the following:

◆ **Salary.com (www.salary.com):** This may be the most popular of the handful of websites that provide sound and solid salary research. Start here.

◆ **CareerJournal (www.careerjournal.com/salaryhiring):** In addition to many salary tables, including upper-level numbers, this website offers an array of calculator tools that may make it easier for you to zero in on an appropriate salary range.

◆ **JobStar (www.jobstar.org/tools.salary/sal-surv.cfm):** This is a very large salary survey site and one not to miss.

Although the free sites are very good, they don't always have the most up-to-date information. Consider investing in Salary Source (www.salarysource.com), which promises the latest.

Online or off, you might also consult the following old standbys:

◆ The most recent report from the *Occupational Outlook Handbook*. Ask for it at the local office of the U.S. Department of Labor, or access it on the Internet at www.bls.gov.

◆ Professional and trade journals in your field or industry. Look for issues that publish annual salary surveys.

◆ *National Business Employment Weekly*. It runs periodic salary surveys, and you should be able to get back issues from the publisher or at your local library.

Nice Save!

If the interviewer offers you coffee, my advice is just say no, thanks—even if you feel you could really use a cup. To begin with, you probably don't need the added anxiety caffeine may generate. More important, in an interview, with your attention tautly focused and your nerves ratcheted up about as far as they can go, a hot, dark cuppa joe is just a catastrophe waiting to happen.

That said, here's what you do if you actually spill coffee on yourself:

1. Don't try to minimize the accident. If the coffee is hot, stand up, and do what you can to get it off of you.

2. Declare, "*This* is embarrassing! Can you direct me to the washroom?" Go to the bathroom and clean yourself up as much as you can.

3. Apologize, but don't grovel and don't put yourself down: "I'm really sorry this happened. I hope I haven't stained your rug." (Do not say, "I'm such an idiot!", "I'm so clumsy!", "I can't believe how stupid I am!", or the like.)

4. Thank the interviewer for his help—even if he did nothing more than direct you to the restroom. (Actually, he'll most likely get you paper towels, make sure you didn't burn yourself, and reassure you that "it could happen to anyone." Insofar as this catastrophe empowers the interviewer by giving him an opportunity to help you, the incident is not as destructive as you might fear.)

5. Above all, get on with the interview. After apologizing, continue: "I'm okay. We were talking about so-and-so. This is what I wanted to say before I so rudely interrupted myself …"

Playing Chicken

Salary negotiation is like a game of chicken. You enter the interview (supposedly) knowing what salary you need and can expect. But maybe they're willing to offer you much more than you expect. If you blurt out a low figure—flinch—first, you lose. But if you too insistently evade answering the interviewer's questions about salary requirements, you lose again—you probably won't get the job.

How to Put Yourself in the Catbird Seat

This is where it gets tricky. Your primary task at the interview is to sell yourself as the answer to the employer's problems. While you're busy doing that, however, you need to remain sensitive to the signals that tell you just when it's time to get into a salary discussion. Ideally, this will come near the end of the interview.

An interviewer could actually try to pin you down to an exact salary figure. This is almost certainly the sign of a power-hungry interviewer, not of any genuine need to get an exact figure. Still, it's a power struggle you will lose if you arbitrarily fail to cooperate. If the interviewer says something like "Look, let's not play games. I really do need a firm figure from you," offer the salary range, and, if that fails, *do* volunteer a figure. Use the lower part of the *top quarter* of your range; for example, the top quarter of your original range of $38,000 to $43,000 is $41,750 to $43,000. You could round that down to $41,000, or even $40,000.

Toe to Toe's Not Time to Flinch

Provided that you can keep your anxiety in check, it's not terribly difficult to avoid raising the salary issue first. However, the interviewer may launch a preemptive strike by asking you point-blank, "How much are you making now, and how much do you want?" Make certain that you have reviewed Chapter 10, which includes tips on evading—in order to delay—the salary issue.

Unfortunately, there is no guarantee that the avoidance techniques in Chapter 10 will work 100 percent of the time. If the employer insists on getting a figure from you, don't alienate him by persisting in evasion. But don't nail yourself to a single figure, either. Come to the interview armed with a broad salary range with which you can respond, if pressed.

Use your workable and reasonable figures to calculate the range. Let's say the workable figure you've arrived at is $36,000. Having researched the industry, you've concluded that the salary range for your target position is $33,000 to $41,000. (That's good! It suggests that your current needs correspond well with the reality of the marketplace.) Now what do you do with these figures? Bracket the salary range you report to the prospective employer so that it interlocks with and slightly exceeds the upper range of the reasonable figures and also exceeds your own workable requirement. In this case, when the employer presses you for a figure, reply that you are looking for a salary in the low forties. If he presses you for something more precise, reply that your acceptable range is $38,000 to $43,000.

Timing Is Everything

Avoid the subject of salary *until:*

1. You're in the final interview—if there is more than one round of interviews.

2. You're satisfied that the interviewer has gotten to know you and fully understands your qualifications.

3. You feel that you've been fully informed of what the job is all about, and the duties and responsibilities it entails.

4. You're confident that the interviewer has reached the "gotta have you" stage.

Gotta Have Me? Act Now!

That last step needs some explanation. The "gotta have you" stage is the point at which the interviewer decides that you are *the* answer to his needs and the solution to his problems. At this point—and not before—is when salary negotiation should take place.

The buy signal that marks the "gotta have you" stage will probably be less subtle and more direct than the buy signals of the "sorta like" stage. Maybe something like this: "I think we see eye to eye about the duties and responsibilities of the position. Now what about salary?" Or: "I believe you can do the job we want. What salary were you looking for?" To be classified as a genuine buy signal, the request for salary information *must* be preceded by a "gotta have" statement ("I believe you can do the job …"). Without such a statement, it's just a premature request for a salary figure.

But don't jump at the buy signal, no matter how tempting. Remember, if possible, get the interviewer to be the first to mention a figure. Try this response to the buy signal/ salary question: "This is the first time we've really broached the subject. Could you tell

Clincher _____

What if the final buy signal doesn't come? In this case, it's time for you to take control by asking a question like this: "Based on what I've told you, don't you think I could give you all that you need in this position?" Review "Get Action Now" in Chapter 12.

me what the authorized range is for someone with my qualifications?" Assuming the interviewer furnishes this information, you can then choose one of four options:

1. Accept the range: "The upper end of this range is certainly what I had in mind and would be acceptable to me."

2. Open negotiations by responding with your own range, the bottom end of which should overlap the top end of the interviewer's.

3. Thank the interviewer for the information, and then ask for additional time to consider the figure.

4. Thank the interviewer for the information, but tell him that the range is well below what you were expecting and what you consider appropriate.

> **Don't Call Us ...**
>
> Don't betray yourself with negative body language. Acquire and practice—in front of a mirror—a *pleasant* poker face, one that displays neither disappointment nor hip-hip-hooray enthusiasm in response to a salary offer. Maintain near-neutral eye contact throughout the negotiation.

Avoid telling the interviewer that his or her offer is not even in the ballpark, unless you are prepared *not* to get the offer. If the employer's figure is substantially below your range, it is better to choose option #3: ask for time to think over the offer.

If you really are pleased with the figures offered, you may respond with the first alternative. Just be aware that most employers don't lead with their best offer. Even if the employer is well within your ballpark, it is usually best to respond with the second option. It may capture for you a figure in a somewhat higher range.

Be aware that option #2 requires some work. It's not likely that the employer will simply cave in just because you topped his or her top range. This is the time to recapitulate and resell. Remind the interviewer of *why* you are worth top dollar. Add to this reminder a demonstration of your knowledge of the industry:

> As you might imagine, I've looked through a number of industry salary surveys. The range I would find acceptable is appropriate to prevailing salaries in the industry. Since we're agreed that I have the qualifications that will more than satisfy your needs, and I can promise you that I'll be up, running, and producing for you from day one, I feel that compensation somewhat above your upper range is appropriate and fair—fair for me and, certainly, a fair value for you.

The Usual Objections—and How to Overcome Them

Generally, for entry-level and lower-compensation positions, salaries tend to be rather firmly fixed, barely negotiable, or totally non-negotiable. That is a hard fact of life. As you go up in compensation, salary ranges increase in flexibility. At the very highest ranges—above $65,000—there is often considerable room for negotiation.

Let's break this down.

An entry-level position that pays $25,000 a year or less will probably offer little or no salary flexibility. For such positions, the pool of available candidates is usually large, and it makes more sense for the employer to find a person who will accept her offer rather than negotiate with someone who won't.

In the middle range between $26,000 and $65,000, there is limited room for maneuvering. It is not unusual for employers hiring in this range to negotiate as much as 15 percent above their stated salary figure. Just don't expect more.

Positions that pay more than $65,000 in annual salary are typically skilled and demanding; therefore, the candidate pool is proportionately smaller. Employers tend to be willing to spend more of what it takes to get the person they want.

With a firm grasp on reality, you can still overcome the following four major hurdles interviewers throw in the path of a salary negotiation.

"Exceeds Range Authorized"

If you're interviewing for an entry-level position, this hurdle may be immovable—that is, the interviewer's invocation of it is not a negotiating ploy, but a simple statement of fact: "Position Y pays *x* dollars, period." Nevertheless, you can try to negotiate a somewhat higher salary—the worst they'll say is "no."

One thing to note is that neither the "exceeds range authorized" objection to higher salary, nor any of the other three we will discuss have anything to do with your value or performance.

This objection—and the others—focus on *cost*. Unfortunately, cost is the single criterion on which most purchases are based, whether the merchandise is a bar of soap or a potential employee. Your task is to get the employer focusing on cost versus *benefit*; that is, shift his concentration from cost to *value*. Sell your special qualifications, talents, and abilities as investments in greater profitability. Sure, you may cost more than what the employer anticipated paying, but the benefits you offer also exceed what the employer anticipated. Your greater value, therefore, outweighs your greater cost:

> I understand. But perhaps a higher figure could be authorized. The value my qualifications and skill represent, I think you'd agree, clearly merit a salary in the range I mentioned. Frankly, I believe that you would have difficulty hiring anyone with qualifications comparable to mine at the salary range presently authorized.

"The Budget Is the Budget"

Confronted by this objection, accept and acknowledge it. Then use the *value* argument to attempt to persuade the employer to rethink his budget:

> I appreciate the discipline of a budget, and I understand that you budgeted under $35,000 for the position, but I know other employers who are willing to pay more. More important, however, I think we're both agreed that I offer exceptional qualifications and skills. I believe my background demonstrates my absolute commitment to high standards of performance. Maybe I cost a bit more than you've budgeted for, but I'm also offering you more *value* than you bargained for. That's why I feel amply justified in asking for the $38,000.

"Others Don't Make as Much"

Attack this objection logically. When you are told that others presently employed in comparable positions at the firm don't make the salary you're asking for, remind the interviewer—politely and tactfully—that what the employer pays others is a matter between the employer and the others. Your salary concerns only the employer and you. Again, begin by appreciating and acknowledging the objection. Don't just ignore it:

> I appreciate your point of view. Nevertheless, based on our conversation thus far, I understood that my salary would be based on my performance and my qualifications, and that it would not be capped by what others in the firm earn.

Do everything you can to separate yourself from limiting factors of precedents.

"But Your Salary History ..."

The best way to prevent the interviewer from using your own salary history to cap his offer is by avoiding the issue of salary history in the first place. Don't volunteer information concerning your current compensation level. This, of course, may not be possible, and if the interviewer tries to use your salary history as a precedent for setting your new salary, you need to separate the past firmly from what you are asking for now:

> Mr. Smith, I don't understand what bearing my past salary has on the work I will do for you. My history is not relevant to salary. What *is* relevant is performance and qualifications, and these we've discussed thoroughly. I believe we're agreed that I offer great value to the company. Moreover, I've looked into how this position is compensated in other organizations, and it seems to me that the figure I'm proposing is not only fair, but represents excellent value for money. Wouldn't you agree that a combination of the qualifications I offer and industry standards is a fair and appropriate way of arriving at a reasonable salary figure?

This Is Negotiable (Isn't It?)

Salary negotiation can become a single-minded tug o' war, at least until either you or the employer cuts the rope by saying no. Salary is a simple figure, all too easy for an interviewer to engrave upon her mind: *This is the number. He shall not have more! This is the number. He shall not have more!* So, at some point, it is likely that you'll hit a brick wall.

Nevertheless, there still may be room for negotiation. After all, salary is not the only part of the compensation package.

Perks Aplenty

Even if the salary figure turns out to be carved in stone, paid vacation time may be negotiable. In addition, you may be able to agree on a *flex-time* arrangement that makes your day more productive and convenient. Child care and day care have emerged over the past decade as key employment issues. You may be able to negotiate for a day-care allowance.

def•i•ni•tion

Flex time is an arrangement that allows employees to adjust their morning start and evening quitting times to suit their preferences, to accommodate family schedules, or even to avoid rush-hour traffic.

Some Bennies from Heaven

If you reach an impasse in salary negotiation, there are other nonsalary benefits you may be able to negotiate. These items include performance-based bonuses, profit-sharing plans, stock-purchase options, payment for special training and career development education, payment of professional membership dues, payment of professional subscriptions, and so on.

You might also negotiate a favorable *golden parachute* severance agreement: a cash payment in the event you are "let go."

Other benefits that may be negotiable include …

- An office of a certain size, location, and description.

- A company car.

- A car allowance.

- A private parking space.

def•i•ni•tion

A **golden parachute** is a liberal severance compensation package that is agreed to, by contract, at the time of the offer. A golden parachute usually includes several months or more of severance pay and other goodies, such as stock or stock options or outplacement assistance.

Money's Not Quite Everything

It used to be that employee benefits—so-called "fringe benefits"—were the employer's last resort for sweetening a deal going sour. It also used to be that such benefits packages were fairly lame, fairly standard from employer to employer, and certainly a disappointing substitute for cash.

It *used* to be. Today, the cost of medical care, for example, is nothing less than terrifying, and good employer-provided medical insurance is a great benefit indeed—one that varies competitively from employer to employer. Not only should this benefit loom prominently in your evaluation of a compensation package, it can also be used as a negotiating chip. Federal law may prohibit the employer from offering you a medical plan that is better than what other employees receive, but you may be able to persuade the employer that his package is not competitive with what other employers offer. This may provide the leverage you need to return to the issue of salary and get a better offer.

Relocation Reimbursement

Relocation costs can be staggering. Let's say you have a modest house, a family of four, and you're relocating 500 miles. Expect to spend $6,000 to $12,000 just to transport your stuff. Then there are storage costs, costs for temporary living arrangements (renting an apartment or staying in a hotel), and costs associated with selling a residence and buying a new one. True, expenses for employment-related relocation are generally tax deductible (tax laws change frequently; consult your tax specialist!), but the outlay can be significant. For this reason, relocation reimbursement is an important area for negotiation:

♦ Negotiate for moving expenses.

♦ Negotiate for temporary housing expenses.

♦ Negotiate a guaranteed purchase of your former residence—the employer agrees to purchase your house at a set price if it fails to sell within an agreed-on period.

Victory in the Gulf War

The Gulf War: Not only can't you and the employer see eye to eye, but you're a million light years apart. What do you do? You could conclude the interview with a thank you, walk out the door, and continue your job search. And maybe that would be your best alternative at this particular time. But what if you really want—or really need—this job?

You have one final item left to negotiate: the future. Accept the employer's best offer now, but be explicit about the proviso that your salary will be reviewed in six months (or some other period you and the employer agree on before the interview concludes) in light of your performance. Don't let overeagerness or genuine desperation lock you into a low salary for the long term.

The Least You Need to Know

♦ Calculate your salary needs and expectations before you go into the interview.

♦ Avoid being the first to mention a salary figure; if pressed to "name your price," offer a range rather than a target figure.

◆ Try to delay the salary negotiation until the interviewer has reached the "gotta have you" stage.

◆ Overcome employer objections to your salary demands by focusing on issues of value rather than cost.

Part 3

"Do You Have Any Questions?" (You'd Better!)

The questions you ask at the interview are every bit as important as those you answer. Of course, you want to find out everything you can about the prospective employer. He may think he's hiring *you*, but it's a two-way street, after all. You're also deciding whether to choose *him*.

But the questions you ask should do more than just gather information. They must provide additional opportunities for you to sell yourself to the employer; to exhibit your achievements; and to demonstrate your skills, your qualifications, your knowledge, and your character. The chapters in this part will help you build such double-edged questions.

Chapter 14

Questions You Should Always Ask

In This Chapter

◆ Getting the interviewer to invest time in you

◆ How to find out what the employer expects from you

◆ Asking questions that reveal you as the answer to the interviewer's prayers

◆ The "official" job description versus the interviewer's version

◆ Questions that produce positive action

Is the glass half-full or half-empty? The litmus test for optimists versus pessimists—the optimist says half full, while the pessimist says half empty—applies to employment interviews as well. You can view the interview as a great opportunity involving some risk, or as a giant risk involving a slim opportunity. But even the pessimist needs to realize that it's the interviewee—that means *you*—who controls the gravest risk: the worst thing that can happen in an interview is that *you* fail to ask questions.

Don't Call Us ...

They say there is no such thing as a stupid question. Wrong. Stupid questions exist in abundance, so be careful not to ask them. What's a "stupid question"? Any question to which you should already have the answer. For example: "So what exactly does Google do?"

Fail to ask productive questions, and the interviewer will assume that you are simply not particularly interested in his or her organization. Even worse, by not asking questions, you'll be passing up an opportunity to get the information you need to decide intelligently whether you really want the job. Most important of all (as any sales professional will tell you), *questions*—not compelling facts or a slick pitch alone—are what finally close the sale. Closing the "sale" depends on getting your "prospect" to respond to you in a positive manner, and thoughtful questions are critical to getting the prospect to verbalize needs and desires, as well as reservations. This chapter will get you started with some of the best questions you should ask.

Big Question #1: "Have You Had a Chance to Review My Resumé?"

As hard as it may be to believe, this is a critically important question. In the first place, a staggering number of interviewers do *not* review—or even read—candidates' resumés before the interview. Understandably, few interviewers will admit this to you, so be certain to phrase the question just this way: *"Have you had a chance to review …?"* The word "chance" communicates your sympathetic understanding that the interviewer is very busy, while "review" lets him know that you assume he has *read* the resumé, but that he may not have had an adequate opportunity to study and thoroughly *review* it. This phrasing transforms the question from challenge to opportunity—an opportunity to present your qualifications and achievements in a powerful point-by-point manner. It's also an opportunity to extend a helping hand to the interviewer—to come across, that is, as a solution rather than a problem.

Nevertheless, because interviewers are loath to admit scant familiarity with your resumé, you're not likely to get a simple "No, I haven't read it" in response to this question. Odds are, the interviewer will respond with something like, "I haven't had the chance to review it as thoroughly as I'd like to" or "Why don't you refresh my memory?" (Both of these may almost certainly be translated as "No, I haven't read it. Not a word.")

Don't be dismayed by such a response. It's not unique or even unusual; in fact, it's more the rule than the exception.

Without missing a beat, and without betraying any disappointment or anxiety in your body language, just continue: "Perhaps, then, you'll find it helpful for me to hit the highlights of my qualifications and achievements."

You'll most likely receive a positive response to this. Congratulations! You've already begun to make the sale. A positive response is the beginning of a commitment, an investment in you. You've made a big step out of the realm of "total stranger." Now in a bright and conversational tone, review your qualifications. If you like, reach into your interview kit or crank up your laptop (see Chapter 4) and produce a copy of your resumé to use as the basis for this review.

Clincher _____

Pause frequently during your review to signal the interviewer that you welcome questions along the way. Remember, the more questions the interviewer asks, the greater the investment—of time and mental energy—he is making in you.

Always Ask the Questions That Set You Up to Make the Sale

When you have concluded reviewing your qualifications and achievements, follow up with:

> Is there anything else I can tell you about my qualifications and achievements?

With each minute that passes in productive conversation, your value appreciates in the interviewer's estimation.

Big Question #2: "What Results Do You Want Me to Produce?"

Asking this question prompts the interviewer not only to start thinking about how you will fit into her organization, but, indeed, starts her thinking of you as somebody who *could* fit into the organization. Moreover, just by asking the question, you demonstrate that your intention is to *do* a job rather than *take* a job.

Your object is to respond point by point to whatever list of results the question elicits. Ideally, this pattern will emerge: *Here's what* you *want. Here's what I'll do.*

You can elaborate on and refine the question by going on to ask:

> What do you see as a timetable for the results you expect from my effort?

Not only does this question allow you to insert yourself into the strategy and operations of the organization—another move toward the status of a candidate the employer feels he has "gotta have"—it allows you to assess how reasonable and realistic the employer's expectations are. If they strike you as unrealistic, it's best not to challenge them at this point, but to allow your assessment to weigh in the balance when you are negotiating salary and when you are deciding whether to accept the offer, should an offer come.

Clincher

Always try to use the phrase *qualifications and achievements* rather than *experience*. The phrase conveys active, real accomplishment, whereas "experience" is more neutral and passive. "Qualifications and achievements" are your property, carried with you as the *value* you offer *this* employer; "experience" is what you gave in the past, to someone else.

Probe Employer Needs

The next question to develop from Big Question #2 works in two different circumstances. If it's clear to you that your qualifications and achievements mesh well with the employer's needs as they were expressed in answering Big Question #2, go on to ask:

> What do you consider to be ideal qualifications for this position?

If your assessment of fit is accurate—and if you are quite lucky—the interviewer will respond with something like "Well, I'd say what you offer is pretty ideal." More likely, however, the interviewer will list some qualifications. It is then up to you to help the interviewer draw the connections between *his* list and *your* qualifications. Your objective here is to guide, not shove, the interviewer toward conclusions that are his, yet (of course) also those you want him to reach. The sense of having made up one's own mind is always a more positive and empowering experience than the feeling of having

been talked into something. In response
to the interviewer's list of ideal qualifications, use guiding remarks such as, "That
seems similar to what I did to increase sales
of widgets at Joe Blow, Inc. Wouldn't you
agree?" Or: "I think you'd agree that my
work with widget analysis would be valuable
in that area." Or: "Managing freelancers has
taught me a lot about such-and-such."

Clincher

The ideal question is double-
edged: it not only allows you
to display your qualifications
and achievements and to present
yourself at your best, it also helps
you assess the job in order to
determine if it's right for you.

Fill the Gaps

Even if you discover substantial gaps between what the interviewer identifies as ideal
qualifications and what you have to offer, make guiding remarks that bridge the gaps
rather than try to pass over them in silence, leaving them to gape. For example: "My
work directing freelance vendors has taught me a great deal about management" is a
great deal more persuasive than "I admit I haven't managed a department, but I have
worked with freelancers."

Only if the gap between the interviewer's
ideal and your actual qualifications really is
too broad to be filled, consider not draw-
ing attention to it. Focus on something else,
some other item on the interviewer's list
that *does* demonstrate a fit with what you
have to offer. If you cannot ignore the item,
respond to it as positively as possible—as
an opportunity for growth: "I'm eager to
develop my management skills." Don't
direct attention to your lack of such skills,
but emphasize your eagerness to acquire
them.

Don't Call Us ...

Avoid showing frustration
or consternation if you
discover that the interviewer's
description of the job differs
sharply from the "official" description. Use these differences as
points of discussion. Make it
clear to the interviewer that you
greatly value her "inside" information.

Questions to Which *You* Are the Answer

Assuming that your qualifications have meshed to what is at least a plausible degree
with what the interviewer says he needs, it's time to ask questions that reveal you as
the answer to the employer's needs. Jump in with the following:

What are the principal problems facing your staff right now?

This question has a dual purpose. First, it helps you understand the employer's problems and gives you an opportunity to define just how you will work to solve them. The second purpose of the question is to help you discover any seriously objectionable situations at this company that might affect your decision to accept or reject an offer. The interviewer might possibly reveal something hopelessly intolerable.

After you ask about problems, ask this question:

> How would *you* describe the duties of this job?

The question should be posed exactly as written here, with the emphasis on the "you." You are not asking for a job description. You should have already done your homework and gathered a solid idea of what the job is about—at least *officially* about. But you'll often find that the interviewer's ideas about the nature of the job differ significantly from the official version.

Even if the interviewer's description harmonizes with the official description, by soliciting her perspective, you may get a better handle on which functions are *perceived* as most important and, therefore, really *are* the most important. Such insight will help you decide whether to accept an offer and will also give you the opportunity to emphasize or reemphasize appropriate skills and qualifications.

Personalize the questioning by asking this one next:

> What would my first project be?

This demonstrates your intense interest in and thorough engagement with the position. It also prompts the interviewer to begin thinking of you as one of the team. In order to answer the question, she will have to imagine you on the job.

The cliché about "climbing the ladder of success" is overused precisely because there is so much truth to it. Few careers are built on lateral moves. Typically, you progress upward, through increasing levels of skill and responsibility. You may, therefore, find yourself interviewing for a position that requires skills or qualifications you don't yet possess. In this case, once you have established your otherwise sound fit with the organization, you might ask:

> What type of training will I receive?

Be careful to ask this in a way that doesn't suggest feelings of inadequacy. Your point is that you want to prepare yourself to do the best possible job for the employer. Your object is to demonstrate initiative, a commitment to acquiring new skills, and an ambition to learn and grow in order to do the job at hand.

Questions That Close the Sale

When you feel that you have made your case, that you have presented what you have to offer and have shown how it all fits the employer's needs, it's time to press the interview toward a close—a *positive* close. If you're lucky, the interviewer will take the initiative in this, either with a strong buy signal—an expression of satisfaction—or by actually making an offer. However, if neither of these is forthcoming, ask the following:

> Based on what I've told you, don't you think I could give you all that you need in this position?

Salespeople are accustomed to asking such questions, but, admittedly, it may be hard for those of us unaccustomed to putting matters quite so bluntly. What should make it somewhat easier is the confidence that this question invites a positive response, or, more accurately, invites a train of thought that is likely to lead to a positive response.

As phrased, the question is heavily loaded. It makes it difficult for the interviewer to answer negatively. The question doesn't just force the issue to a conclusion, it coaxes that conclusion toward a *yes*.

No guarantees, of course, and if the "closing" question produces an objection rather than the positive response you'd hoped for, do your best to address the objection. If, however, the interviewer fails to formulate an objection that you can address, prompt her:

> What do you see as my greatest strengths—and my most significant weaknesses?

This should give you an opportunity to build on the strengths, using them to resell yourself, even as you address the weaknesses. Don't make excuses, but do acknowledge the interviewer's assessment and deal with it. While you should not rush to agree with the weaknesses she may identify, do express your willingness to learn, improve, and grow.

If the interview does not conclude with an offer, find out how long you'll be waiting to hear:

> When do you expect to reach a decision?

The next best thing to an offer is a question that puts the interviewer on notice that you are not prepared to wait indefinitely for an answer.

The Least You Need to Know

◆ Your objective in an interview is not to get a job, but a job offer. Work toward that goal, and don't worry about whether you will ultimately accept the offer (if one is forthcoming).

◆ Ask questions that encourage lively conversation—a commitment of time and an engagement of intellect from the interviewer.

◆ Even if, partway into the interview, you realize that this job isn't for you, continue to focus on making the interview a success. *All* contacts with *any* prospective employer are valuable.

◆ Ask questions to obtain the interviewer's perspective on the duties, responsibilities, and problems the job involves. Discuss major differences between the "official" job description and the version the interviewer gives you.

◆ Conclude with questions aimed at closing the sale—at moving the interviewer to positive action.

Roll-Up-Your-Sleeves Questions

In This Chapter

- Asking questions that demonstrate your *immediate* value to the employer
- Inserting yourself into the employer's mission
- Demonstrating your bottom-line impact
- Sounding like a leader without stepping on any toes
- Making sure you get the vital information

The questions in the preceding chapter give you an opportunity to tell the employer what kind of a person you are and what kind of portable skills and general qualifications you offer. The questions in the next chapter address issues specific to certain fields: sales, marketing, service, financial, R&D (research and development), and production. The present chapter applies to any field, but is aimed at giving you questions that demonstrate your readiness and ability to jump right in, to flatten the learning curve—in short, to hit the ground running.

Show Them You Can Hit the Ground Running

Most of the time, you can hardly go wrong by being polite, but there is a tendency among job candidates to be politely tentative at a job interview, peppering the conversation with such phrases as "if I get the job," "if you make the decision to offer me the position," and "assuming there is an offer." It's understandable not to want to appear presumptuous—or foolish—but if you are politely tentative, it's the tentative part that will come through more strongly than the politeness. Better to be a little presumptuous. Walk into the interview *assuming* you will be offered the job.

Ask questions that embody enthusiasm as well as ability and willingness:

> How soon do you want an employee in place?

If (and only if) no start date has been mentioned, this is always a good roll-up-your-sleeves question. Although you should assume you will get an offer, it's still better to refer to "an employee" rather than use the personal pronoun *me*. But the real secret is in the phrasing of the question: *how soon*, not *when*. The emphasis is on speed, rapid delivery of the goods, eagerness to begin, and readiness to serve.

Nothing is more hands-on than being there. It is said that people vote with their feet—that is, the strongest expression of interest, eagerness, and willingness to pitch in is an expression of action rather than mere words. Indicate that you want to *see* and *experience* the workplace for yourself:

> Can I visit the department?

Or:

> Can I get a tour of the facility?

There is a great advantage in asking for a tour or a visit rather than waiting to be offered one. It shows that you are excited and that you know how to take charge of a situation. Even more important, of course, a plant or facility tour will tell you a lot about the job, which should help you decide whether to accept an offer. It may also give you an opportunity to talk to some people at the site. Not only will this teach you more about the job, but, by "spreading you around" the prospective workplace, it will give more people a stake, however modest, in your candidacy. Indeed, the time the interviewer spends physically walking

Don't Call Us ...

Don't ask questions to which you already have the answer. If you know when the proposed start date is, don't ask the employer when he wants the new person in place.

you around, taking you from office to office or workstation to workstation, builds up a greater investment in you and increases your value in his estimation.

Can you tell me why this position is open?

This question serves a dual purpose. It may reveal some good or some bad things about the job. Perhaps the position is open because the current employee has been promoted—which suggests that this is a position from which it is possible to grow. On the other hand, perhaps the position is open because someone quit or was fired. Perhaps the position is thankless or a dead end.

Whatever the answer to the question, the fact that you asked it demonstrates your practicality and sense of professional reality. It shows that you look before you leap, and that you are not one to snap at the first job that comes your way.

Depending on the response you get, you might want to follow up with something like this:

What's turnover like in this position? How many times has the position been filled in the past five years?

If the turnover is high, ask where the previous people went. If they were promoted into other positions within the company, great; if not, the indication may be that this is not such a desirable position, and you may want to think twice before accepting an offer.

 Clincher

Take the opportunity to translate "I" and "you" into "we" or "us" as often as possible in the course of the interview conversation.

If the line of questioning concerning the history of the position proves fruitful, you could continue with something more provocative:

What did you like best about the person who held this position previously?

Notice that the question is phrased positively—not *what didn't you like* or even *what did and didn't you like*. Let the interviewer volunteer any positives or negatives, to which you may respond accordingly.

Interviewer: Joe was a real self-starter. I liked that.

You: I can appreciate how important that is in this position. That's one of the things that appeals to me about it. It's an opportunity to take charge, to see projects through to completion, to take pride and satisfaction in a project.

Should you pick up on any significant negatives about the most recent holder of the position, follow up with this:

What would you like to see the next [job title] do differently?

This does not directly criticize an incumbent or a predecessor, but it does give you an opportunity to mine leads that signal directions in which the interviewer would like you to go.

Interviewer: Bill was a nice guy and a very hard worker, but I do wish he had developed a better tracking and reporting system.

You: That's good to know. It's awfully important to capture vital information with each sale. That's not information we'd want to squander.

Avoid negativity, which means that you should not criticize the person who had the job before you—especially since you are in no position to judge him firsthand. Notice in the example that the answer is nothing so graceless as "I would do a better job than Bill," but the message is unmistakable nevertheless: you agree and understand that the task, which Bill left undone, is important. Note the use of "we," which begins to integrate you into this organization's community.

Embrace the Mission

Stop talking about yourself, and start using your questions to address the company's *mission*. This is not only the last thing the interviewer expects you to talk about, it is the very thing of greatest concern to him—even if he never actually uses the word "mission" himself.

Your pre-interview research (see Chapter 2 and Appendix B) should tell you something about the mission of the target organization and provide a platform from which you can address your mission-related questions. However, you will find that most such questions fall into one of three categories:

1. Line extension

2. New lines

3. Market-share growth

def•i•ni•tion

Mission is the more or less concise formulation of the purpose, goals, and objectives of an entire organization or department.

Line Extension

All companies produce a product(s) or service(s). A fruitful course of questioning may concern *line extension*—new products or services that are not radical departures from what the company already does, but, rather, logical developments from current lines. Asking questions about line extensions will demonstrate to the interviewer that you are inventive, imaginative, yet grounded in reality. You understand the company's product or services; you're not suggesting radical new products or services unrelated to the company as it is currently set up, but logical extensions of what the firm already does. Try something like this:

> I noticed that you've extended your line of [product A] into the [product B] market. Is line extension an important part of the company's mission?

Or:

> I really admire your [product A]. Is the company planning to extend the [product A] line into [products B and C]?

def·i·ni·tion

A **line extension** is a new product or service that is a continuous, logical development of the products or services a firm currently offers. For example, a maker of breakfast cereal may introduce a line of snack foods (such as chewy bars) based on the cereal.

New Lines

Questions in this area require more caution. If the company you're interviewing with is clearly conservative, living off long-established product/service lines, you may simply want to steer clear of new-line questions altogether. However, if the company has a track record of innovation, pick up on it. Avoid storming in with a let-me-show-you-how-it's-done attitude. Instead of trotting out your own new-product ideas, engage the interviewer by allowing him to talk about his brainchild:

> Acme Industries has such a stunning track record of innovation. What new product line are you most excited about?

Then, respond to the interviewer in a way that keeps the conversation going. This is a subject that the interviewer probably enjoys talking about. Show him that you're interested. Let him feel good speaking with you.

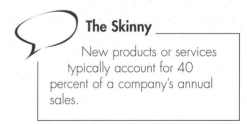

The Skinny

New products or services typically account for 40 percent of a company's annual sales.

Market-Share Growth

If nothing else—even if the company does not define its mission in terms of line extensions or new lines—the mission is usually defined in terms of making organized efforts to increase the firm's share of the existing market. Engage this issue:

> What steps are being taken to increase market share, and how does this position fit into that effort?

Reveal Yourself as a Prophet of Profitability

Although you want to avoid making promises that ring as hollow as they come on bold—"Hire me, and I'll make you untold millions!"—it is never amiss to ask questions aimed directly at the bottom line. Go ahead, put yourself on the spot:

> How would my performance be measured?

Once this question is answered, shift briefly to an apparently selfish mode:

> Obviously, I intend to perform at top level. It will keep us profitable and competitive. But, in addition to this, how is performance usually rewarded here?

The question shows that you have the common concerns of the company uppermost in mind, but that you are also a realist when it comes to yourself. You don't want to give the interviewer the impression that you are too good to be true (and too good to be truthful). However, you do want to demonstrate that your self-interest coincides with the interests of the company.

Demonstrate Proficiency

At some point in the interview, insert a question or two that demonstrates sheer proficiency. If you've never been given a full, written job description, ask for one now:

> Is there a written description of this position? May I see it?

Study it quickly and offer whatever intelligent comments you can on the duties as described. Demonstrate your essential understanding of the job.

If the position for which you are interviewing involves knowledge of special procedures or techniques, try to ask questions related to these. For example:

> Do you report on a cash basis or an accrual basis?

Don't get into an argument over the merits of one versus the other. If you agree with the choice of method, discuss its merits. If you disagree, ask more questions:

> That's interesting. Why do you use that method?

If you are genuinely concerned about the firm's choice of policy or methodology, ask if there is room for flexibility:

> Is there any room for flexibility on that?

> **Don't Call Us ...**
>
> *Ask* for a job description. Never *demand* one. Many employers, especially in smaller companies, do not prepare formal job descriptions. If the interviewer tells you that a job description is not available, drop the request without further comment.

Ask Questions That Show You're a Leader

Tread softly in this area. Questions that convey leadership may also be interpreted as challenges to existing authority. The last thing you want is to present yourself to an interviewer as a potential threat to his or her job.

Matters of Clout

A relatively nonthreatening question to assess the level of authority you'll be accorded is this one:

> Can you give me an idea of what range I'll have in determining my own work objectives, schedules, and deadlines?

Anything beyond this type of question risks being too aggressive. Feel your way carefully.

Take-Charge Attitude

There is a difference between taking charge and mounting an invasion. Here are two questions that demonstrate your willingness to give direction and take responsibility without stepping on any toes—or gunning for anyone's job:

> How many people would I be supervising? What are their backgrounds?

This takes up the gauntlet of responsibility while framing a question that merely asks for information. Continue:

> I'm curious as to why you are looking outside for candidates for this position rather than promoting from within. Is that something we could discuss?

The answer to this may provide just the launching pad you need to discuss the role of leadership in the position under consideration.

Highlight Diversity

Increasingly, employers view diversity as an asset rather than as a challenge or a burden. This said, you should never present yourself as a black candidate, a white candidate, a Polish candidate, a Hispanic candidate, a Catholic candidate, a female candidate, a gay candidate, or a disabled candidate. Race, ethnicity, national origin, religion, gender, sexual orientation, and so on should have no bearing on your suitability for the position. It is illegal for an employer to consider any of these things, and you should not bring them up, either.

This said, it is still possible to promote diversity as an asset. As questions that focus on the employer's needs. For example:

> Alphaville is a very diverse community—the kind of place I grew up in. Are you looking for employees who can take advantage of the diversity of the market in which you do business?

Or:

> The widget market has expanded rapidly and has, I believe, become increasingly diverse. Is hiring account executives who understand that diversity important to you?

Craft questions that assume diversity is an asset—and an asset you understand and are prepared to enhance and augment.

Clincher

Link questions about authority and clout to questions about responsibility: "Will I be *responsible* for setting my own schedules and deadlines?" *Not* "Will I have the *authority* to set my own schedules and deadlines?"

The Nitty-Gritty

In addition to asking the strategic questions—questions intended to convey as much information about you as they glean about the employer and his firm—don't leave the interview or proceed to the salary negotiating stage without having obtained a full understanding of the duties, responsibilities, and reporting levels the job entails.

Duties and Responsibilities

If no job description has been furnished, ask:

> What are the chief duties and responsibilities of [job title]?

Even if a description was made available to you, it pays to ask:

> Are there any duties and responsibilities listed in the job description that you see as especially critical?

And:

> Does the job description cover all the duties and responsibilities you think are important? Is there anything else I should know about?

Reporting Levels

Assess your relative position in the organization by nailing down an official version of the hierarchy:

> To whom would I report in this position?

When you've secured the answer, inquire about your prospective supervisor:

> And he/she reports to ...?

This should be sufficient to provide a quick sketch of the organizational structure of the department or firm. Some authorities suggest requesting a formal organizational chart, but this could be seen as an imposition. Never make the interviewer work on your behalf.

Above All, Know When to Stop

Don't ask questions just to hear yourself talk. Each of your questions should either say something about yourself or obtain the vital information you need to make your decisions. Ideally, each of your questions is aimed at accomplishing both objectives. When you sense that you've transmitted and received all the information that is important to you and to the employer, stop asking questions. You should also stop anytime the interviewer indicates that the interview is at an end.

The Least You Need to Know

- ◆ Ask dual-purpose questions, aimed at gathering information while conveying your qualifications and skills.

- ◆ Train yourself to walk into the interview *assuming* you will get the offer.

- ◆ Ask questions that always allow you to demonstrate your value to the prospective employer.

- ◆ It's important to ask questions, but never ask them for the sake of hearing yourself talk. Know when to stop.

Real-World Questions

In This Chapter

- Tailoring your questions to specific fields and functional areas
- Getting to the nitty-gritty that gets you the job
- Questions that show your grasp of real issues
- Questions relating to major functional areas

All employers look for the same things some of the time, and some employers look for the same things all of the time, but not all employers look for the same things all of the time. Certain needs and problems not only vary from one employer to another, but also from one industry to another. Pre-interview research will help you assess the issues specific to a company, and such research is also valuable for scoping out the needs of an industry. This chapter also suggests some key questions to raise when you interview in any of six major fields: sales, marketing, service, financial, R&D (research and development), and production.

One Size Does Not Fit All

You should not fail to ask the kinds of questions covered in the preceding two chapters. They apply to virtually any employment situation, because they relate to your portable skills, the skills that you carry with you and apply to whatever you do, rather than specialized skills required by a particular job. This said, jobs are not *all* about portable or transferable skills. They are also very much about those specialized skills and qualifications that are specifically targeted to certain tasks. Before your interview, take the time to research the functional areas of the target position and prepare some relevant questions.

If You're in Sales ...

Interviewing for a sales position is unique in that the entire interview process is in itself an opportunity to display your sales prowess. The emphasis is on performance, on selling yourself, and that is how it should be, but—and this is critical—not to the exclusion of other key considerations.

If you concentrate exclusively on selling yourself, on deliberately demonstrating your salesmanship at every turn, on focusing attention on yourself as merchandise, you risk coming off as self-centered, insecure, and, ultimately, unaware of a number of important realities that a sales position entails.

The questions that follow assume that you have been conducting the interview as a "sale," and that you have *answered* questions that demonstrate your aptitude for the position. Now it's your turn to ask questions that go beyond an eager—maybe overeager—desire to exhibit your skills. Ask questions that reveal your sophistication and savvy, that in some degree require the employer to sell *her* organization to *you*.

Client Load

You can make claim after claim about your selling prowess, but if you don't base what you say in the hard ground of reality, each of your claims will be perceived as just so much hot air.

For experienced salespeople, that hard ground is made of two principal substances:

1. The product itself

2. Client load

The interview is not the place to argue the merits of the product—although you could ask something like, "What do you see as the major selling points of the Acme Widget?" Instead, the interview is very much the appropriate venue for discussing client load:

What is the average client load per salesperson?

Once you have an answer to this, continue:

> How does that typically break down in terms of contact hours?

Then, open up the question:

> What kind of support do you give your salespeople in terms of assistants, secretarial help, and customer service?

You could then explore the functional links between sales and service:

> How do sales and service function together?

> **The Skinny**
>
> Both retail and whole-sale sales positions typically have great potential for income growth. Successful retail sales-people can expect to earn 200 percent more than their entry-level income within the same basic position after a few years. Successful wholesale salespeople can expect almost 300 percent growth.

This question is critical for two reasons. It not only demonstrates your strategic understanding of sales—the necessity for follow-through and customer support, which requires a strong customer-service operation—but also provides an X-ray view of the organization. Is the target employer a place that logically and logistically supports its salespeople and its customers, developing ongoing business rather than putting the emphasis on one isolated sale after the other? Or is it a place content to leave its sales force—and its customers—to twist slowly in the wind?

Reporting Structure

Your prospects and customers need to know that you have the *authority* to make deals, and that the deals you make are definitive. It is, therefore, vitally important for you to learn about the reporting structure of the organization that may hire you:

> To whom would I report in this position?

Expectations

Let's say you went to college, got a business degree, did pretty well at that, but just barely scraped by in those Science 101 requirements. That physics course almost killed you! Now knowing what you know about your interests and aptitude where physics is concerned, you wouldn't apply for a job as a rocket scientist. You know that you could never meet the employer's expectations.

Yet many job candidates fail to clarify issues of expectation during the interview. While this is a most consequential omission, it is an understandable one. You may fear that bringing up the subject of expectations is somehow a confession of your limitations. It's easier just to make claims and promises (truthful or not) and, for the present, assume that you'll meet them (which you'll then put off worrying about until you find yourself drowning in the job).

But the fact is that reality is always more persuasive than empty claims. Frame your questions about employer expectations as positively as possible, with an assurance that you are asking the questions in order to ensure that you will satisfy the employer:

> What do you consider a good, solid level of productivity for an incoming sales-person?

Only after you have this figure, should you establish whether or not there is a *minimum* requirement:

> Do you have an absolute minimum target?

Clincher _____

Try to obtain a statement of expectation expressed in numbers—sales volume, units sold, clients contacted, and so forth. Vague, subjective expressions of expectation are of little help to you and may lead to mutual disappointment later.

Wrap up with something like this:

> Ms. Smith, I want to make certain that I can satisfy your needs in this position. Are there any other expectations you'd like me to know about?

Avoid phrasing a question about expectations this way: "I want to make sure I can do the job." Never say anything that prompts the interviewer to question your ability. Instead, frame all questions regarding expectations in terms of ensuring that you will provide satisfaction.

Compensation Basis

Don't confuse questions concerning compensation basis with salary negotiation. Certainly, it's important to negotiate the level of your compensation, but it's also of crucial importance to clarify the *basis* on which that compensation will be determined:

> Can we review the subject of commissions?

That question may be all you need. However, you may also need to clarify:

◆ Balance between salary and commission

◆ Varying levels of commission—depending on product, price, terms, and so on

◆ Policies on splitting commissions

◆ Performance bonuses and other incentives

If You're in Marketing ...

Marketing continues to be a growth area for employment opportunity; however, few functional areas are subject to as much variation in definition and expectation as marketing. The consequences of such confusion range from a botched interview to a disastrous employment situation.

Mission

Certainly, it would be a mistake to start a marketing interview by asking, "Yes, I have a question. Just what is marketing?" It is very savvy, however, to ask *this* question:

How would you define the mission of marketing in this organization (or department)?

Relation to Other Departments

Another area of ambiguity and wide variation from organization to organization is the relation of marketing to other departments.

Establish just where marketing stands in relation to other components of the organization:

How does marketing work with other functions here?

If necessary, sharpen the focus of the question:

Would you say that marketing leads or follows the other departments?

Role of Innovation

That last question is a natural entry point into the issue of innovation. You will want to determine what role innovation plays in the target company and what role marketing plays in innovation.

> Is innovation a significant part of your program?

If your pre-interview research has already revealed that innovation is a significant aspect of the firm's strategy, don't ask a superfluous question; just leap in to clarify the role of marketing in innovation:

> From what I've learned in researching the firm, innovation is a vital part of your corporate mission. Where does marketing fit into this? Does it lead the innovation effort? Does it follow the lead of R&D?

Reporting Structure

Find out to whom you report, and to whom he or she reports in turn:

> To whom would I report in this position?

If You're in Service ...

In recent years, customer service has reached a crossroads. Some organizations have decided to view it no longer as a kind of necessary evil, something that has to be provided, but that drains rather than generates revenue. Traditionally, customer service was classed strictly as a support service, not a profit center. Lately, in some organizations, customer service has been seen as an important part of the value customers purchase. Just think of the role a reputation for good customer service plays, for example, in your decision to purchase one brand of personal computer over another. Even more, some companies now regard customer service as an extension of the sales function: the customer-service specialist can use his or her customer contact to educate the customer about new products and accessories and to *upsell* accessories and related products.

def•i•ni•tion

To **upsell** is to use the customer-service function as an opportunity to offer customers accessories and other products related to their original purchase.

It is also true that many organizations have made a very different turn at the cross-roads, effectively separating the company's core operation from the customer service function by outsourcing as much of it as possible. Outsourced customer-service operations are not necessarily bad, but they rarely reflect an attitude that sees customer service as an opportunity. Typically, the firm that outsources service regards it as an obligation.

If you are interviewing for a customer-service position, it is crucially important that you ask the questions that define the target employer's approach to customer service and the firm's attitude toward it.

Mission

Precisely because the mission of customer service represents a crossroads for so many firms these days, you will want to ask questions that define it:

> How would you define the mission of customer service in this organization?

The Skinny

When you ask about workload, be certain to frame your questions to focus on the needs of the employer, not on your desire to be out the door by five each day: "My concern is to have ample time with each call to ensure customer satisfaction."

Client Load

Client load is an area you need to probe thoroughly in the course of the interview:

> What is the typical per-hour, per-representative client load?

You may define this further:

> The average customer-support call lasts how long?

And:

> Typically, how long are callers put on hold?

Outsourcing Issues

In recent years, many customer-service operations, either in whole or in part, have been outsourced, often to offshore service providers. This book is not the place to debate the desirability of outsourcing from the point of view of the firm on the one hand and the customer on the other, but it is absolutely necessary that, when you interview for a customer-service position, you ask questions about the issue. Unless your pre-interview research has provided the answer, a good question to start with in this area is simply this:

What is the department's position on outsourcing?

Depending on the response, you may ask questions to clarify and expand on the issue:

What customer service functions are outsourced?

How do those within the department interface with the outsourcing service?

What control and direction does in-house customer service exercise over the outsourcing provider?

Is there a procedure in place for escalating a customer's issue from outsourcing help to an in-house supervisor?

Also probe the in-house role in creating customer service procedures and policy:

How are procedures and policies formulated?

How are procedures and policies communicated to the outsource provider?

How are procedures and policies monitored and enforced?

Outsourcing is a reality, and like any other reality it presents liabilities as well as opportunities. The questions you ask should help you to determine not only the nature and scope of the position for which you are interviewing, but its likely future—or, indeed, whether there is even likely to be a future in it.

If You're in Financial ...

Financial positions vary widely. If it's not clear from the job description, your major objective will be to determine to what degree the position is an accounting function—essentially financial reporting—and to what degree it is an analytical function—predictive and heavily involved in creating financial projections.

Mission

Ask questions that define the mission of the financial department in general and the nature of your prospective job in particular:

Is the mission of this department primarily reporting or analytical?

Or:

Approximately what percentage of the position's responsibilities deal with financial projection, and what percentage deal with financial reporting?

Reporting Structure

In financial positions it is of critical importance to understand the reporting structure that is in place.

To whom does this position report?

Follow up with:

And to whom does [position's supervisor] report?

Income and growth potential are typically proportional to the degree of discretionary authority you are given. The more layers of management that stand between you and the top, the less authority you will enjoy.

Special Goals

While the mission questions should define the broad goals and objectives of the department, it would be thoughtful to add a question about any special goals. For example:

Are there any special circumstances that call for the department to capture certain kinds of data for specialized purposes?

If You're in R&D (Research and Development) …

Typically, interviews for R&D positions involve specialized technical issues that are beyond the scope of this book; however, you should not neglect the following, more general subject areas.

Mission

It's likely that your pre-interview research will have revealed the thrust of R&D's mission—at least in historical terms—in the target organization. If not, you could begin with:

How would you define R&D's mission in this organization?

If you do come to the interview with some idea of the department's mission, ask questions that build on your knowledge:

It's apparent that, historically, R&D has been involved in XYZ. Do you see that involvement continuing, or is the mission developing in different directions?

Autonomy and Reporting Structure

Creativity and accountability are not always easy to balance. Be sure to craft some questions that address issues of creative autonomy versus the department's reporting structure. Try something like this:

How are work groups organized in this department?

You will also want to ask the usual "To whom do I report?" question.

Expectations

Clarify issues of workload and the measures by which progress and achievement are judged:

How does the department evaluate—and reward—accomplishment?

If You're in Production ...

As is the case with R&D, the primary issues in production-oriented interviews are likely to be technical and specialized. Beyond this, the most central issues are likely to revolve around expectations.

Don't Call Us ... _____

Reserve comment if you discover that the employer's expectations are unrealistic. Avoid shaking your head, gasping, laughing, or muttering "Impossible!" Instead, ask the employer what she is currently achieving. Get more information. Discuss—do not judge—the employer's unrealistic expectations. Remember, you can always turn down a job offer—but only *if* the interview produces one. Don't mislead the interviewer, but do keep the discussion upbeat.

Expectations

You don't want to leave the interview without a clear idea of what is expected in the production function in terms of volume and quality of work. Quantify expectations as much as possible:

> I understand that this position has been created to increase efficiency. What is your target increase?

Or:

> What is our goal above and beyond the current rate of production?

Reporting Structure

Like customer service, production is a function in which you can either shine or be buried. To a significant degree, the fate that awaits you hinges on the reporting structure in place. Ask the usual questions:

> To whom does the person in this position report?

And:

> [Job title's] supervisor reports to whom?

Regulatory Issues

Your pre-interview research, combined with general knowledge and common sense, should tell you whether or not government regulatory issues have significant impact on R&D at the target company. Some industries and products are more closely regulated than others. Asking questions that relate to regulation demonstrate your understanding and appreciation of real-world research and development issues.

Precisely what questions to ask depends entirely on the nature of the field, the product, and the position you are seeking.

Outsourcing Issues

If your pre-interview research has raised questions of the degree to which R&D is outsourced in the target company, don't leave the interview without pursuing the issue. Be straightforward:

> Is all of your R&D handled by in-house staff?

If the answer is no, continue:

> About what proportion of R&D is outsourced?
>
> What kinds of projects are outsourced?
>
> What aspects of R&D are outsourced?
>
> Can you give me an idea of how the in-house person [that is, the person holding the job for which you are interviewing] works with the outsource provider?

Depending on where the answer to the last question leads, you may want to continue the discussion by asking about control and monitoring of the outsource provider, control of trade secrets, and issues of reporting and responsibility.

As in the case of customer service, outsourcing is a reality of R&D—and, these days, a growing reality. It is not something to be feared, let alone shunned, but rather understood.

The Least You Need to Know

- ◆ Although you should not become bogged down in questions related to the details of a specific job, do tailor your questions to fit specific fields and functional areas.

- ◆ Real-world questions reveal your practical grasp of a field or functional area.

- ◆ Be careful to ensure that your nitty-gritty questions are not phrased as challenges to the interviewer. Their purpose is both to gather information and to demonstrate your grasp of the position in question.

- ◆ Ask questions that assess the future of the position, including the prospects for advancement and the role of outsourcing.

Part 4

Special Settings and Challenging Circumstances

Often—and, these days, more often than not—the interview is a combination of variations on the traditional, one-on-one scenario. The chapters that follow show you how to initiate an "informational interview," and how to avoid being screened out in a preliminary interview. With more and more preliminary interviewing being done online or on the phone, it is essential to know how to put yourself across when you're not face to face. Here, you'll find advice on interviewing online as well as on the phone.

Then there are the special situation interviews, including mealtime interviews, panel interviews, sequential or serial interviews, and automated or computer-assisted interviews.

Chapter 17

Creating an Interview

In This Chapter

- How to get an informational interview
- The online informational interview
- How to evaluate employment and career potential within an industry or company
- Identifying the person with the power to hire you
- Questions to ask at the informational interview

You know the routine. Answer an ad or send a letter of inquiry and your resumé, and, if all goes very well, you'll get a call for an interview. It's like a dance party 50 or 60 years ago: the boy's job was to ask the girl to dance. And the girl's job? She was supposed to do nothing but wait until asked.

But just as all that began to change in the 1960s, so has the etiquette of the interview. You no longer have to wait for someone to respond favorably to your resumé before you secure an interview. You—yes, *you*—can take the initiative and *ask* for an interview. Here's how.

Wallflower No More

Begin by understanding this: the interview you ask for is not an employment interview, at least not directly. It is instead an *informational interview*, an attempt to collect information about specific careers and companies. And it's important that you approach the informational interview this way, rather than as a thinly disguised effort to "get a foot in the door" and land a job. The informational interview is a step in a process. To be sure, if you're offered a job during this interview, consider it. But don't expect it, and don't push for it. Your objectives are:

◆ Information gathering

◆ Information broadcasting

Let me explain. It's important to learn as much as you can about your target company and your target industry. The informational interview is valuable for this. But it's also important to make yourself known to the people who matter—people within potential target companies as well as within your target industry generally. Eventually, you have every reason to hope, these contacts may pay off in terms of employment, but the object is not an immediate ticket to a job.

def·i·ni·tion

An **informational interview** is an interview you request in order to gather information about a particular company or an entire industry. The purpose of such an interview is to enlarge your business network, to meet potential employers, to learn from them, and to allow them to make your acquaintance. Immediate employment is not an objective of the informational interview.

When to Go Online and When to Commit to Real Life

"Face time"—a one-on-one, in-person interview—is always potentially valuable. There is no substitute for it. Or, rather, no 100 percent satisfactory substitute for it. A telephone interview is a weak substitute, but better than nothing. An online interview, especially with a real-time video component, is stronger than a phone interview, but still not the same as real, live face time. An alternative to all of these informational interviewing modes is e-mail or instant messaging.

Any good contact with a potential employer—or someone who may lead you to an employer—is better than none; however, if possible, bid for in-the-flesh face time.

Five Steps to an Informational Interview

The informational interview won't come to you. That's because it doesn't exist until you create it. The informational interview is an opportunity to take control and to *make* things happen.

Step 1: Identify Your Targets

The first step is to identify your targets. You'll need to decide just what it is that interests you. Perhaps you already know; perhaps you arc still looking. If you need help—or need to stimulate your career thinking—resources abound. Here are some "general outlook" books that may start your creative juices flowing:

- *The Adams Jobs Almanac, 9th ed.* Holbrook, MA: Adams Publishing, 2006 (updated frequently).

- Bolles, Richard Nelson. *What Color Is Your Parachute? 2008: A Practical Manual for Job-Hunters and Career-Changers.* Berkeley, CA: Ten Speed Press, 2007.

- Farr, Michael, and Laurence Shatkin. *Best Jobs for the 21st Century.* St. Paul, MN: JIST Works, 2006.

- *Occupational Outlook Handbook 2008-2009.* St. Paul, MN: JIST Works, 2008 (updated frequently).

- Zichy, Shoya, and Ann Bidou. *Career Match: Connecting Who You Are with What You'll Love to Do.* New York: AMACOM, 2007.

The web bristles with career-guidance sites, ranging from sites that offer interactive diagnostic quizzes and tests to job outlook sites. Check out the following:

- Princeton Review Career Quiz (www.princetonreview.com/cte/quiz/)

- The Career Key (www.careerkey.org)

- Career Briefs (www.soicc.state.nc.us/SOICC/info/briefs.htm)

- While you are scouring the web, log on to "Informational Interviewing" at http://danenet.wicip.org/jets/jet-9407-p.html, which discusses at length the whole subject of informational interviewing—and has plenty of good ideas to consider.

Once you've narrowed your focus to a particular industry, search for and read news articles concerning the target industry online and in the general as well as business press. You might also contact the publicity offices of various firms in the industry. Get copies of speeches by the CEO and obtain industry-related press releases.

Clincher

A readily accessible way to identify growth companies, growth industries, and growth markets is to read the stock quotation pages in your daily newspaper. Track companies that show a pattern of upward movement in stock prices. These are likely to be the firms engaged in promising growth. If they are bristling with opportunity for the investor, they probably offer opportunity to the potential employee, too.

Step 2: Evaluate Your Targets

After you've determined where your interests lie, you'll need to evaluate the industry and firms within the industry. You'll want to look at two dimensions:

1. Where the action is.

2. Where the action is likely to be.

Look for industries and firms that are hiring now. More specifically, look for industries and firms that are currently hiring people with your skills. Remember, however, that just because an industry is "hot"—frequently mentioned in the press, and often the topic of conversation—does not necessarily mean that jobs are plentiful. Hot industries may indeed require many new hires, but they may also be relatively closed or glutted with applicants for a few plum positions.

This brings us to the second dimension of your evaluation. The savvy investor never devotes large sums to "mature" companies—those that have done about all the growing they're going to do. Follow this investor's lead, and look for industries and companies poised for growth and expansion in expanding markets. It is a very good idea to log on to Google News and set up "news alerts" keyed to the industries, issues, and companies that interest you. When relevant news appears online, an alert will be sent to your e-mail address.

Don't limit your research to books, magazines, newspapers, and online sources. If your target career or industry produces something sold in retail stores, start window shopping. Look at the product or products in question, and ask the store manager or assistant manager or the cash-register clerk how the merchandise has been moving and what people say about it. Log on to online retail sites (such as Amazon) and check out the product's sales ranking, a piece of information that many sites provide.

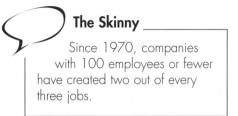

The Skinny

Since 1970, companies with 100 employees or fewer have created two out of every three jobs.

Step 3: Identify the People with the Power to Hire You

Face it: no company will ever hire you.

Now that I have your attention, read on: no company ever hires anybody.

A *person* hires you. People hire people. You'll never get an interview with General Motors, or Verizon, or Dell Computer, or General Foods, or Microsoft. What you will get is the opportunity to speak with a human being associated with one of these firms. And the real trick is finding just the right human being among the 5,000, 10,000, or 20,000 employees who work for the typical mega-organization.

The *real* trick? Actually, it's easy to decide on the right person to talk to. Choose the one who has the authority—the clout—to hire you.

The easiest way to find the person with the clout to hire you is to apply exclusively to companies with fewer than 50 employees. Call such a place and ask for the name of the boss. That's the person who can give you a job.

But maybe you can't—or just don't want to—limit yourself to small firms. Researching the larger firms should begin to turn up names of the people in charge. Log on to Networking for Professionals (www.networkingforprofessionals.com). This site may well you connect with some of the people who have the authority to hire you—or who can guide you to those who do.

Now is a good time to review the discussion of networking in Chapter 2. Start building up and working your network. If you get a name and phone number from one of your network contacts, secure permission to use his or her name: "May I tell So-and-so that you recommended I call?"

The next step is to make the call (preferable) or send the e-mail (second best). Explain that you are interested in scoping out career opportunities at Such-and-Such Corporation and that So-and-so recommended you call. Ask: "Who would I contact who has the authority to hire me for a [job title] position?"

Step 4: Make the Call

Once you've identified the person who can hire you, pick up the phone and bid for an in-person interview, if possible and practical. (If an in-person interview cannot be arranged—for example, if the target employer is located in another city, and you don't want to invest in the travel expenses—try to arrange for a later online or telephone interview.)

If all you have is an e-mail address, send an e-mail rather than make a phone call. Just remember that everyone in business gets a ton of e-mails every day. They are easy to overlook and even easier to ignore. A phone call is Plan A.

If you obtained the person's name from one of your contacts, make certain that you secure permission to use his or her name. You might even ask your contact to call ahead on your behalf. If, however, you obtained the name through your own research, let that be your lead-off point:

> Mr. Crawford, my name is Sarah Ferguson. I've been doing quite a bit of reading about your company, and, in just about everything I've read, your name appears prominently.

Step 5: Explain Yourself

So much for the opening sentence or two. Next? Well, don't ask for an interview. Indeed, *ask* for nothing. Instead, make an offer:

> I am the assistant controller at International Widgets, where I've been involved in upgrading our audit systems. I've been able to cut general audit turnaround time by 20 percent here, and I would be grateful for the opportunity to discuss with you how what I've learned at International might benefit Such-and-Such Corporation.

Appealing in some immediate way to your target's self-interest is a far more effective way to begin the conversation than by asking him or her for something.

If you're just starting out or, for some other reason, feel that you have no special infor-mation or insight to share, you can still make an offer. Offer the opportunity to help:

> Mr. Blank, Mary Wheeler suggested that you might be willing to help me with some informal advice. Mary spoke very highly of your expertise in the direct mail marketing of widgets. I've been with Acme Widgets myself for the past

two years. I'm now assistant sales manager, but I would like to move into the marketing side. The move is getting a bit urgent. You may be aware—since you're apparently aware of just about everything that goes on in this industry—that Acme is beginning a downsizing program. While I don't seem to be in immediate danger personally, I know my department is going to be reduced, along with opportunities generally.

Here's how you could help me. I am hoping that we could sit down together for a few minutes—at your convenience—to discuss direct-mail approaches to widget marketing. Your insights into where the industry is going and whom I should contact would mean a great deal to me. I'd also be grateful for any feedback you might have to offer on my own background and experience.

Is this request really an "offer"? After all, what does the employer get out of it? The fact is that most people welcome an opportunity to be helpful. It's not only flattering, but also gratifying. It feels good. You are offering an opportunity to feel good.

Only if your target expresses interest, either in what you have to offer or in helping you, should you set up an interview.

It would be nice if it were always this easy. Unfortunately, it's possible that your target may turn you down flat, claiming that he is too busy for a meeting. If that happens, reply politely: "I understand that you're busy …" Or: "I understand that you're not hiring at present and that your schedule doesn't give you much leeway just now." Then continue: "Circumstances do change, however, so may I send you my resumé for your reference?"

Don't Call Us …

Beware of offering proprietary or privileged information that belongs to your present employer! It's not only unethical, but it may be illegal or expose you to a civil suit. At the very least, such disclosure is grounds for dismissal.

What *Are* You About, Anyway?

But let's assume you're in, that you've scored at least a few minutes of face-to-face contact with someone who has the power to hire you. Congratulations!

Now what?

Offer Something

Make good on the promise that got you the interview. If you have certain insights, experience, skills, or knowledge to share, begin by sharing them. If you are "offering" an opportunity for the employer to help you, follow through and reiterate that. Whatever you do, do *not* begin by putting out your hand for employment.

Don't Call Us ...

Beware of renewed resistance if your conversation partner suspects you are just trying to get a foot in *his* door. Fend this off with preemptive assurance: "I want to emphasize that I am not here to hit you up for a job. At this point in my job search, I'm just looking for information—surveying the nature of the marketplace. Of course, if you know of any specific opportunities, I'd appreciate hearing about them. But I haven't come here with that expectation."

The Questions to Ask

While the face-to-face phase of the informational interview should be informal, don't leave it unstructured. After thanking the person for seeing you, reiterating who recommended that you call, and reminding him of the reason for your visit—including a quick review of your situation and interests—begin the conversation. Provide a thumbnail sketch of your background. Prepare it beforehand and pare it down to no more than a three-minute presentation.

After you've presented the thumbnail sketch, open up the discussion with the following questions:

- How did you get started in this line of work?
- What do you like most about it?
- What do you dislike most about it?

Then broaden the discussion:

- What are your views on the present state and future prospects of the industry?
- Can you recommend anyone else I might speak with?

Limit the Time

In a formal job interview, it's up to the interviewer to end the session. He or she decides when your time is up. In an informational interview, however, you should serve as timekeeper. Unless the conversation clearly warrants more time, try to limit the interview to no more than 15 or 20 minutes. If the other person shows any impatience, you should pick up the cue and signal that you are ready to wrap things up:

> Ms. Smith, I know you're busy, and I appreciate your having given me this time. I have just two more questions.

Nice Save!

Televised Academy Award and Emmy Award ceremonies used to feature a set with a sweeping staircase, down which the award presenters would walk to the podium. Who could watch presenter after presenter walk down those stairs without thinking, *What if she trips?* It rarely happens, but it *can* happen. And when you are nervous, your feet may feel like lead and your legs may be knotted and reluctant to move. If you obviously stumble while making your entrance into the interview, it's important to get the incident behind you and the interviewer *pronto*. Neither ignore it, nor berate yourself as a clumsy, worthless oaf. Try something like this: "I always try to make a memorable entrance. Maybe I've succeeded this time." Then, offer your hand for the greeting shake: "Hello. I'm John Smith."

Don't Look for a Job Here (at Least, Not Now)

As you bring the interview to its concluding phase, reiterate that your purpose has not been to find immediate employment at this firm; nevertheless, you should ask some or all of the following questions:

- ◆ "Would you happen to know of any openings available now?"

- ◆ "Would you personally know any employers who might want to see me?"

- ◆ "Have you heard of any developments that might suggest a particular company would be interested in what I have to offer?"

- ◆ "What's the best way for me to get connected—to get into a position to hear about employment developments?"

Finally, take a leaf from the book of Ed Koch, New York City's colorful mayor from 1978 to 1989. His trademark tag line was "How'm I doin'?" Ask for a similar report card on yourself:

- "Is my background clear to you? Do I present it effectively?"

- "Are my objectives clear?"

- "Do you think my objectives are feasible?"

If you sense that the partner in your conversation is willing to continue, you might ask a few more specific and challenging questions:

- "Are there certain skills or credentials I need to acquire?"

- "Do you see any problem areas for me, given my background?"

- "Is there anything in my background that is particularly appealing or strong, that I should emphasize?"

The last question is important because it ends on a positive note. Not only might it secure valuable information for you, but it will also leave this individual with an impression of you based on strengths rather than problems and areas that need improvement.

The Least You Need to Know

- Do not expect immediate employment from an informational interview. Its purpose is to obtain information while getting yourself known in an industry or at a company. It is but one step in a process.

- E-mail, real-time texting, and videoconferencing are viable alternatives to the face-to-face interview—and they are easier to set up.

- Do not seek informational interviews at random; research the target industry and employer beforehand.

- Companies never hire people. People (who work for companies) hire people. Identify and seek the person with the power to hire you.

Chapter 18

Getting Through the Gatekeeper Interview

In This Chapter

- What is a screening interview?
- Who conducts the interview?
- The screening interview versus the selection interview: How do they differ?
- Objectives of the screening interview
- What the screening interviewer is looking for
- Questions to expect and how to answer them

Officially, it may be called a preliminary interview. Internally, it's probably referred to as a screening interview. In fact, it's a gatekeeper interview. Its purpose is not to identify and harvest talent, but to eliminate "unacceptable" candidates in order to conserve the high-end time of the senior executive—the person with the power to hire you.

Screening interviews are inherently frustrating for the job candidate because the object is not so much to win as it is not to lose; that is, the object is to evade the screen. This chapter shows you how.

The First Cut—So What?

You open your morning e-mail. There's a message from XYZ Corporation. Your finger hesitates over the mouse button. Will the click reveal good news or bad? In? Or out? At last you get up the nerve. Click.

The message begins with the pronoun "we." Now that's usually bad news. Employers prefer to frame rejection in terms of a collective "we" rather than a personal and individual "I." But you read on.

And—hold it …. Yes! XYZ wants to interview you! They were impressed with your resumé, your background, your qualifications. But, just another minute, the e-mail is *not* signed by Ms. T. J. Krumm, Manager of Sales, to whom you had addressed your cover letter and resumé, but by one Larry Larson, Human Resources Associate.

What gives?

This is your signal that you've been selected for a *screening interview*. Sure, you've made the first cut, but so what?

def•i•ni•tion

A **screening interview** is a preliminary interview typically conducted by a junior-level Human Resources staffer. Its purpose is to screen out unqualified job candidates, so that (theoretically) only qualified candidates are interviewed by the supervisors who are actually authorized to hire. A **selection interview** is the in-depth interview conducted by the person or persons who have the authority to hire you. In larger organizations, this interview is often preceded by a screening interview.

A Lesson from the Hippocratic Oath

Upon taking their medical degrees, many graduates still recite the Hippocratic Oath, composed by the most famous physician of ancient Greece, Hippocrates (ca. 460 B.C.E.–ca. 377 B.C.E.). Its initial precept is "First, do no harm."

This rule shouldn't apply exclusively to doctors. It's also a cardinal principle for those who suddenly find themselves suddenly thrust into a screening interview.

Remember, first and foremost, the screening interviewer is looking for *negatives*—reasons to weed you out—not positive reasons to take your candidacy to the next step. Once you understand the nature of a screening interview, you'll need to adjust your objectives and interview strategy accordingly. To "do no harm," observe the following:

- During in-depth interviews (or *selection interviews*), it's a good idea to take the initiative, but in the screening interview it is best to follow the interviewer's lead.

- Respond to questions as directly and as concisely as possible. Do not digress. Do not evade the question. Do not shoot the breeze or otherwise make small talk.

- Avoid introducing negatives or potential negatives. Emphasize positive qualifications, strengths, and skills.

- By all means, be courteous, pleasant, and polite, but don't make an extra effort to put your personality in the spotlight. Stick to the facts.

The screening interviewer's supervisors judge his performance by the volume of candidates he screens out and by the absence of complaints about unqualified candidates slipping through the initial screen. Therefore, the screening interviewer is actually *motivated* to err on the side of screening out too many candidates.

Foot in the Door (Not in the Mouth)

What, exactly, is the screening interviewer's mission?

- First and foremost, to find reasons to keep you on the far side of the gate

- Second, to note a solid background and promising levels of qualifications and skills

As a rule, candidates are summoned to screening interviews because a resumé, cover letter, colleague's recommendation, telephone conversation, or query letter has roused the interest of the person who actually has the power to hire—or has roused the interest of the person delegated to review incoming resumés. Since interest at this point is based on the alleged facts of the resumé or some other equivalent, the screening interviewer will likely ask questions designed to uncover inconsistencies in your background and possible discrepancies in your resumé. In other words, the screening interviewer is looking for …

- Glitches in your employment history.

- Gaps in your employment history.

- Evidence of lying about the "facts" you have presented.

This is not a very friendly approach to the task of interviewing. Now I'm not saying that the screening interviewer is an evil person. He has a tough job, and, in a large organization that may be flooded with job applicants—many with dubious qualifications—he may even have a worthwhile job. But it *is* just that: a job. The screening interview is mainly a clerical function. Only the most rudimentary judgment is being exercised:

◆ Does the candidate's background raise blatant questions about her suitability for the job?

◆ Is the candidate lying?

Getting Through Online Gatekeepers

These days, you may not even be called to an in-person screening interview, but asked to participate in a telephone or online interview. Review Chapter 6, but also take in all the advice I am about to give. On the phone, online, or in real life, the gatekeeper interview is aimed first and foremost at screening you out.

Many online screening interviews do not even take place in real time. Instead, you may be sent an e-mail with questions to answer or you may be directed to sign in to a dedicated website, where you will find a form to fill out. As with answering any other screening questions, be direct and concise. Avoid providing information that has not been specifically requested. Instead, aim to give the target employer the information he wants—nothing less, to be sure, but nothing extra, either.

If a question or form asks you to specify your "salary requirements," leave this blank or write something like "dependent on duties and responsibilities." If the form demands an answer in numbers—some interactive online forms will not allow themselves to be sent unless every line is filled in—supply a salary range, as discussed in Chapter 13.

Brevity

The screening interviewer's assignment is to get facts. Your objective is to get past the screening interviewer and move up to the next stage. While the screening interviewer's purpose and yours may seem to conflict, you can, in fact, find common cause. It is this: both of you want to get through the interview quickly, efficiently, and with the facts clearly expressed.

The Challenge

The challenge in the screening interview is ...

- To furnish no piece of information that will get you screened out.

- To provide the facts for which the interviewer is hungry.

- To provide these facts clearly and without evasion (apparent or actual).

- To provide these facts concisely.

- To be brief, without being terse or curt.

Don't Call Us ...

Never preface your answers with "As I mentioned in my resumé ..." or "As my resumé states ..." Just answer the question, as if it were fresh.

Let's talk a little more about the last two points. Answer the interviewer's questions as fully as possible *without* digressing; that is, without going on to other subjects. Whereas the in-depth or selection interview (the interview conducted by the person who can actually hire you) resembles a conversation, in which one subject naturally leads to another, the screening interview is strictly Q&A: question and answer. It is not a conversation.

Clincher

Be aware that while the screening interviewer's mission is overwhelmingly fact-oriented, he or she is a human being who responds to the way you act and to your appearance. Present yourself in a polite and pleasant manner and dress appropriately, as you would in any other interview situation. See Chapter 5 for advice on appearance.

But, in your effort at brevity, do not cut your answers so short that valuable information is omitted. Except where obviously called for, avoid simple yes or no answers. Avoid one-word answers altogether. Yes/no and one-word answers tend to bring an interview to a premature end.

Painting Broad Strokes

Here is another fact you should know about the screening interviewer: he will probably never see you again—especially if he is an HR functionary. This has some important implications:

- He doesn't have to be concerned about how he will get along with you.

- He doesn't have to assess how you'll get along with others.

- He doesn't have to concern himself much with your personality.

- He doesn't have to assess your problem-solving ability.

- He doesn't have to probe how your mind works.

- He doesn't have to gauge the level of your creativity.

- He doesn't have to possess a specialist's knowledge of the open position.

All he has to do is verify facts and, perhaps, elicit additional facts. Not only are the screener's intuitive feelings about you irrelevant to his mission, he has probably been "professionally" cautioned against allowing his personal feelings to interfere with his job.

Don't Call Us ...

Do nothing to alienate the screening interviewer. Although he is not supposed to evaluate personality, any serious personality conflict that develops during the interview could well result in your being screened.

None of this means that you should come across like a machine, impersonally churning out fact after fact. Always, in any business contact situation, be courteous and pleasant. Being businesslike doesn't mean you can't smile. Go ahead: smile. Just don't waste time.

As to your personality, render it in broad strokes. Make a positive impression as a decent, friendly, outgoing, eminently cooperative person. You're not one who'll make waves. You're a team player. That's all the screening interviewer needs to know about your personality.

Say This

Difficult as it may be, you should strive to avoid overt creativity in the screening interview. Follow the interviewer's lead. Expect questions relating to …

- Your job history.

- Your skills, including transferable skills.

- Apparent inconsistencies in your resumé (i.e., lies).

- Work-history gaps.

Be prepared to answer such questions directly and forthrightly. Being prepared means that you should have clear answers prepared and ready to trot out. Even more importantly, act preemptively by creating a resumé that is free from inconsistencies. Fill chronological gaps in your work history as fully as possible. Here are some tried-and-true tips for making your between-jobs activity sound most convincing:

◆ If you worked as a *freelancer* or an *independent contractor*, be sure to list your most important clients or projects.

def•i•ni•tion

A **freelancer** is someone who offers services for hire, independent of a regular or permanent employer. An **independent contractor** is an individual or company hired by another firm to perform certain services. The independent contractor is not a regular, permanent employee of the hiring firm. Whereas a freelancer works independently of an employer, an independent contractor may be an entire company or an individual employee of the company (other than the hiring firm).

◆ If you took time out for training or special study, cite where and why. If you did not attend a formal institution for this study or training, call it "independent study" or "independent training" or even "independent research," and state clearly your area of concentration and your purpose. This will probably elicit questions from the screening interviewer, but it's preferable to leaving a gap that denotes unemployment.

◆ Don't *excuse* planned employment gaps. Celebrate and capitalize on them. If you took a half year off after your last job to see the world, present this as a deliberate and worthwhile act. Do not call it a "vacation," "time off," or "goofing off." Say that you thought it important to see the world. Speak—briefly—about what you learned, especially what you learned that may be of value to the employer.

◆ At the very least, be prepared to account for any employment gap in a positive way: "I knew that I didn't have to be desperate for a job, and I decided to take adequate time to research and identify a position in which I could offer excellent value to the employer and in which I could grow professionally."

Finally, don't get caught short. If you hem and haw, looking flustered or stymied, the interviewer will conclude that he has hit pay dirt: a reason to screen you out. Be prepared with a positive answer for any and all gaps or apparent inconsistencies.

Don't Say That

If you want your hand held through the screening interview, hold tightly to this commandment: *Thou shalt give positive answers only.* Do not …

◆ Volunteer modesty or doubts about your skills or qualifications.

◆ Speculate on whether a particular skill or qualification is relevant to the job.

◆ Criticize your current or past employer(s).

◆ Criticize a supervisor, coworker, subordinate, or customer.

◆ Talk extensively about your family or the "burden of" your family responsibilities.

It is possible that the screening interviewer will address issues of salary: "What salary level are you looking for?" This can be a sticky situation. You already know from Chapter 13, that it is decidedly not to your advantage to be eager to volunteer a salary figure. You can be sure that any figure you mention in the screening interview will be passed along to the supervisor at the selection interview. That will make negotiation difficult. Even more serious, however, is the possibility that mentioning either too high or too low a figure will get you screened out, if the figure you give falls outside of the salary range authorized for the position. You have several choices:

◆ If you answered an ad for the position, and a salary range was mentioned in the ad, respond this way: "The announced salary range seems a reasonable place to begin negotiation."

◆ If no salary or salary range has been mentioned, ask for one: "What salary range has been authorized for this position?" If you get a response, respond in turn: "That certainly seems like a good place from which to negotiate."

◆ If the screening interviewer cannot or will not give you the authorized range, you may answer that you "expect a salary commensurate with my skills and qualifications and with the duties and responsibilities of the position."

◆ If the interviewer presses for a figure, respond with a salary range. See Chapter 13 for a method of calculating the range. Come to the screening interview prepared with this information—just in case.

If the salary range the screening interviewer mentions is significantly below what you had expected, don't comment or express disappointment—or, for that matter, agreement. Your sole objective is to get to the next stage, the selection interview. You can always discuss salary there. You're free to reject an offer. But first you must get an offer. Keep your options open. Even if you get nothing else from the selection interview, you'll get one more contact to add to your professional network.

Don't Call Us ...

Avoid hedging your salary requirement by stating a figure, only to add, "Of course, I can be flexible on that." If you can, avoid stating a figure in the first place. If you cannot avoid this, state a range without any qualification whatsoever.

Turn "Goodbye" into "See You Later"

The screening interviewer will signal or tell you when the interview is over. If that signal comes in the form of his asking if you have any questions, respond this way: "Yes. When might I expect to hear from you about the next step?" This communicates your clear understanding of the process and puts you in charge of closure of the interview. It also elicits the most positive response possible in a screening interview—a promise of further action or further communication.

Once you have the answer to your question, *thank* the interviewer and tell him that you enjoyed the experience. Without getting mushy, praise the interviewer for doing his job well: "Thank you. I enjoyed meeting with you, and I appreciate the clarity with which you conducted this interview. You gave me a great opportunity to present myself. Thanks." Leave the interviewer feeling good about what he has done. The idea is to have him associate that good feeling about *his* job and *his* judgment of you.

The Least You Need to Know

◆ In contrast to the purpose of the selection interview, which is to find new talent for the company, the objective of the screening interview is to identify and screen out "unqualified" candidates.

◆ The screening interviewer is usually a junior staffer in the target firm's Human Resources department. He or she is not a specialist in the position for which you are a candidate.

◆ The screening interviewer does not have the authority to hire you, but does have the power to screen you out.

◆ The screening interviewer is a fact verifier and, to a lesser degree, a fact-checker. He or she is not interested in you as a person.

Chapter 19

The Telephone Interview

In This Chapter

- ◆ The purpose of a telephone interview
- ◆ Advantages and disadvantages of the telephone interview
- ◆ The telephone interview vs. the online interview
- ◆ Taking control by dodging the call
- ◆ Preparing for the call
- ◆ Answering questions and projecting confidence

In the preceding chapter, we discussed screening interviews, focusing primarily on those conducted live and in person. These days, such preliminary interviews often take place on the phone. Preliminary (screening) interviews—and even selection interviews—are sometimes also conducted online (see Chapters 6 and 18), but the telephone is still used more commonly for the screening interview, and so this chapter will show you how to prepare for such an interview and how to make the event a success.

Welcome to a Process of Elimination

Ask yourself this: why would an employer telephone you rather than fly you in, put you up in a hotel, feed you a meal or two, and take half a day or more to sit down and converse?

Even if you've never taken an economics course, you know that it's because calling is a lot cheaper.

The Skinny _____

Many employers don't even conduct the telephone interviews themselves, but outsource the job to recruiting firms specializing in telephone interviews.

The Role of the Phone Interview

But that's not the whole answer. Think it all the way through. *Why* does the employer want to save money on you? Answer: the employer doesn't have sufficient interest in you to make much of an investment. At least, not yet. The employer wants to make a minimal investment—of money and time—in screening candidates.

The Good News: It's a Signal of Interest

If this sounds pretty grim, there *is* an upside. While it's true that the telephone interview is usually a screening interview, it is also an expression of interest.

The Bad News: It Isn't Face to Face

The fact is that the telephone, even as it allows communication, stands in the way of contact. The impression you make is blunted by the phone, which delivers nothing more than a disembodied voice.

Observe these rules:

- ◆ Understand that the telephone interview is an attempt to screen you out. Review the preceding chapter for guidance on avoiding the screen.

- ◆ Unless she identifies herself otherwise, understand that the person on the other end of the line is most likely an outsourced recruiter or an in-house Human Resources staffer, in either case someone who does not have the authority to hire you, but does have the power to eliminate you from the running.

- Also understand that the telephone interview is an opportunity to secure an in-person interview, which may well be a final or selection interview conducted by the person who actually has the authority to hire you.

- Psych yourself up for the call. Assume that the call is a prelude to a face-to-face selection interview.

- Do not fixate on getting the job as the objective of the telephone interview. Focus on using the telephone interview to secure a face-to-face meeting.

> **Don't Call Us …**
>
> When you answer a call, don't start speaking until you have the telephone handset to ear and mouth. Think this advice is too basic? How many times have you made a call to the firm of Dewey, Cheatham & Howe only to be greeted by a voice announcing " … am and Howe?

Telephone Interviewing vs. Online Interviewing

A growing number of firms are making use of e-mail, web-based interactive forms, and online conferencing to conduct screening interviews. Some companies even conduct selection interviews at long distance via this technology. (Review Chapters 6 and 18 for advice on making the most of the online interview.) Be aware, however, that most firms that use a two-stage interviewing process—a screening interview followed by a selection interview—use the telephone for the screening portion. In any case, most of the advice that applies to the telephone interview can be readily adapted for online scenarios. But, please, read the next brief section.

The Webcam Dimension

Interviewing with target employers located at a great distance from you, including international employers, can be a time-consuming and expensive process. The advent of online interviewing using real-time video-audio technology, such as Skype, has greatly extended the reach of both employers and job candidates. Just a few years ago, a company based in Tokyo would have thought long and hard before paying thousands of dollars to fly in a candidate from Chicago, but now with video-audio conferencing commonplace, interviewing internationally no longer requires breaking any budgets.

If you are slated for an online video-audio conference, now is the time to review Chapter 6 and "A Webcam Wardrobe" in Chapter 5. Add this to the telephone-oriented advice that follows.

A Welcome Call at an Unwelcome Time

The interview call—eagerly anticipated, possibly momentous—may come at the most awkward of times and places. Like when you're seated at your desk, with your boss hovering over you. *Ringgg!* It's a recruiter. Or it may come at a time when you are simply unprepared for it.

> ### Clincher
>
> Even if you reschedule a call so that you call back from the comfort of your home, consider dressing for the part. Dressing as you would for a webcam or a face-to-face interview helps you to "get into character," even though the person on the other end of the line cannot see you.

Taking Surprise in Stride

Fight the impulse to render unthinking compliance. Just because the call has come in, you are under no obligation to conduct the interview right there and then. Without panic, without seeming flustered, without an air of urgency, welcome the call, but seize the opportunity to reschedule it.

- Reschedule so that *you* are the one who makes the call. The caller always has a psychological advantage over the one who is called.

- Reschedule so that you can make the call at an advantageous time and from a convenient place. If possible, make the call from your home rather than the office—especially if your office is not private.

Bidding for Time

You need not offer elaborate excuses for rescheduling the call. After all, you are a professional whose time is valuable. The easiest thing to say is that you are in a meeting: "Yes, Ms. Deacon, I look forward to speaking with you, but I'm in a meeting just now. I can call you back at 10 o'clock tomorrow. Would that work for you?" Once you have agreed on a time, be certain to get the phone number and the name of the contact person.

If the recruiter insists on calling you back, don't fight over the issue. Agree quickly, but exercise control over when that call will come. If you can arrange to take the call at home, make certain that the recruiter has that number: "I'll be working at home then, and you can reach me at 555-555-5555."

The vast majority of potential employers and professional recruiters will respect your "in a meeting" excuse. After all, no one wants an employee who drops the business for which he is being paid in order to take an outside call.

A Telephone "Interview Kit"

Beyond preparing yourself personally, assemble the following items next to the telephone or telephones you plan to use for interview purposes:

◆ Your resumé.

◆ An "executive summary" of your resumé, highlighting your most important skills, qualifications, and accomplishments.

◆ A crib sheet that gives the answers to the questions you anticipate.

◆ An up-to-date calendar listing all of your obligations; you don't want to fumble if you are asked about your availability for an in-person interview.

◆ Copies of any correspondence to or from companies you have queried or to which you have applied. Keep a separate folder for each firm. Be sure to keep copies of any relevant employment ads.

All of these items can be stored on your computer. Just make sure you know how to find them quickly.

Let the Caller Do the Talking (Mostly)

While you should cordially keep up your end of the conversation, let the recruiter or company representative do most of the talking. Let him or her ask most of the questions. Follow his or her lead in the direction of the conversation. For the most part, limit your own questions to those that will illuminate and expand on what the interviewer asks. For example:

Interviewer: How would you rate your problem-solving skills?

You: Very highly. Are there any particular problems your firm is facing now? Any challenges that stand out?

Don't expect a Human Resources interviewer to answer such a return question, but the fact that you asked it suggests that you are, indeed, a roll-up-your-sleeves problem solver.

Repeatedly demonstrate that you are listening carefully and analytically. An effective technique is to give the interviewer feedback in the form of paraphrasing some of his or her key statements or questions. For example:

Interviewer: How would you rate your problem-solving skills?

You: So problem-solving is a key aspect of this position?

Interviewer: Yes.

You: Great! I would rate my problem-solving skills very highly. For example, in my current position …

While you're listening, take notes. (But do so unobtrusively. If your computer keyboard is not truly silent, use a pen and pad. The sound of clicking keys is both distracting and irritating over the phone, and it may give the impression that you are not devoting your full attention to the interview.) This will not only help you identify topics of concern and topics for further conversation—whether it occurs now, on the phone, or later, in a face-to-face meeting—but will help you later to evaluate the company, the position, your performance, and the general situation.

Don't Call Us …

Taking notes during a telephone interview is good idea, but doing so if you are on a video connection is not. You don't want the interviews to see you scribbling or typing away.

Giving Answers

Because the telephone interview is usually a screening interview, it is generally best to keep your answers brief, yet thorough. How do you satisfy both requirements? Answer factually. For example, the interviewer asks you about your experience in customer service. But you've been exclusively in sales. Here's your response:

You: Customer contact is important to the position, then?

Interviewer: Yes, it is.

You: My approach to sales has always been customer-oriented, with an emphasis on service. For example, a recent customer needed …

In interviews for positions that involve extensive customer contact by telephone, you might encounter something more than the usual cut-and-dried, screening-interview, fact-finding/fault-finding questions. The interviewer may engage you in role play. For example, she may play the part of a disgruntled customer. Your assignment: satisfy the customer without giving away the store.

This task is less threatening than it sounds. In any telephone role-play scenario, it's less likely that you will be judged on the basis of every word you say than on your ability to keep your cool, to respond in a generally creative manner, and to keep the conversation going. A significant portion of your score will also be based simply on your willingness to go along with the game.

If the interviewer comments critically on your role play, thank him for his suggestions, criticism, and advice. Do not defend or explain your words or actions, just make it clear that you are listening to and learning from the interviewer's comments.

Finally, consider this ploy. Answer just about every question that comes your way. But when a major question comes up toward what you sense as the impending end of the interview, defer it or defer part of it:

> I can answer A, B, and C, but D is such a large subject that it can be answered adequately only in person, with give and take. Can we set up a meeting? I'll be prepared to discuss this issue in detail, as well as anything else of interest to your firm. I'm free at the end of the week—Friday all morning. Would that be good for you?

Deferring an answer like this takes a certain amount of nerve, but no interviewer will criticize you for it. On the contrary, this maneuver will probably elicit admiration of your initiative. It might even prompt an in-person interview. Of course, if the interviewer insists on an answer over the phone, don't fight him: "Well, I'll do my best to do the issue justice." And proceed with your answer.

Don't Say "Yes," and Don't Say "No"

However you answer the telephone interviewer's questions, try to avoid giving yes or no answers or one-word responses. These say very little about your skills and qualifications. Instead of making you sound direct and forthright, excessively terse answers give the impression of evasiveness or out-and-out lack of knowledge.

Make a Note of This

Keep a legal pad and pen handy for taking notes or, if you have a truly quiet keyboard, use your computer. Jot down key points, but don't become so intent on your note taking that you fail to concentrate on what's actually being said. Your notes should serve two purposes:

1. They are a record of key issues and questions to study prior to a subsequent face-to-face interview. It's rather like getting the exam questions before the midterm.

2. They will help you keep focused. As a question is asked, jot down the points you want to cover. Having a record of these will not only make your answer more complete, but will significantly reduce your anxiety. You need to worry less about becoming confused or leaving out something important.

An added bonus of good note taking: if the interviewer is interrupted or for some reason distracted, you can jot down his last question. When the interviewer gets back on the line, you can jump in with "We were just discussing …" or "You were asking …." In any interview, it's always to your great advantage to be perceived as a practical problem solver.

The Least You Need to Know

◆ Most of the time, a telephone interview is a screening interview—more a process of elimination than an effort at recruitment.

◆ Your objective in a telephone interview is not to get a job, but to get an in-person interview.

◆ Feel free to reschedule calls that come at an inconvenient time. Try to arrange it so that *you* call back; the caller always has the psychological advantage over the recipient.

◆ Make it your business to be prepared for telephone interviews; create a "telephone interview kit" and make sure that it's ready, by the telephone, at all times.

◆ Give concise, factual answers. Don't wander.

◆ Take notes during the telephone interview; these will be invaluable in preparing for a subsequent in-person interview.

Chapter 20

Expecting the Unexpected

In This Chapter

- ◆ Surviving—and shining—in the group or panel interview
- ◆ Avoiding the "Ancient Mariner" syndrome in sequential interviews
- ◆ Turning the computer-assisted interview to your advantage
- ◆ Making the right impression in mealtime interviews
- ◆ Coping with the out-of-town interview
- ◆ Handling drug-test issues

The interview as performance. You enter, stage left, lines memorized, fully prepared, well rehearsed. A peachy idea!

Too bad reality doesn't always oblige. True, many interviews are the classic one-on-one (or two- or three-on-one) encounter, but there are variations on this "standard" interview format. Especially in cases where the employer is paying for your long-distance travel and lodging, expect to be interviewed by a number of people, maybe together, all at once, or maybe one after the other. The employer will be eager to get his money's worth by giving you maximum exposure. You should also anticipate more complex interview situations in large organizations and those with elaborately developed bureaucracies. This chapter will help you to prepare.

Panel Interviews

People have nightmares about stuff like this. You walk into a room, and a dozen shiny-suited inquisitors put you on the spot and pin you to the wall. The *panel interview*, also called a group interview, typically consists of five to a dozen interviewers, assembled at one time and in one room, usually around a conference table, asking the candidate questions. The purpose of this mass interview is to expose the candidate to as many decision-makers as possible in a short time.

"We're Not Ganging Up on You ..."

The main object of the panel interview is probably not to expose you to stress (although there may be an element of this), but rather to allow the greatest number of decision-makers to see and talk to you at one time. In theory, this is an efficient and cost-effective interviewing strategy. In practice, it can be highly inefficient and, for you, intimidating. For what too often emerges in panel interviews is a distressingly broad spectrum of private agendas among the interviewers. Not only do different members of the "executive committee" want different things, but what one member wants may conflict with or contradict what another insists on. Too often, the panelists start performing for one another, and the interviewee is suddenly relegated to a role in the supporting cast. Sometimes, these meetings degenerate into a debate among the interviewers. This may actually take the pressure off you temporarily, but it's *your* show that's being stolen, and, when it comes time for the "executive committee" to review candidates, what they'll recall is a candidate who sat silently watching the debate.

Clincher

The upside of any interview challenge is that, while posing a difficulty, it gives you a chance to demonstrate your problem-solving skills by actually solving a problem.

Basking in the Barrage

If you're lucky, the group interview will proceed in an orderly fashion, with interviewers asking questions in turn. In effect, you'll be speaking to one person at a time. More likely, however, questions may come from several directions, perhaps several directions at once. It is this barrage effect that makes the panel interview so intimidating.

What do you do?

Some candidates believe that the best strategy is to try to identify the leader of the group and play to him or her. If this means responding most often to the person who asks most of the questions, well, you have little choice. However, the most talkative panel member is not necessarily the person with the power—or the most power—to hire you. Sometimes the boss keeps herself in the background, quietly listening. Worse, you risk offending other group members by directing your comments and your eye contact to a single, apparently dominant individual.

Identify a leader if you wish, but make an effort to distribute your attention and your remarks to as many members of the panel as possible. Don't risk leaving anyone feeling frozen out.

A greater challenge is making yourself productively heard over the din of competing agendas. The most effective approach is to address the panel members as individuals, asking each what he or she wants or expects or needs from the position in question. As a result of such patient questioning—*on your part*—you may be able to define areas of consensus and address those. This, of course, is the ideal outcome. You may be unable to gather a consensus, either because your *group dynamics* skills aren't quite up to the task or, more likely, because the opposed points of view among this group are fundamentally irreconcilable. One possible outcome of a panel interview is your realization that the job these folks require is simply impossible or that you are being invited to join a group of fundamentally incompatible people. Better to learn these things sooner than later.

def•i•ni•tion

Group dynamics is the systematic study of how groups operate, how members persuade one another and fail to persuade one another, how conflicts develop, and how consensus is reached.

The most brutal form of the panel interview involves a dozen questioners or even more, some of whom may actually come and go during the course of the interview. Don't let such traffic rattle you. In fact, force yourself not to think of more than one panel member at a time. You *are* playing to an audience, but, as all great actors learn or instinctively know, you must play to them one at a time, person to person.

Sequential Interviews

In the panel interview, you stay put, and the questioners assemble before you. In a *sequential interview*, also called a serial interview, you are passed from interviewer to interviewer, to be met with privately in the office of each.

"The Rime of the Ancient Mariner" Revisited

At some point in your high school or college career, you probably read a narrative poem by the Englishman Samuel Taylor Coleridge, about the old seafarer doomed to tell his woeful tale seagoing guilt and redemption to everyone he meets, over and over, mainly because he thoughtlessly killed an albatross. The business about the albatross may not have made much sense to you back in high school (I bet you'd never even been *tempted* to kill one), but once you embark on a serial interview, you'll gain a profound insight into what it's like to be cursed with the task of churning out your life story again and again. That is the principal challenge of the sequential interview: to treat each encounter as if it were absolutely fresh.

Keeping It Fresh

The easiest way to keep each interview in the sequence fresh is to begin each as if it were a screening interview, keeping your answers straightforward and factual until you feel your way into the interviewer's needs and interests. Only then should you engage in an in-depth discussion. The Ancient Mariner was obliged to pour out his heart and soul to all comers. Why make an already demanding task more difficult by voluntarily taking on his burden? Don't *start* with your soul; focus on business first, and then share your personality as each interview session ripens.

Tying It Together

While you should not comment extensively to Interviewer B on your conversation with Interviewer A, you can seek advance information from Interviewer B concerning Interviewer C. As Interviewer B wraps up his time with you—"Well, I'd better send you on your way to Ms. C"—you might take the opportunity to probe for some key company issues: "Does Ms. C share your concerns about cash flow and collections procedure?" The answer to this provides a lens to help you focus the next interview and allows you to present yourself as a problem solver who has materialized as the perfect solution to the company's problems.

A word of caution: never criticize one interviewer to another, even mildly—"Gee, your Mr. Thomas is sort of an odd guy." To begin with, such criticism is not your province. More important, you don't know how Interviewer B feels about Interviewer A. They may be best friends or mentor and protégé. You could end up knocking yourself out of the running in a single stroke.

Booting Up

In Chapter 6 and, more briefly elsewhere, we have addressed the growing use of online interviewing techniques. Computers are rarely used as a full substitute for human-on-human interviewing (though this may take place online), but a growing number of large employers are using computers to automate the main phase of the screening interview. When you find yourself in such a situation, what can you expect and how can you make the best of it? The fact is that, depending on your feelings about computers, the automated screening interview can be a daunting or offensive process, or one that is refreshingly stress-free. Some of us have an easier time relating to a nonjudgmental machine, a virtual person, than to a flesh-and-blood human being.

Multiple-Choice Scenarios

At its most basic and impersonal level, computer interviewing begins when you answer a want ad directing you to call a certain number. You are not even asked to sit in front of your own computer, but instead to use your touch-tone phone to answer a series of prerecorded multiple-choice questions, using your touch-tone keypad to respond. The sophisticated interviewing programs will ask you to forward your résumé or will arrange for a company callback if your answers fit a certain profile programmed into the machine's software. You may be asked to record your name and phone number, and then answer multiple-choice questions relating to job title, responsibilities, years on the job, and salary. Beyond this, you may be asked *any* other kinds of questions that can be answered by multiple choice. Many of these questions are intended to gauge intelligence and aptitude.

The secret here is to answer quickly, since you are probably being timed, and to make certain you get the question right the first time. While you may be offered an opportunity to have the question repeated, requesting such a repetition may be counted against you.

The Skinny

Despite appearances, the computer is rarely used as a substitute for human interviewers, except sometimes in the initial screening stage. Usually, the computer serves merely as a tool to gather, sort, and flag data that will help human interviewers structure useful, probing questions during a subsequent selection interview.

Computer-assisted screening interviews are aggressively impersonal. You have every right to be aggressive in return. Take as much control as possible. If you dial a phone number in response to a want ad and find yourself confronted by Robo-Interviewer, hang up without leaving your name or a message. Next, dial *67 (in the United States) to temporarily block Caller ID, so that your number will not be identified. You want to remain anonymous when you call back. If asked to give your name, simply make one up, so that you can get to the questions and listen to them. Jot them down. Then, hang up without leaving your real name, phone number, or any other message. Study the questions and prepare answers to them. Now—without blocking Caller ID—call back and proceed with the interview, "spontaneously" furnishing the full and accurate information you have carefully prepared.

Not all computer interviews are conducted by phone. You may be asked to log on to a website using your PC, or you may even be asked to come to a recruiting center or to the employer's offices, where you will be offered a seat in front of a terminal and be left to answer 50 or more multiple-choice questions. If you find this less stressful than talking to a person, fine; just don't relax *too* much. Remember, your responses may be timed.

Open-Ended Approaches

Computer-assisted interviewing is not limited to multiple-choice questions. You may encounter situations in which you are asked to compose, in your own words, brief narrative answers to a battery of questions. In this case, the computer is probably not being used to evaluate your responses, but is acting merely as a word processor. Your answers will be read and evaluated by human beings. It is generally advisable to keep your responses concise and to the point, but take care to use good grammar and appropriate vocabulary.

Honesty—Not Always the Best Policy

Funny thing about the computer: it invites more candor than any human interviewer. Wedded as most of are to the Internet, we've gotten on very intimate terms with computers. Besides, there is no living, breathing human presence to please or to displease, no one there to smile or frown at you, and the result, for many candidates, is an attitude better suited to the confessional or the psychoanalyst's couch than to a job interview. Answer the computer as you would a human interviewer, whose job, after all, *is* to judge you. Don't confess your flaws or express your doubts. Respond as positively as truth and credibility permit. Your objective is to make yourself look great. Period.

Mealtime Interviews

The good news is this: being asked out to lunch or dinner is a very positive sign. Indeed, you may take it as a strong "buy signal," a clear expression of significant interest in you. The employer is imagining you as part of the team and wants to get to know you in a setting less formal than the office. Moreover, you are justified in seeing the invitation to lunch or dinner as a gracious act: the employer regards you as a human being, not some anonymous working stiff.

Clincher

Do you want to get hired, or do you want to lay aggressive claim to your rights under the law? Sure, employers are barred from asking you potentially discriminatory questions. But if you are interested in gaining employment, you should try to answer any questions you do not find intolerable—even those that may tread the edge of what is appropriate or legal.

Focusing the Conversation

If the conversation strays into the personal arena, try to answer whatever you feel comfortable with and whatever you feel creates a positive image. If the questions encroach on areas you consider inappropriate, respond firmly but politely and as inoffensively as possible:

> **Interviewer:** So you live in the Brighton area. What church do you go to?

> **You:** I consider religion a family matter, and I never discuss it outside of our family.

The best way to avoid having to answer a lot of questions that get too close for comfort is to steer the conversation as much as possible to matters directly related to business. However, don't dwell on the daily routine—"Do you use #1 paperclips or the premium jumbos?"—but talk about issues and trends that really excite you. Make it *interesting* business conversation.

Dangerous Passages

Openness and candor are qualities we greatly prize in our friends. But your prospective employer and colleagues, while friendly, are not your friends. Present yourself in an open and straightforward manner, but don't open up too far, confessing heavy credit card debt, say, or the fact that your spouse "just doesn't appreciate me," or that your child has "a mild drug problem." Nor should you volunteer opinions concerning public figures, politics, religion, or morality. Your host's views may be very different from yours.

What do you do if the employer is insistent on probing areas that are inappropriate? For example: "It is very important for us to know how you stand on the issue of abortion."

◆ You can insist—gently but firmly—that your views on this subject are private and can have no bearing on your job performance.

Don't Call Us ...

One time-honored mealtime interview ploy is to offer the candidate salt and pepper. If she takes it and seasons her food without first tasting it, she flunks the test. Her host concludes that she is a person who makes hasty, thoughtless, premature decisions.

◆ You can ask—again, gently but firmly—how the question relates to the job: "It's not clear to me how my opinions about the abortion issue relate to this job."

◆ You can claim that you have no opinion.

◆ You can state your opinion—and hope that it is the answer the employer wants to hear.

◆ You can decide that the question is so offensive that you wouldn't take the job if it were offered to you.

Mind Your Manners

Your table manners are on display. If you eat like a pig, that fact will be duly recorded. Beyond this, your hosts, consciously or not, will take note of what and how much you order. Err on the side of modesty and moderation, ordering neither the most expensive nor the cheapest dishes. Also, this is not the time or place to experiment with new foods, especially highly spiced items. Order food familiar to you and food that is easy to eat. No lobster, please. And hold the spaghetti. They're stain bombs waiting to explode.

Nice Save!

Despite prudence in ordering easy-to-eat foods, accidents happen. If you spill some-thing on the table, *handle* the situation. If your host does not immediately summon a waiter, you should do it. If you spill food or drink on yourself, wipe yourself off, summon a waiter, and ask for club soda. Dab a little on the stain. This time-honored method may or may not minimize the damage to your clothing, but at least it will demonstrate that you know what to do in a minor crisis. Apologize simply and quickly to those at the table. Don't apologize profusely or at length. This is an employment interview, not a seminar on mealtime catastrophe. You might, however, poke gentle fun at yourself: "Well, I hope this job doesn't require much eating!"

If you spill food or drink on one of the interviewers, you do have a more serious prob-lem. Chances are, the "injured party" will be gracious and a good sport, but there may be unspoken resentment, and you will certainly look foolish. Accept the catastrophe as a test of your grace under fire. Apologize quickly, and then *ask* what you can do to help. Do not start wiping down your fellow diner. Suggest the club soda treatment: "Let me call the waiter over and get you some club soda for that." Do not add insult to injury by offering to *pay* for dry cleaning, but do offer help: "I have a marvelous dry cleaner. Can I send you there—or take your suit there myself?" Finally, give voice to your embarrassment: "This is *really* embarrassing. I'm very sorry." Then get on with the interview meal.

I'll Drink to That!

The best approach to liquor during a mealtime interview is to avoid it. Even if your hosts drink, you are best advised to order sparkling water. If you feel you must have a drink, order a glass of wine or a light drink, such as a white-wine spritzer.

Don't Call Us ...

No smoking. Even if the interviewer smokes, it is best not to do so yourself. These days, with antismoking legislation and escalating health-insurance premiums, no company wants to go out of the way to hire another smoker.

When You're in from Out of Town

Traveling any distance to an interview presents nagging logistical concerns. Be pre-pared for the unexpected. Formulate alternative plans if weather seems likely to delay your flight (a real possibility if you're interviewing in Minneapolis in January, for example). What will you do if your luggage goes astray? How will you find your way around in a strange city?

Scheduling and Logistics

At the time the interview is set up, be certain that you know …

- ◆ Who is responsible for arranging for travel and accommodations.

- ◆ Who is paying for transportation and accommodations.

- ◆ How to get from the airport to your hotel.

- ◆ How to get from your hotel to the employer's office.

- ◆ How long it takes to get from the hotel to the office.

Clincher

If the weather looks doubtful either where you are or where you're going, call your airline. If the situation looks dicey—a storm front looming or heavy snow in the forecast— consider flying in a day early and picking up the extra day's hotel tab yourself.

Make certain that you are prepared with sufficient cash or a major credit card to cover your out-of-pocket expenses. Remember: most hotels require a credit card imprint when you check in, even if the room is prepaid by your host. Always assume that your luggage *will* go astray, so bring along a fresh suit, shirt/blouse, and shoes in your carry-on luggage, just in case. Also ensure that any essential papers—such as extra copies of your resumé, CDs or DVDs, letters of recommendation, and so on—are in your carry-on bag or briefcase. Of course, your laptop computer should always be treated as carry-on luggage.

Jet-Lagged

Long flights, either transoceanic or coast-to-coast, can leave you jet-lagged. If you're in for a long flight, schedule your arrival for the day before the interview, if possible. At the very least, try to arrange to have time to freshen up at your hotel before the interview. This includes a shower, a change of clothes, and, if possible, a nap.

Speaking of sleep, be certain to pack your own alarm clock *and* arrange with the hotel desk for a wake-up call. Even if you are one of those lucky people who *never* oversleeps, a change of time zone can wreak havoc on your body's internal clock.

Drug Testing

You don't need me to tell you that drug abuse is a serious problem in our times. Certainly, most employers believe this, and more than half of the Fortune 500 companies include some form of drug testing either during or after the hiring process. The odds are good that you may be asked to take such a test.

Is It Legal?

Being asked to take a drug test is neither an inappropriate nor an illegal question. Worse, if you indicate that you would not be willing to take a drug test, you will almost certainly be assumed guilty without a trial. ("What is she hiding?") You won't be hired.

Sign on the Dotted Line?

If you answer that you are willing to take a drug test, the chances are only about fifty-fifty that you will actually be given one. But if you do find yourself submitting to a drug test, don't assume that, just because you're clean and sober—perhaps have never used a controlled substance in your life—you will pass the test. At least 5 percent of drug tests routinely yield false positives due to the presence of such innocuous substances as certain foods and over-the-counter as well as prescription medications.

Obviously, it's critically important that whoever performs the testing—usually an outside firm hired by the employer—fully explains the test in advance and provides you with a complete list of items that may cause false positive results. Avoid these substances if at all possible before taking the test. If you must take medications that may yield a false positive, report this fact *in writing* to the testing company, with a copy sent directly to the prospective employer.

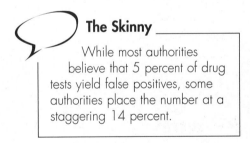

The Skinny

While most authorities believe that 5 percent of drug tests yield false positives, some authorities place the number at a staggering 14 percent.

If you are the victim of a false positive, insist on being given a backup test of a different type. Document your request in writing and be sure to send a copy of this document to the president or CEO of the firm to which you have applied.

The Least You Need to Know

◆ Although you should pay attention to everyone in a group interview, remember that you are speaking to individuals. Relate to them all, but do so one person at a time.

◆ Maintain a high level of enthusiasm and energy in sequential interviews by feeling your way into each interview session. Let the interviewer identify his or her areas of special concern, and then pursue these.

◆ Answer computer-assisted interview questions quickly and as positively as possible.

◆ Don't let your guard down at mealtime interviews. While the conversation may stray to social and personal topics, remember that you are still being evaluated.

◆ Employers have the legal right to ask you to take a drug test; be certain that you have some protection against possible false-positive results.

Chapter 21

"Nice to Be Here": Mastering the Mid-Life Interview

In This Chapter

◆ The aging workforce

◆ The "second career" phenomenon

◆ Rethinking your career at mid-life

◆ Turning age into an asset

If you make it to age 65, the so-called "traditional" retirement age, you can expect, on average, to live 18.7 more years. This number is up from 13.9 in 1950, 15.2 in 1970, and 17.2 in 1990.

But let's go back from age 65, which, based on the latest data, no longer seems quite so old, to 40 (make it this far, and you can expect to live another 39 years). According to federal law, namely the Age Discrimination in Employment Act, anyone 40 or older belongs to a "protected class" of workers who have the right to sue for age discrimination. So these days, you can have your cake and eat it, too. The stats say a 40-year-old truly is middle-aged—at the mathematical midpoint of life—but the government says that, at 40, you can call yourself an "older worker" and gain special protection under law.

Thanks a lot, Uncle Sam!

Trouble is, at 40, you do have about half your life ahead of you—a lot of years to fill and to finance. No wonder that, these days, mastering the mid-life (and the later-life) interview is more important than ever. This chapter will give you a hand.

Mid-Life Crisis or Mid-Life Opportunity? (Pick One)

As 2008 comes to a close, the U.S. economy is in recession after years of unprecedented prosperity. Throughout much of the 1990s, inflation was low and employment was high. In fact, as economists define things, America was just about at full employment. As we make our away somewhat nervously into the second decade of the twenty-first century, however, nobody is harboring illusions about full employment. The numbers of those out of work—or only marginally employed—are not soaring, but they are climbing. True, entry-level jobs continue to be plentiful in many fields, and a lot of firms are committed to training, mentoring, and developing employees.

Up to a point. The fact is, corporate commitments begin to wear thin once an employee passes 40.

The Skinny

Economists agree that 0 percent unemployment is impossible, because, at any moment, about 4 percent of the workforce is between jobs, in transition, or otherwise briefly and temporarily unemployed; therefore, most authorities define "full employment" as 4 percent unemployment. During the late 1990s, U.S. unemployment was about 4.3 percent, just a third of a percentage point shy of theoretical full employment. As of January 1, 2008, the U.S. Bureau of Labor Statistics pegged the rate at 4.9. In Idaho, the rate was just 2.7 (virtually full employment), whereas in Michigan it was 7.4 (a high rate).

Doubts and Direction

Now before you become too anxious or depressed to read any further, there *is* some very good news. *Baby boomers* have moved into their 40s, 50s, and 60s, and, with this, the nation's average age has also been climbing. As this trend continues, more and more candidates for each job opening will be 40 or older.

This should help ease worries over losing your job in middle age, but that isn't the only angst mid-life has to offer. Now is the time many of us begin to question (and doubt and even regret) the career choices we've made. Am I on the right track?

Where is that track going? Have I reached my goals? Can I reach my goals? Have I set the right goals? Have I set any goals at all?

Such thoughts can be chilling. Or they can be invigorating. Before you worry about preparing for a job interview, maybe the time is right to rethink your career and retool your skills.

The Second Career: A New Trend

Morning TV talk shows and news networks with 24 hours to fill have lately jammed the airwaves and cable broadband with lots of stories about 40- and 50- and even 60-somethings embarking on marvelous "second careers" after leaving (voluntarily or not) their first.

The fact is that most 40-somethings who test the waters of a second career end up asking for their old jobs back within a few months. This said, second careers are, for increasing numbers of older workers, a new and viable reality.

Don't count on just jumping on some second career bandwagon. Think and plan before you leap. Begin by evaluating what you like and don't like. If you are passionate about some new career path, by all means start there. But if you just feel that you need a fresh start, but don't know where to go, take careful stock of your skills, achievements, and interests. Look for a new path that will allow you to transfer your portable skills readily. If you need some help brainstorming your next move, log on to Careerpath.com and Monster.com, both of which offer helpful interactive self-assessment quizzes.

Develop and use your network. Get a sense of the fields that are open to you. For advice on building and working employment networks, review Chapters 2 and 3.

Understand—and be sure you can undertake—whatever is necessary to upgrade your skills and education for the second career.

def•i•ni•tion

A **baby boomer** is anyone born during the sharp increase in birth rate following World War II, that is, between 1947 and 1961.

Clincher

Mid-life is an ideal time to return to school, because you not only have a wealth of experience to bring added meaning to the training you will receive, but also enough work years ahead to make the investment of time, money, and effort worthwhile. Besides, employers respect mid-life learning.

Family Values

An honest self-evaluation may either encourage you to move toward a second career, or it may dissuade you altogether.

If you have children, you are probably already struggling to juggle work and family time. Adding reeducation to the mix may seem out of the question.

It *is* possible that full-scale retraining is not a viable option for you right now. But this doesn't mean that you can't shoehorn in some significant time to devote to career development. Schedule just one hour each week for career development. Use this time to do the following:

- Revise your resume. Don't just update the facts—though you must do this—but hone and sharpen the document. Think about it. How effectively does it sell what you have to offer?

- Have lunch with a friend or colleague outside of your workplace. Learn about what's going on in his or her shop or field.

- Look for relevant short-term or one-shot training seminars to attend.

- Invest some time reading about new developments in your field.

- Surf the Net. Identify websites relevant to your interests, and devote some time to monitoring these.

Investing time is like investing money. Over the long run, small investments, made regularly and with discipline, add up and pay off.

The Spirit Is Willing ...

Many industries are undeniably youth oriented—at least on the surface. Scratch that surface, however, and you may find that the corporate climate is not so much youth directed as it is health conscious. Exercise, eat properly, get plenty of rest, and stay emotionally engaged with life, and you will retain more of the health that employers value in youth.

It has been said repeatedly in this book: at the core of most successful job interviews is the transmission of energy. If you can make the interviewer perceive you as a vibrant presence, you will deliver a highly positive impression. Keeping yourself fit and presenting yourself as such are keys to transmitting this most effective personal energy.

To Boldly Go?

There was a time when a man—and in those days, it *was* almost always a man—"built" a career over an entire working life. Having done this, he didn't dare change careers, nor was he asked or required to do so. These days, however, most workers can expect to change careers—not jobs, but *careers*—three or four (or more) times in their working lives. While this means that employers no longer regard "career hopping" with nearly as much suspicion as they once did, it is also true that you may have trouble matching your set of skills to the level of the job for which you are interviewing. In moving from one field to another, you are not precisely a neophyte (because you have been working a long time), even though you may be a beginner in the new field. This can make for some awkward application and interview situations. To overcome problems, consider these two strategies:

◆ Get your foot in the door: set as the objective of the interview persuading the interviewer that you are willing to take a step-down position in exchange for early performance reviews and likely promotion.

◆ Build a bridge before you interview. Prepare for the transition to a new field by acquiring special training or by acquiring special experience. Perhaps you can do consulting work that allows access to higher-level projects in your target field. Perhaps you can arrange for intern or volunteer work in order to build up your resumé prior to making applications and bidding for interviews.

To Square One

For most job hunters, a resumé is a prerequisite or, at least, a prelude to an interview. *The Complete Idiot's Guide to Getting the Job You Want, Second Edition* (Alpha Books, 1998)—by Marc (yours truly) Dorio—will help you create a winning resumé, but, for now, take note of these special tips for the mature candidate:

◆ Don't give your date of birth or age on the resumé.

Let's pause a moment. Your age is nothing to be ashamed of, but remember this: resumés are used as much to *screen out* job candidates as they are to *find* or *select* applicants. The first object in preparing your resumé is to avoid anything that may serve only to screen you out. Age is rarely a positive reason to hire someone, but, unfortunately, it may be a reason to screen a person out; therefore, avoid making reference to your age.

Even if you are careful not to disclose your age, many employers will look for clues. For this reason, don't include your graduation date from college. Just list the degree and the name of the school. Although you may list 10, even 15 years of experience, put the focus on the past 5.

◆ Highlight relevant, up-to-date skills, such as proficiency in certain technical areas and the like.

◆ Remember the subject of "portable skills" from Chapter 2? Don't assume that a prospective employer will, without prompting, recognize them. For example, it may not occur him that your customer-service experience at an air conditioner manufacturer will also serve you in the high-tech customer support position you've applied for. Point out, very explicitly, just how your past and current experience are directly relevant to what you hope will be your future employment. There is nothing sacred about your resumé. Revise and rewrite it specifically to suit each position you apply for.

Get Ready, Get Set

At least one important prerequisite for interview success is the same for a "mature" job candidate as it is for one just out of college: *preparation.*

Never "wing" an interview. Spontaneity is fine, valuable, and charming—as long as you thoroughly prepare for it. Review the chapters in Parts 1 and 3 for advice on preparing for the interview.

Also be aware of the following special considerations for the candidate who is over 40:

◆ Don't worry about your age and don't bring it up. Don't allude to it or draw attention to it in any way.

◆ It is against the law for the interviewer to raise the subject of age, unless you raise it first. Hence, don't.

◆ Practice substituting such words and concepts as "experience," "achievements," "accomplishments," "successes," and "judgment" for "age" or "years on the job."

◆ Be prepared to discuss highly relevant examples of your achievements and accomplishments.

One final interview aspect to prepare for: spend some time thinking about the negative stereotypes that are attached to older employees:

◆ They are inflexible.

◆ They are worn out, tired.

◆ They are hopelessly out of date.

Now think about what you can do; how you can look; how you can act, behave, and move; what you can wear; and what you can say to shatter these stereotypes.

Nice Save!

What do you do if the interviewer lacks the legal savvy to avoid bringing up the issue of age? What if he asks you how old you are? Or what if he asks, "Aren't you a little old for this position?" You would be within your rights to point out that such questions are illegal. But, then, you'd probably fail to get the job, and while this might give you grounds for litigation, do you want to spend your time and money in court or in a rewarding career?

Assuming that you still want the job—that the question doesn't simply turn you off to this employer—direct your answer away from the negative aspects of the age issue, but without obviously evading that issue. Here's how:

◆ First, quickly dismiss the negative issue: "It's not a question of age …"

◆ Next, focus on the positive aspects of age by translating age into experience, judgment, achievement, track record, and wisdom. Demonstrate that your years in business have raised your performance level well above the standard.

Some interview experts call this the "5/55 Rule": spend just 5 seconds answering the negative part of the question, and then invest 55 seconds in focusing on the positive. Whatever you do, *end* with the positive. That is what the interviewer will remember.

Go for It

Go into the interview with your mind made up not to hide your age, but to reveal it as an asset. The value a young person brings to a company is youth—which is really more of an asset to the employee than to the employer. It's great to be young, isn't it? But what does the employer get out of it? The benefit of inexperience? In contrast, the assets a mature employee brings to the enterprise are of greatest benefit to the employer: the wisdom and judgment born of experience and proven track record.

Go Ahead, Play the Age Card

Avoid "age" as a word and a concept, but sell *maturity*. Discuss specific ways in which your experience has enabled you to make faster and better decisions than younger co-workers, whose experience in the real world is no match for yours.

Broadcast Positive Attitude, Positive Appearance

You are 55 years old. You keep in shape. People say you look 40. That's nice. However, they don't say you look 20. Why not? Well, because you are 55 years old.

Clincher

In the short term, prepare for the interview by anticipating key questions, formulating answers, and thinking of examples to share with the interviewer. In the longer term, prepare by eating well and exercising. If you are unaccustomed to exercise, consult your physician before embarking headlong on a strenuous physical fitness program.

Our years are written on our faces and hands. Eyes get crow's feet, hairlines recede, hands acquire the marks of "character." Perhaps plastic surgery and dye can trim a year here or there, but not 20 or 30.

◆ Decide what you can change and what you cannot.

◆ Keep fit.

◆ Develop and project a winning attitude.

◆ Walk into the interview briskly. Smile. Make eye contact. Give a firm handshake. In other words, broadcast energy and good health.

Up to Speed

Review Chapter 5 for advice on interview dressing. Don't dress like a teenager or even a 20-year-old, but do look around you. What is fashionable *for your age?* Be stylish in clothing and haircut.

It is also important to assess the "dress code" of the company or industry in which you are interviewing. If you are bidding for a job with a new high-tech firm and you come calling dressed like an old-line banker, your look will scream *generation gap.* Get in touch with the prevailing look, and then leaven it according to what makes you comfortable.

Women need to pay special attention to the amount of lipstick and other make-up they apply. As mentioned in Chapter 5, with make-up and perfume, the principle of less is more should be rigorously followed. As you age, avoid using make-up as an obvious cover-up. The effect of this is likely to be overly harsh. The object is to soften your look. It is also a good idea to avoid dark, somber-colored clothing. Choose lighter and more cheerful hues.

Watch Your Language

Learn the language of the industry, and use it. In some fields, terminology changes rapidly, and some words go out of date quickly. Know what these are and avoid them.

- A subject to avoid? *The Good Old Days.*

- An interview for a job tomorrow is no place to reminisce about the working world of yesterday.

- A word to avoid? *Old.*

- If you need a synonym, use *mature, seasoned,* or *experienced.*

 Don't Call Us ...

Like it or not, packaging is important. You have a matter of minutes to make an impression. *How you look* amplifies, for better or worse, the impact of *what you say* during those minutes. You can devote a lot of time to keeping up with the trends and technology in your field, but if you present yourself at an interview *looking* outdated, your words will have little positive effect.

Get in Touch

If you're trying to work with 20-somethings or 30-somethings, tune in to their world. What issues interest them? What books do they read? What television shows do they watch? What celebrities appeal to them? What music do they listen to? What blogs do they log on to?

Add It Up

Remember: an interview works both ways. You may feel as if it's you who's under the microscope, but, really, the interview gives you, as well as the prospective employer, an opportunity to evaluate one another.

You've come to this company for an interview. Use the occasion to ask questions, to look around you, and to listen.

Do the place and the pace excite and energize you? Or does the prospect of huffing and puffing to keep up with a flock of newly minted college graduates, single, wildly ambitious, determined to work an 80-hour week, seem discouraging and daunting? Sure, it's important to be flexible, but before you say yes to a job offer, make sure that it has at least the possibility of feeling right for you.

The Least You Need to Know

♦ Despite federal law, there is, in some industries, prejudice against the mature worker; however, it is also true that the workforce as a whole is maturing.

♦ It is no longer either foolish or uncommon to rethink and revise your career in mid-life.

♦ You don't have to fake youth to get a good job, but you usually do need to present yourself as in touch with relevant current trends, in synch with current technology, generally energetic, vigorous, and in good health.

♦ Look for opportunities to present age as an asset by translating "age" into "experience," "maturity," and "sound judgment."

Part 5

On the Spot

The chapters in this part are devoted to understanding how to succeed in two of the toughest kinds of interview situations: the performance interview and the (dreaded) stress interview. Also, I deal with the most common—and thorniest—objections, doubts, and other obstacles an interviewer is likely to hurl your way. The assumption is that most "objections" are really pleas for help: the interviewer wants *you* to help *her* say yes. The trick is to avoid feeling discouraged or intimidated, so that you can transform challenge into opportunity, using objections as points of persuasion.

Hey, You're On! The Performance Interview

In This Chapter

◆ How to prepare for an "audition" and set up your performance

◆ The art of radiating confidence

◆ The K.I.S.S. principle

◆ Preparing for tests

◆ Doing well on psychological tests

◆ Scoring high on integrity

All jobs require performance. You have to *do* something. That's what you get paid for. In many jobs, the performance takes place over time: you do accounting, you design airplanes, you analyze the profit potential of new companies. Whatever. In some jobs, however, performance can be seen and evaluated almost instantly. "Do you see this pen?" the interviewer, brandishing his fountain pen, asks the hopeful salesperson. "Sell me this pen." Or the chairman of the English department asks the candidate for a teaching position at a private school "to teach a class on the poetry of Emily

Dickinson." Or the customer-service manager is asked to "handle" some hypothetical customer-service scenario.

Even if the job you're up for does not lend itself to a here-and-now, real-time audition, you may still be tested to measure aptitude, knowledge, or your psychological profile. Here's a chapter to help you perform at your best, whether in a vocational audition or on a test.

The Show on the Road

Time for some tough love. If a demand to perform comes as a surprise, shame on you.

Expect it. Think about the nature of the job for which you are interviewing. Does it lend itself to performance on demand? *Expect* a performance component if you are interviewing for jobs that involve any of the following functions:

- Customer contact
- Customer service
- In-person or telephone sales
- Client or staff training
- Counseling
- Hands-on management
- Human resources
- Diagnosis and repair
- Troubleshooting

If your target position involves any of these, expect and prepare for an "audition."

Run Through Your Network

Whether or not you've been alerted to performance as a component of an upcoming interview, work your network to find out all that you can about the target company, the interviewers, and what you can expect at the interview. If you can obtain information on what the company is looking for, you can be certain to showcase key issues in your performance.

Play to Strengths

In preparing for a performance interview, there is a natural tendency to try to repair your weak areas, even to the exclusion of fully exploiting your strengths. Don't know much about subject A, but excel in subject B? You'll have the urge to "cram" for subject A to the exclusion of any thought for subject B.

To a degree, the impulse to address weak areas is healthy and necessary. You don't want to be caught short, after all. But a day or two before the interview is not the time to attempt to acquire expertise you do not have. Your precious hours are better spent honing to an even sharper edge the areas of your greatest strength. If you are asked to come to the interview prepared to give a "training session" on some aspect of personnel management, work up a presentation in your strongest area. If you are big on risk management, but less interested in, say, mentoring techniques, you'd better prepare a session on risk management and leave mentoring alone. This is true even if you have not been *told* that you will be expected to make a presentation. If you suspect that an audition may be sprung on you by surprise, have your strongest area prepared to present.

Clincher

If possible, practice your presentation in front of a friend. And I do mean *friend*. This is not the time to seek out your harshest critic. Find someone who is honest, but also supportive. You want positive comments and genuinely constructive criticism.

Props and Digital Aids

If you have been asked in advance to prepare a presentation of some sort, of course you will need to ensure that you have any necessary props available. If you need a blackboard, whiteboard, projector, or computer audiovisual setup, make certain—in advance—that whatever you need will be available to you. If you can conveniently carry any necessary props yourself, do so.

Nice Save!

What if you forget to bring a key prop to the interview? Let's back up. You shouldn't let this happen, and it won't if you make a checklist of items you *must* bring to the interview. But if your failsafe system somehow does fail, you have two choices: either improvise without the missing item, or try to obtain the item in a hurry. If you do improvise, do not apologize for having failed to bring the equipment you should have brought. You need to be able to perform so well without the missing item that the interviewers never realize there's anything missing. If, just before the interview, you decide to buy a replacement for your missing item, do it fast. This, of course, may be neither practical nor even possible, and, in that case, you'll have to depend on the kindness of strangers. Ask the employer if you can use whatever item you need.

Take It Away!

Once you're on stage, cast all modesty and doubt forcibly aside. Your mission is to radiate confidence and self-assurance. Smile. Try to look as if you are enjoying yourself. Also …

- Pace your presentation. Don't rush.

- Open your mouth when you speak. Give full value to each word.

- Review Chapter 8 on body language. Be certain that you are not broadcasting mixed messages—saying one thing verbally and with confidence while communicating doubt and uncertainty through your nonverbal gestures.

- Don't waste time by digressing. Make certain you and your audience know the objectives of your presentation, and then focus the presentation exclusively on those objectives.

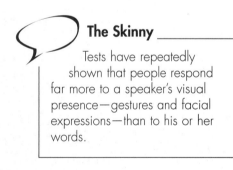

The Skinny

Tests have repeatedly shown that people respond far more to a speaker's visual presence—gestures and facial expressions—than to his or her words.

Framing the Show

That last point bears repeating. Set up your performance by telling your audience *exactly* what you intend to achieve. You don't have time for the luxury of subtlety, and why entrust a career opportunity to the intelligence and imagination of your audience? *Tell them what you are going to do.* Think of this as half of a frame in which you set your performance. Those who have mastered the art of public speaking will tell you that one key to successful public speaking is to set the presentation in a solid frame. It works like this:

1. Tell your audience what you are going to do and say. (That's half the frame.)

2. Do and say what you said you were going to do and say. (That's the presentation.)

3. Conclude by telling your audience what you did and said. (That's the other half of the frame.)

Remember: your goal is not so much to provoke thought among those who are reviewing your performance as it is to communicate crystal-clear and unambiguous messages. Above all else, the performance interview is about communicating. Whatever your area of expertise, whatever kind of performance you give, you are committing an act of communication. The clearer and more vivid that act, the better.

K.I.S.S.

Most of us say that we enjoy seeing movies that are "true to life," but is this really the case? Think about it. If movies were true to life, they'd be very long, tortuously meandering, intolerably complicated, full of contradictions, and mostly boring—though punctuated by a moment of excitement here and there. If movies were really true to life, nobody would pay to see them.

So take your cue from the movies when you think about your performance. You don't have to make it *too* true to life: complex and contradictory. Instead, take the message of this acronym to heart:

> **K**eep **I**t **S**imple, **S**tupid

Simplify the presentation, giving it a clearly stated objective, a beginning, a middle, and an end. Then, for good measure, tell your audience what you just—successfully—did. The performance in a performance interview is an artificial demonstration. It is not a slice of life.

Clincher _____

The average business speech is no more than 25 minutes long.

Leave 'Em Wanting More

Keep your performance as brief as possible without skimping or seeming evasive. Stimulate the interviewers' collective appetite, don't sate it.

Surprise!

Despite your best efforts, it's certainly possible that a "command performance" will take you by surprise. You may have even expected an audition and have prepared a fine presentation on subject A—only to be asked to deliver something on subject B instead.

What do you do? This *is* a tough one.

Grace Under Fire

When an employer springs a surprise demand on you, he is looking for two things:

1. How well you can think on your feet

2. How you react to pressure

That there are two objectives actually puts you at an advantage. If you can at least *act* unruffled—calm, cool, and in control—you will have successfully met challenge number two. This requires no knowledge, no expertise, no particular thought. It's an act and an attitude. Demonstrate grace under pressure, and you've automatically earned the first 50 points out of the 100 required to pass the test.

Never Apologize, Never Excuse

But it is all too easy to lose those points. This is precisely what will happen if you make apologies or excuses for your performance: "Oh. I'm not really prepared …" Or: "I wasn't expecting to …" Or: "This would be a lot better if I had been given some warning …"

Don't prepare your audience for a bad show. If they *expect* to see a poor performance, they will almost certainly interpret whatever you show them—good, bad, or indifferent—as a disaster.

Respond to the surprise demand with pleasure: "I'd be happy to do that!" No apologies, excuses, or other qualifiers are necessary or helpful.

Test-Taking Tips

Employment-related tests come in six types:

♦   *Knowledge tests.* How much do you know in a given area?

♦   *Skills tests.* How proficient are you at certain tasks—typing or data entry, for example?

- ◆ *Aptitude tests.* What is your performance potential, based on natural abilities?

- ◆ *Career interest inventories.* What jobs interest you most?

- ◆ *Personality or psychological tests.* How do your traits and character stack up against those of others?

- ◆ *Integrity tests.* How honest and trustworthy are you?

You may be asked to take any one or a combination of these tests.

The Skinny

Polygraph (lie-detector) tests were once popular employment screening tools. In 1988, however, federal legislation was enacted barring lie-detector tests as an adjunct to employment screening for most federal jobs, and, currently, about half of the states severely limit the use of the polygraph in all employment situations.

Do Your Homework

If you know—or suspect—that you may be tested on your knowledge of a subject area, or that your skills may be tested, the best advice is to do what you did (or were supposed to do) to prepare for exams when you were back in school: study. Review the essentials of your field of interest. If there are skills involved in what you do, practice them.

While you can't really study for psychological or integrity tests, you can prepare for them. Make a list of language that communicates positive traits:

achievement-oriented	honest
agreeable	realistically optimistic
communicative	reliable
conscientious	responsible
dependable	stable
imaginative	tolerant
intelligent	trustworthy
inventive	willing

Commit this list to memory. Choose answers that contain these and similar words. By the same token, avoid answers that contain language like this:

angry	stressed out
dishonest	temperamental
prejudiced	violent
rigid	narrow-minded

Pop Quiz

Even if a test takes you by surprise, you can arm yourself with the test-taking skills that will help you to perform at your best:

◆ Avoid extreme or absolute answers. "Never say never," the cliché goes, and that is sound advice. Don't hem and haw in your responses, but do make them reasonable.

◆ Skip what you don't know. Play to your strengths by answering first the questions you know best. Then, as time permits, tackle the ones you are less sure of.

◆ Imagine yourself scoring high. This isn't magical thinking, but if you can picture yourself as successful—as a high scorer—you have a better chance of performing well.

◆ Imagine the ideal employee. Now try to answer the test like one.

The Skinny

The most common personality tests you may encounter include Personnel Decisions, Inc.'s Employment Inventory (seeks to identify stable, responsible, motivated applicants, while weeding out those who are nonconforming or hostile); the Hogan Personnel Selection Series (seeks to measure conscientiousness while identifying hostility and "problems" with authority); the Wonderlic Personnel Test (a broad-based personality test that emphasizes measurement of the candidate's attitude toward challenge); and the Minnesota Multiphasic Personality Inventory (seeks to evaluate a broad spectrum of traits relevant to job performance).

"Beating" a Psychological or Integrity Test

The single most important thing to do is always to think before responding. Beware of giving knee-jerk answers. The next most important point concerns honesty. You should approach this issue in two ways:

◆ When asked for factual information, be absolutely honest, giving true answers about your name, your address, your background, and so on.

◆ When asked to rate yourself, always rate yourself very highly, even if you feel this is not completely honest. Never express self-doubt, even if you "honestly" have doubts about yourself and your abilities.

Beyond these basics, take four steps to psych yourself up for a psychological test:

1. Don't view the test as psychotherapy. This means that you should not plumb the depths of your soul to come up with an answer. Answer positively. Make yourself look stable and happy—whether you *feel* that way or not.

2. Related to the first step is this: be prepared to give the answers you think the employer *wants* to get. Look at yourself from the employer's point of view. Answer as the ideal employee.

3. Think of people you know who have failed in the workplace. What are they like personally? Avoid answering questions as you imagine they would.

4. Conversely, think of your friends who have succeeded in the workplace—people whose success you may even envy. How would they answer personality questions?

Integrity tests are easier to handle than personality inventories. Answer each question in a way that paints you as a 100 percent honest, trustworthy, and responsible person. Leave absolutely no room for doubt. For example, if asked if you "ever thought of stealing" from an employer, you could be honest and answer yes. Who hasn't *thought about* stealing? "Yes" is almost certainly the most honest response you could make. Unfortunately, it won't get you hired; therefore, just answer "No, of course not."

 Clincher

You don't have to be "you" when you answer questions on a psychological test. Instead, be—at least for the duration of the test—the person you imagine the employer wants.

Kudos and Lumps

If your performance or test interview concludes with an on-site evaluation, critique, or commentary on how you did, listen carefully and with obvious attention. Try to maintain a pleasantly neutral expression, nodding occasionally to indicate that you are taking in all that you are being given. Do not defend yourself or make excuses. Do not argue with the evaluation. Do not protest it. But you do not have to remain silent in the face of criticism, either. Hear the interviewer out, and then, instead of defending yourself, thank him for his comments. Go on to ask: "Do you have any suggestions for improving _____?"

You also need not agree with the criticism. If you believe that it is unfair or that you have been misjudged, respond this way: "I appreciate what you're saying, and I agree that I could improve my _____. However, I don't agree with you concerning _____, and I'd like to point out _____, _____, and _____."

If you are praised at the end of the session, accept the compliments with warm thanks and an expression of pleasure: "Well, thank you very much. This has been very interesting for me—just a great experience."

If you are neither criticized nor praised, don't assume that you have failed to make an impression. Most interviewers do not rush to evaluate you or to make their opinions known. After all your hard work and sweat in the performance or test interview, you'll most likely receive nothing more than thanks and a promise that "We'll be in touch." Return the thanks, express pleasure over the event ("I really enjoyed this!"), take your leave, and do the *really* hard part: wait.

The Least You Need to Know

◆ The performance interview is about handling stress and communicating clearly.

◆ In most performance interview situations, how you behave is even more important than what you say.

◆ The key to performing well on psychological tests and personality profiles is to imagine yourself as the ideal employee and answer the questions from that perspective.

◆ Answer questions concerning integrity in one way only: so that you seem 100 percent honest and trustworthy. Leave absolutely no room for doubt.

◆ Should you answer all questions with brutal honesty or should you give the answer you think the employer wants to get? No contest. Give the employer what he wants.

Chapter 23

You're on Fire! The Stress Interview

In This Chapter

- ◆ What is a stress interview?
- ◆ Motives for conducting a stress interview
- ◆ How to show that you have "the right stuff"
- ◆ A catalog of stress-interview strategies
- ◆ Typical stress questions—and how to answer them

Welcome to your worst nightmare. The stress interview is to the world of employment what "plebe" hazing is to a military academy: part rite of passage and part trial by ordeal, an attempt to assess how the candidate handles pressure, and an attempt to weed out the weak from the strong.

Stress interviewers may pose abrasive questions; adopt an unpleasant or outright hostile tone; indulge in long, uncomfortable, staring silences; rapidly fire one question after another, without giving you time to complete an answer to any of them; ask impossible, riddlelike questions; put you in an uncomfortable role-playing situation; or simply show up a half-hour late to the interview, leaving you all alone in a small room. Fortunately, few interviewers employ all the stress techniques in any one interview, and few interviews are stress interviews from start to finish. However, a significant minority of interviewers employ one or two stress techniques—just to see how you'll respond—and, in certain high-pressure work environments, the stress interview is *the* interviewing style of choice. It pays to be prepared. This chapter will show you how.

No More Mister Nice Guy

An interviewer who scowls, doesn't offer a handshake, sits down and just stares without speaking, and then begins with a question like this: "What's the stupidest thing you've ever done?" can throw you for a very serious loop indeed.

Body language? What kind of impression do you think you're making now, with your mouth gaping open like that?

Stress Interview Motives

You'll have an easier time handling the *stress interview* if you understand the interviewer's motivation. It has nothing to do with you. The interviewer doesn't *know* you, after all. The stress interview is motivated by one of two things:

◆ The interviewer considers the position he is trying to fill high pressure and stressful and wants to fill it with an employee who can handle whatever curves the job throws his way.

◆ The interviewer is a twisted little fellow who has heard somewhere that you can tell what a person is "really made of" if you abuse him (and besides, it's kinda fun).

def•i•ni•tion

A **stress interview** is characterized by strings of difficult questions, "trick questions," demanding role-playing assignments, and even verbal harshness on the part of the interviewer—all with the objective of assessing the candidate's performance under emotional pressure.

To Reveal the "Real You"?

If the target position does fall into a high-pressure category, you'll just have to accept stress interview tactics (if they are used) as part and parcel of the territory—and, if you can't take the heat, consider the possibility that this particular kitchen isn't the place for you.

Now if you're applying for a high-pressure position, assume that the motive behind all this stress interview unpleasantness is to find out just who you are. But don't just show him who you really are. Show him that "who you really are" is the very person he wants on his team.

Address the issues the stress interviewer throws at you, but avoid matters of personality and emotion. For example, if you are asked to describe your most serious weakness, avoid discussing a personality defect; instead, tell a story about some event that shows how you overcame a weakness. Defuse emotion by focusing on acts and actions.

To Let You Shine?

That certainly *sounds* like a good idea, but how do you pull it off? To begin with, don't worry about "who you really are." Think instead about who this employer wants you to be. That he is subjecting you to a stress interview tells you that he wants you to be a person who handles stress well. So concentrate on being that person.

What the interviewer is really looking for, whether he realizes it or not, is not so much the words you give him in return for his questions, but how you behave, how you act in response to *his* questions, *his* actions, *his* behavior, and *his* demonstration of attitude. The image you manage to create and convey—of unflustered calm, stability, coolness, and the willingness to tolerate and even play along with the stress interview game—is far more impressive than any single answer you may give.

The real you? That may be the interviewer's agenda. For you, the stress interview is your finest hour: a chance to shine. Just play the part, don't respond emotionally, keep your voice low and even, maintain eye contact, think before you speak, and don't give in to fear, nervousness, irritation, or exhaustion.

Stress Interviewer Strategies

The stress in the stress interview may be created by the interviewer's apparently hostile, certainly unpleasant demeanor. It may be intensified by long silences. The response to either of these techniques is simple: don't react to them at all. If the interviewer is curt or unpleasant in tone, uphold your end of the conversation calmly and politely. If the interviewer is silent, you can be silent, too. Don't let your eyes wander. Just maintain a pleasantly neutral expression.

Overload

Beyond these brutally simple stress tactics, the interviewer may try to overload you by heaping one question after another on you or by *layering* them, like this:

Interviewer: Do you work well in a high-pressure environment?

You: Yes, I do.

Interviewer: Fine. Give me an example of a time when you experienced pressure.

You: (You manage to come up with an incident. After you are halfway through your story, the interviewer interrupts.)

Interviewer: Okay. I get the picture. Look, why did this situation come about?

You: (Now you have to come up with an analysis. You begin … only to be cut off with another question.)

def•i•ni•tion

Layering is an interrogation technique that rapidly builds, piles, or "layers" one question on top of another.

Interviewer: Now when did all this happen?

You: (You pin down the date.)

Interviewer: I see. What kind of mistakes did you make in that situation? What would you have done differently?

You: (Now you've been maneuvered into saying something negative about yourself. Refuse to move into the negative corner. Instead, show that what you did was the best thing that could have been done in the situation.)

Interviewer: Well, what about the others? How did your supervisor create a stressful situation?

You: (This is not only overload, but entrapment. The interviewer wants to see if you'll start telling tales against your current employer. Resist the temptation.)

Interviewer: Then who was responsible for that situation?

You: (The interviewer refuses to let you off the hook. You'll have to come up with an answer.) I'd say it's just all part of doing business in a high-pressure environment. You take the pressure. You handle the pressure. Nobody goes out of their way to create the pressure. It comes with the territory.

It takes a certain amount of imagination to fire one question after another, but any interviewer can layer questions, simply by insisting on knowing the who, what, why, when, and how behind every answer you give. In answering, you have two objectives:

1. Refuse the bait tempting you to launch into negative remarks about yourself or others.

2. Answer calmly. Don't let yourself get rattled. Don't adopt the questioner's rapid-fire rhythm. Don't protest ("Would you give me a chance to answer?!"). Remember, what you actually say is less important in the stress interview than how you say it. The interviewer is prepared to judge behavior more than words.

Brainstorm

Another stress technique puts you on the spot by asking questions that are off the wall and of absurdly sweeping scope:

◆ "Tell me what's wrong with my company and how you'd fix it."

◆ "I want to sell more widgets. Tell me what to do."

◆ "Why should I hire you?"

The first mistake you'll be tempted to make is to respond by remarking on the scope of the question: "That's an awfully broad question." Of course it is. Don't waste time remarking on the obvious, or worse, dropping a suggestion that the question is too big for you to answer. Pause several seconds to organize an answer. The interviewer has revved up the pace, but you don't have to keep step. Collect your thoughts and begin an answer whenever you can. Remember, the most important aspect of your answer is its tone—calm, straightforward, unrattled. Only after you have established the tone, bring in the substance.

Set Up for a Fall

Finally, there is the heavy artillery of the stress interview. It begins with an innocent-sounding question:

> **Interviewer:** You are currently a [job title]?

> **You:** Yes.

> **Interviewer:** How long have you been in that position?

> **You:** Three years.

Hey, all of this is on your resumé. What gives? *This* gives:

> **Interviewer:** How do you account for your failure to advance?

Bang! This zinger is calculated to make you feel bad, to tear you down, to provoke a negative, disheartened response.

Understand the game. This kind of cruel question is specifically calculated to simulate a circumstance in which, say, a client tries to tear you down. How will you handle it?

You handle it by refusing to accept the criticism, the negative appraisal the remark proposes:

> I don't see my progress as slow. The position I have is challenging and has prepared me to move on to even greater responsibility.

Twenty Stress Questions (and Answers)

Now that we've surveyed the landscape of the stress interview, let's zero in on a few of the typical questions.

> 1. *Tell me what your greatest weakness is.*

Stress interviewers love to ask *When-did-you-stop-beating-your-dog?* questions—that is, questions that invite negative answers. The secret to fielding these is to reject the negativity. Don't deny that you have failings. No one will believe that you are perfect. Instead, go ahead and identify a *minor* weakness or *slight* flaw, then put it in the past. Show how you overcame it: "I used to have some difficulty staying organized on the road. But then I got into the habit of taking the time to make really thorough notes immediately after each customer call. I just learned to take the time to do it—then and there. Since then, I've always had it together, in the home office or out on the road."

Clincher _____

Asked about your "greatest weakness," offer a flaw that is really a strength in disguise: "Often, I get a little *too* focused on my work." Or: "I'm a perfectionist. I don't settle for halfway measures. Or: "Well, some people tell me that I demand too much of myself." Be careful, however, that you don't make yourself sound like a humorless grind or give the impression that you really are neurotic—a hard-driven individual doomed to burn out.

2. *What skills do you need to improve?*

The trouble here, once again, is that you can't simply proclaim your perfection, yet if you admit to areas that need improvement, the stress interviewer will respond like a shark to blood. Sidestep the question by redefining it: "Based on our conversation thus far, I'd say I have all the skills necessary for the position. That's what excites me about the job." You could then take the opportunity to review the highlights of your resumé.

3. *What kinds of decisions do you find especially difficult?*

If you answer this question using the terms that the question offers, you can only answer negatively. Then, the interviewer will pounce. The secret here? Reject the negative terms: "I don't find any decisions particularly 'difficult,' but it is true that some demand more thought and analysis than others. Perhaps you might call this 'difficulty.' I call it doing the job you're being paid to do."

4. *How do you manage to live on an entry-level salary? You must be in debt. It must be tough.*

Here's an attempt to trick you into confessing personal problems or difficulty managing your own finances. To be sure, there may be more than a grain of truth in what the interviewer implies. Sidestep the issue nevertheless: "Have you ever met anyone my age satisfied with their salary? Sure, I want to advance. Obviously, that's one of the reasons I'm talking to you. As for now, I budget my expenses, and I pay my bills."

5. *You've been with your current employer quite a while. Why haven't you advanced with him?*

Let's assume the interviewer has struck a nerve. What he says is all too true. That doesn't mean you have to agree with the negative terms of the question. "What I like about my present position is that it is both stable and challenging. But it's true that

Clincher _____

The stress interview is not a court of law. You need not deliver yes or no answers. Bend the questions to deliver the answer you *want* to give.

I've grown about as much as I can in it. That's why I'm here. I'm ready to offer more to a different company." Note that this response turns the issue of salary on its head, transforming it from "*What more can I get?*" to "*What more can I offer?*"

6. *I know I can't ask how old you are, but it's apparent that you're no teenager. Shouldn't you be in a more advanced position by now?*

This is meant as a dig, a goad, something to bruise you. But you need not take it that way. Why not look at it as a compliment paid to your skills and level of achievement? "I am in this for the long haul. I'm willing to pay my dues, and that is what I've done. I've gained a great deal of experience and a solid background. I'm here to offer those assets to you."

7. *Are you a risk-taker?*

A trap for the unwary. If you simply answer yes, you open the door to questions about your prudence: "So you're impulsive, even careless sometimes?" Before answering any wide-open question, ask for qualification: "How would you define 'risk'? What do you see as an example of a possibly acceptable risk? I'd need to know the upside and downside. This is not a question I would answer without thorough knowledge of all the elements involved." Whether or not the interviewer pursues the question, you have demonstrated that you won't take mindless risks. You look before you leap. If the discussion of risk does continue, be sure to leave the impression that you are neither timid nor impulsive: "Look, I'm not interested in doing anything that would put the company at risk. Sure, there is no reward without risk, but risk can be managed, and management takes information and assessment. With the right information, I might be prepared to take certain risks."

8. *I have a "reputation" in this industry. Tell me, what's the worst thing you've heard about me?*

The last thing this person wants to hear is that you've heard nothing at all bad about him. Obviously, he relishes his tough rep. On the other hand, you certainly don't want to volunteer that you heard he was, say, an [insert organ of elimination here]. Smile: "What I've heard is that you're a tough interviewer. The word on the street was sure right on that one!"

9. *I'm considering promoting from the inside to fill this position. Why should I hire you instead?*

You'll be tempted to respond incredulously: "Why the heck did you invite me out here if you're going to promote from within?" But recognize that this question is just a particularly intimidating way of asking you to persuade this person to hire you. Take a breath and review your resumé highlights, always painting yourself as the answer to the employer's needs. Having concluded this, accept the question at face value for a moment: "If you haven't found someone to promote from within, I'd have to assume that you are looking for something you don't yet have in this company. What benefits are you looking for?" If you can get a straightforward answer to this, you should be able to shape your pitch even more sharply, precisely tailoring it to what the employer says he needs.

> **Clincher** _____
>
> Whenever possible, punctuate the interview with positive feedback. Don't praise the interviewer for being a nice guy or a brilliant person, but comment on his performance: "You certainly know how to get to the heart of the matter!" Or: "That is a thoughtful question. Give me a moment."

10. *How do you handle rejection?*

Rejection is part of just about any business. People don't always buy what you have to sell. The trick here is to separate rejection of your product from rejection of yourself: "I see rejection as an opportunity. I learn from it. When a customer takes a pass, I ask him what we could do to the product or price or service to make it possible for him to say yes. Don't get me wrong: You've got to make sales. But rejection is valuable, too. It's a good teacher."

11. *Tell me about a time when you said something really embarrassing.*

Don't dodge this one, but don't make yourself look like an oaf, either. Offer as innocuous a faux pas as you can dredge up: "A colleague of mine came to a party with his wife. She had put on a good deal of weight. Well, my colleague had been talking quite a bit about starting a family—and I just naturally put two and two together. 'So when is the big day?' My colleague's wife just looked at me, 'What big day?' 'The baby!' I said. 'I'm not expecting.' Well, you can bet that's the last time I put two and two together like that! Fortunately, she took it all graciously—and seemed concerned that *I* was embarrassed. But I learned a lot about never assuming something without getting the facts first. I mean, she could have been a client or a client's spouse. The stakes are often higher than you think. It was an embarrassing but valuable lesson."

12. *Why do you want to leave your current job?*

This is a basic question, hardly peculiar to the stress interview, but it is all the more difficult to answer in the context of other stress questions. Fortunately, employment advisers have come up with a neat acronym to cover this one. It's easy to remember, even under pressure: CLAMPS. The acronym stands for **C**hallenge, **L**ocation, **A**dvancement, **M**oney, **P**ride (or **P**restige), and **S**ecurity. Expressed singly or in combination, any of these motivating factors should persuade the interviewer that you have a sound, intelligent, thoughtful reason for wanting to leave your current position.

Don't Call Us ...

Resist the temptation to "open up" to the interviewer. A skilled interviewer will put you at ease and may even come on more as a friend than as a potential employer. Don't kid yourself. The interviewer is not your friend. She's not your enemy, either. But keep the relationship businesslike and always present your best: show the qualities that make you a great employee, minus the various failings and foibles you as a person share with the rest of humanity.

13. *What do you most dislike about your current job?*

Typical of the stress interview, this question is expressed in negatives. But even when you are *invited* to be negative, avoid negativity. The interviewer will discount that *he* invited you to be critical, and he will remember only that you were a complainer. Worse, his or her overall impression of the interview will be negative. Moreover, while dissatisfaction with your present position may seem to *you* a very good reason to change jobs, it fails to address the needs of the target employer. Your answers should always address the needs of the employer. Remember, a successful used car salesman doesn't pitch you with, "Buy this car so that *I* can pay *my* mortgage and put *my* kids through college." He sells the value and benefits of owning this particular car.

How should you answer then? Consider something like this: "I like everything about my current position." Then, go on to list some vital skills, qualifications, and achievements associated with the position. Conclude with: "I'm now ready for a new set of challenges and an opportunity for greater advancement and greater responsibility, an opportunity to bring all that I have learned to a more challenging and rewarding position."

14. *How many hours a week do you need to get your job done?*

In the context of a stress interview, this is a trick question. The "trick" is that if you reply with something like 40 hours, you risk labeling yourself as a clock watcher, yet if you say 60, you might be implying that you're slow, inefficient, and easily over-whelmed. Even worse, you may be setting yourself up for nothing but 60-hour work-weeks.

How do you avoid the trap? Whenever you are invited to mount the horns of a dilemma, simply decline the invitation. Instead of pinning your answer down to a specific number ("I work 47.2 hours each week."), reply, "I make an effort to plan my time efficiently. Usually, this works well. However, as you know, this business has crunch periods, and when that happens, I put in as many hours as necessary to get the job done."

It's not likely that the interviewer will press beyond this answer, unless she is "layer-ing" questions as part of her high-stress tactic. If she persists, demanding that you furnish a number, turn her question around with a question of your own: "That really does depend on the project and the priorities. What's typical in your business/ department?"

15. *What do you consider an acceptable attendance record?*

This question demands little or no thought at all, depending on whether you are inter-viewing for a management/supervisory position or an entry-level job. If you're in management, be careful that your answer does not seem to evade responsibility. "I demand perfect attendance from my people" is not only an unrealistic response, it places the responsibility for good attendance entirely on the staff. Answer in a way that puts you front and center in the picture: "I believe that attendance is a function of motivation and management. If I do my job right, my staff will be motivated, and atten-dance won't be a problem."

Clincher

The objective of the stress question is to lock you into a difficult, negative, or impos-sible set of answers. Reject this by redefining the question. "What *don't* you like?" can be answered by simply turning the *don't* into a *do*. "I like every-thing."

If you are up for an entry-level position rather than a management post, simply answer that you are strongly motivated, are excited about the job, enjoy working, and are rarely sick.

16. *What's the most difficult situation you ever faced on the job?*

Do *not* search your soul to find an answer for this one. The last thing you want to do is to dredge up a situation so difficult that it resulted in personal failure or general disaster. Expect a question like this—even if you're not in a stress interview situation—and come to the interview prepared with a story that has a *happy* ending—not just happy for you, but for your company as well.

Some tips: do not discuss personal or family difficulties. Do not discuss problems you've had with supervisors or peers. You may discuss a difficult situation with a subordinate, provided that the issues were resolved inventively and to everyone's satisfaction. You could also answer this question by relating a situation that was particularly challenging for you; for example, the time you had to learn a whole new piece of software before you could write a how-to article about it. It was difficult, but one of the most rewarding assignments you had.

17. *What kinds of people do you find difficult to work with?*

Now that you are thoroughly indoctrinated in the avoid-negativity-at-any-cost school of thought, you might answer this one quite simply: "I don't find it difficult to work with anybody." Or: "I get along with everyone." Neither of these is a bad answer, but they are not very convincing. Use the question as an occasion to show that you are a team player: "The only people I have trouble with are those who aren't team players, who just don't perform, who complain constantly, and who fail to respond to any efforts to motivate them." The interviewer is expecting a response centered on personality and personal dislikes. Surprise her by delivering an answer that reflects company values.

Clincher _____

Even in a stress interview, you are not trying to beat the clock. Take the time you need to formulate a response. A brief silence between question and answer is better than hemming and hawing. If you need to buy more time for thinking, repeat the question back to the interviewer in a thoughtful tone: "The most difficult situation I ever faced on the job ..." Just don't use this dodge too often. If you do, you risk sounding like a parrot.

18. *Evaluate me as an interviewer.*

Here's one out of left field, and it can throw you for a loop. This person has been applying the pressure for a half hour or 45 minutes, and now he's asking you what you think of *him?* What is he after? A pat on the back?

Hardly.

This is your opportunity to signal to the interviewer that you understand and appreciate what he's trying to do. "Frankly, this has been the toughest interview I've ever had. But I understand and appreciate what you're after. You want someone who can think on her feet, who works well under pressure. What kind of interviewer do I think you are? Well, I believe you've succeeded admirably in seeing how well I perform under pressure."

19. *How would you respond if I told you that your performance in this interview has been poor?*

A body blow? The knockout punch? Only if you overlook the "if" in this question. The interviewer is not telling you that your performance was poor. He's asking you what you would say *if* he told you that. The key to responding to criticism is neither to ward it off nor to embrace it, but to learn from it. Here's an effective answer to the question: "I would ask you what it was that you didn't like. Where do you feel the problems were? If your response led me to conclude that I had miscommunicated with you, I would try to make myself clearer. If, however, you identified a deeper difficulty, I would ask your advice on how to correct it. Certainly, I don't relish being told that I have failed in any way. But even failure is valuable as a learning experience."

20. *I'm not convinced that you're right for this job.*

You have nothing to lose by taking the phrase "I'm not convinced" as an invitation to convince the interviewer once and for all that you *are* right for the job. Yet again, the experience of veteran salespeople can serve to guide you. When a salesperson meets resistance, she probes for soft spots through that resistance by asking questions. You should do the same: "Why do you say that?" Or: "What will it take to convince you?"

Let the interviewer tell you what he needs, then give it to him:

Interviewer: I'm not sure that you have enough supervisory experience.

You: Of course, you can find people who have been supervising longer than I have, but if you look at what I've accomplished in my department—a 15 percent reduction in costs, a record for high customer satisfaction—wouldn't you agree that I am an effective supervisor?

Clincher _____

"Sucking up" is an ugly synonym for dishing out empty flattery. *Empty* flattery has no place in an employment interview. Flattery, however, is another story. Take the opportunity to provide positive feedback to the interviewer—not empty flattery, but flattery based on the interviewer's actions, questions, and comments: "That's hardly your run-of-the-mill interview question. You've obviously given this issue a great deal of thoughtful consideration."

Probe with your questions, invite the interviewer to review his needs, and respond to each of those needs. Each time you present your qualifications, invite agreement: "Wouldn't you agree?" In a stress interview, the interviewer's expressions of doubt are challenges—or requests—to you for more information, more reasons for him to say yes.

The Least You Need to Know

- ◆ Exploit the stress interview not to reveal "the real you," but to reveal the person the prospective employer wants "you" to be.

- ◆ The employer is less interested in the specific answers to his stress-producing questions than in how you behave—your tone and body language—under stress.

- ◆ Avoid making emotional responses to emotionally provocative questions.

- ◆ Try to translate the stress interviewer's negative questions into positive responses.

- ◆ Defuse difficult questions by turning them around as questions you ask the interviewer.

Chapter 24

What to Do at a Brick Wall

In This Chapter

- ◆ Recognizing the "red flags"
- ◆ Preparing for objections
- ◆ What are the most frequent objections?
- ◆ Tactics for overcoming objections
- ◆ Dealing with illegal or offensive objections

Here's the good news: a prospective employer isn't going to summon you to an interview to tell you you're wrong for the job. If you're invited to fly into his air space, he's not likely to *try* to shoot you down.

But it does happen. And that's the bad news.

In the course of the interview conversation, objections can and do arise. Sometimes the objections loom large enough to overshadow the areas of agreement. Your objective is to turn objections into opportunities that demonstrate why the employer was right to call on you in the first place. This chapter discusses the typical interview killers and not only how to beat them, but how to use them to help make your case.

Call to Action

The range of employer objections is at least as great as the range of reasons an employer may find to hire you, and a determined interviewer can turn any positive into a negative. For example, a common red flag is a resumé that reveals a history of frequent job changes. If that's the case with you, you'd better prepare some answers to overcome the inevitable objection. However, if you've been with the same company for many years, you may well run across a potential employer who will object to that: "Why have you stayed with Acme Widget so long? Is security more important to you than challenge?" Other common objections you should prepare yourself to deal with include …

- Gaps in your resumé.

- Insufficient experience.

- Inadequate or inappropriate educational background.

- Apparently sluggish career progress.

- Overqualification.

- Being fired from a job.

- Concerns that you won't "fit in."

Objections in these areas can come at any time during the interview, but they typically come toward the end and may be triggered by the very effort you make to bring the interview to a positive close. As you may recall from Chapter 14, the most effective way to bring an interview to a conclusion is to move the interviewer to some positive action: "Based on my background and all I have to offer, wouldn't you agree that I bring to the position everything you need?" While such a question invites a positive reply, it may also provoke objections.

And that's okay. The objections, after all, are in the employer's mind and will figure in her decision whether or not to make an offer. Isn't it better that you know—*now*, before you leave the interview—what objections remain active? At least this will give you an opportunity to confront and perhaps overcome them.

Five Steps to Overcome Any Objection

If you're lucky, the employer will raise an objection that is easy to overcome: a simple misunderstanding, perhaps, or something somehow left out of the interview discussion.

Such objections can be addressed straightforwardly by restating the misunderstood item or by supplying a missing piece of data.

Other, more complex objections involve the employer's feelings and his perception of you and your background. Overcoming these requires a more systematic, exploratory approach.

1. The Rephrase Step

The first step in overcoming a complex or difficult objection is to make that objection your own by restating it in your own words. This not only helps to ensure that you understand the problem, it shows the employer that you are eager to take on responsibility for problems, and that you are willing to make the employer's concerns your concerns: "So you are worried that, having managed the department at Acme for two years, I have insufficient supervisory experience?"

Clincher _____

"What's in a name?" Shakespeare asked. While most may call an employer objection an *obstacle*, you should think of it as an *opportunity*. An objection is an opportunity to demonstrate your problem-solving skills—right on the spot.

2. The Confirmation Step

Don't leave your rephrasing of the objection out there all by its lonesome. After you've rephrased it, confirm your understanding of the objection: "Do I understand you correctly?"

Two responses to this question are possible:

1. "No, that's not quite what I said."

2. "Yes. You understand me correctly."

Either response serves to keep the doors open, to prevent the interview from grinding to a negative halt. If the employer tells you that you have misunderstood his objection, *he* will restate it, thereby investing more time in you—which, in and of itself, is valuable to an interview. Second, in the course of restating the objection, both of you may come to a clearer understanding of just what it is the employer wants and needs. Finally, it's also possible that restating the objection may drain some of the fuel out of the objection, or at least put it into a context that makes it look less absolute.

If, on the other hand, the employer replies that you have understood his objection, you've accomplished two things. First, you've established that the two of you have communicated successfully—in itself a positive achievement. Second, you've gotten the interviewer to speak again, which now means that it's your turn to talk. This will push the imperiled interview forward.

3. The Concession Step

Tread carefully here. Your next move should be to acknowledge the validity of the employer's concern even as you disclaim actual liability. You do this by conceding the feelings, not the facts: "I can see why you feel that way. It's certainly important to have an experienced leader in this position." All that has been conceded is the validity of feelings. There is no agreement as to the validity of the facts that have been asserted.

4. The Neutralizing Step

Having acknowledged the employer's negative feelings, it is now up to you to neutralize them by providing new information or by reintroducing vital information that the employer may be overlooking or discounting. If you managed to wedge in a fact when you rephrased the objection, you already have a leg up: "In my three years in sales at Acme, I've taken on increasing levels of responsibility. As I mentioned, the sales force at Acme always had a great deal of autonomy. We were free to sink or swim. I swam, and I made it my business to mentor others. I understood that my success depended on the success of the entire team. Team building—that's the single greatest leadership lesson I've learned over the past three years."

Clincher _____

Don't think of an objection as criticism or doubt, but as a cry for help. The employer is having trouble making the decision to offer you the job. Help him make that decision.

5. The Storytelling Step

Having set up a fresh approach to your information—an approach you hope will overcome the employer's objections by making him see your skills and qualifications from a more favorable angle—state some *specific* accomplishment to support what you've just asserted. As always, your message will come through most clearly if you deliver it in the language of business—namely, dollars: "In the last quarter, my own sales were up 26 percent. But what I'm most proud of is having played a role in bringing up sales for our entire unit—up 14 percent. This is what I mean by building a team. That improvement was due in no small part to my mentoring efforts."

The Charge Is Job Hopping

Objections about your employment history are the most common concerns interviewers raise; frequent job changes are especially likely to raise an eyebrow.

An objection to job hopping should never take you by surprise. *You* know whether or not you've held several jobs over a relatively brief span of time, and, if this is the case, you should know that you must have an explanation ready.

Preparing the Defense

You need to study your finished resumé, not just with an eye toward tweaking and improving it, but in order to see it as a prospective employer might. If it becomes apparent to you that the duration of each of your positions has been relatively brief, you can be sure that this impression will be made even more vividly on the prospective employer. Think about how you will meet—and make the most of—the objection that will almost certainly be raised.

The Best Light

Don't concentrate on making excuses for job hopping. Don't defend it. Don't justify it. Above all, don't talk about the personal problems or restlessness or feelings of dissatisfaction that may have motivated you to move from position to position. Instead, find an explanation that puts it all in the best possible light. For example:

> You're right. I have held a number of jobs during the past five years. You know, most people stumble upon their careers by default. They start a job, and they stay in it just long enough so that it becomes "what they do"—their career.
> I don't like things to happen just because they happen. I try to operate from firsthand knowledge and experience. Because of that, I've been willing to explore a number of job possibilities over the years. Now, at last, that experience has paid off. I've discovered, through firsthand experience, what I want to commit myself to: a position as widget control analyst with Smith Widgets. That's why I'm here.

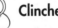 **Clincher**

"An ounce of prevention," goes the cliché, "is worth a pound of cure." Try to structure your resumé so that there are no gaps. See Chapter 3 for gap-filling strategies.

Gaps, Gulfs, and Gaffes

Anything that doesn't look 100 percent positive is likely to trigger an objection. Again, there is little excuse for letting yourself get ambushed by one of these situations.

There's a Hole in Your Resumé

For most employers, the ideal candidate is one whose career shows continuous employment and an uninterrupted upward trajectory. If there's a hole in your resumé, you'd better be ready to account for it.

Unless the gaps in your employment history correspond with a coma, you *did* do something with that time. Talk about your volunteer work, study, special training, travel, freelance employment, consultant work. Express in the most productive terms possible whatever you did during those gap periods.

Perhaps you left "regular" employment to strike out on your own as a freelancer, an independent contractor, or a consultant. If you enjoyed any tangible degree of success in this endeavor, use it as your reason for having left a past employer and feature the "gap" prominently on your resumé and in interviews. List your most prominent clients and/or projects on your resumé.

 Don't Call Us ...

Confronted with an objection that you lack experience, it's perfectly proper to respond by putting the experience you *do* have in the best possible light—showing, for example, how your experience in customer service applies productively to sales as well. However, resist the temptation to fabricate experience you don't have. If you're ever found out, fraud is a cause for summary dismissal.

Not Enough Experience

This is probably the most common objection of all, and the one that's hardest to overcome. After all, your experience is your experience: a matter of record.

But what is "experience?"

Few employers insist on your making a lateral move from Job A at Company A to Job A at Company B. Most appreciate your wanting to step up from Job A to Job B—maybe even to Job C. A leap to Job D will probably take a more earnest effort at persuasion, and, beyond this, most employers will, with justification, protest that you lack sufficient experience.

When you meet with an objection that you don't have Job C experience, you might concede that, yes, you haven't done Job C before, but your experience with Job A and certain other elements of your personal background, education, and personality give you a strong foundation on which you can quickly build the skills necessary for the job. "Besides, it's a challenge. I'm motivated. I wouldn't want a job that didn't challenge me."

In Chapter 2 we talked about portable skills—the skills you carry with you from job to job, in contrast to skills that are demanded by a particular job. When you meet an objection relating to experience, it's your cue to trot out your portable skills. Show how the skills you have developed on your own, as well as those you use and have honed in your current or most recent position, are portable, readily transferred, and applied to the requirements of the target position: "Customer service is about people and about selling the company and the company's reputation with each and every service call I handle. So while I've not had 'sales' in my job title, the skills I've honed these last two years have been sales skills. I really see no difficulty making the transition from selling the values of the company to selling particular products."

> **Clincher**
>
> One last alternative: Get more education. If you find that doors are repeatedly slammed in your face, it's a pretty certain signal that you should consider going back to school.

Wrong Degree, No Degree

Face it: If you want a job as chief of surgery in a large metropolitan hospital, you're going to need that M.D. degree, and no amount of talk about "portable skills" or "related experience" is going to be accepted as a substitute. There *are* certain positions that require specific educational credentials. In business, however, educational requirements are not always carved in stone. Confronted with an objection concerning your education, you have three options before you throw in the towel and walk out the door:

1. Say "Yes, but …" and present the strengths you do have, including practical experience, qualifications, and portable skills. If you can make a convincing case, you may be able to circumvent the formal degree issue.

2. Agree that you would be happy and eager to pursue the required degree—with the target employer's assistance. Perhaps this firm is willing to assist you with a professional development program.

3. Using a polite, nonconfrontational tone, ask the interviewer just what he expects the degree would do for you and the company: "I have a Bachelor's, majoring in the field. What benefit would I—and the company—derive from my holding a Master's?" Depending on the response, you may be able to make a strong case for the greater value of your practical experience in the field.

Climbing Down the Ladder of Success

Prospective employers like candidates with simple lives and simple careers, careers that might be represented graphically as a straight line rising at a 45 degree angle. Always up. Never down.

Life is not always like that.

Explaining a Salary Reduction

One way to avoid having to explain a salary reduction is to avoid volunteering salary information in the first place and certainly not listing it gratuitously on your resumé. If, however, you do somehow find yourself in the position of having to explain a reduction, show how you traded opportunity—or something of real value—for money. For example:

- "The opportunity to work independently on special projects was more than worth the 14 percent reduction in salary. I learned a great deal."

- "The opportunity to live in Chicago was worth a modest pay cut to me."

- "This is the industry I want to be in. Breaking in came at a price—a fairly substantial reduction in salary—but it's been worth it."

Explaining an Apparent Demotion

More difficult to explain in terms of an exchange of value for value is an apparent reduction in responsibility. If you were, in fact, demoted, you should either do your best to hide that fact or be prepared with a very good explanation. Try to ascribe the reason for the change to "staffing needs"; don't suggest that you failed to deliver satisfaction.

If the "demotion" is only apparent, go ahead and explain it:

◆ "I was excited about working at the Smith Company. When an opening occurred there, I grabbed it, even though it meant a title change from manager to supervisor."

◆ "For family reasons, I wanted to move to Chicago. I was willing to take a somewhat lower-level position to make the move possible."

I'm Overqualified!?

What objection can be more stupefyingly frustrating than the opinion that you are *"overqualified* for the position?" In responding, take your cue from your own sense of frustration. You need to understand the objection. You need more information. Respond to the objection with a request for clarification. If possible, couple that request with a mini-review of the highlights of your practical qualifications:

I'm frankly bewildered by that statement. My understanding was that you needed someone to manage customer service. I've been running customer service departments for 15 years. I can meet the challenge—and it's a challenge I don't think anyone could be "overqualified" for. During my tenure at the Smith Company, I reorganized the customer service departments, so that costs were reduced by 13 percent, while reported customer satisfaction rose by 21 percent …

def•i•ni•tion

To be **overqualified** means that you have too much experience or too much education to "fit into" a given position. The employer's assumption is that you'll become bored with the job and soon quit.

This should coax the interviewer into rethinking his position. If it doesn't, he's going to have to work that much harder to justify to himself—and to his supervisors—why you should *not* be offered the job.

You Were Fired

First of all, be certain to distinguish between being laid off—termination due to circumstances entirely beyond your control, such as corporate downsizing or a workforce reduction—and being dismissed due to what your employer perceives as your failure to perform or to some transgression your employer determines that you have committed. If you have been laid off, ensure that the target employer understands this and does not believe that you were fired.

But what if you really were fired?

When asked about the circumstances of termination, don't lie. Deceptive answers in an interview or on a job application are always grounds for summary dismissal a day later or 10 years down the road. If you are caught in your lie, you will be fired—again.

Be honest, but don't strip naked. Don't volunteer the information that you were fired. If you're asked, though, give a full and forthright reply that puts the event in its best possible light:

> I have to say that my termination was my fault. I had personal problems at the time, which are now completely resolved. But, at the time, I was frequently late. My supervisor—with whom I am still very much on speaking terms—was under orders to reduce the workforce, and, quite honestly, my attendance record at the time gave him the reason he needed to let me go.

Unless you can make an ironclad case that you were fired unjustly, don't blame other people for what happened to you. You will not be believed. Try to put that event in perspective. If you can, find out how many others were fired, laid off, or even left voluntarily during the period in which you were dismissed. After responding forthrightly to the interviewer's question, add: "I am one of 38 people who have left so far this year."

Avoid wallowing in guilt. Just take responsibility, and, along with responsibility, take the opportunity to demonstrate that you understand how you failed and, more important, how to avoid repeating the failure. Create the impression that getting fired taught you about commitment and responsibility, taught you the "hard way," a way you'll never forget, a way that will benefit any company that employs you. You will not repeat your mistakes.

Of course, going into the interview, *you* know if you've got an unpleasant termination in your employment history. You must prepare a solid response to any objection this fact may elicit. One aspect of this preparation may be to contact your former employer. Ask her what she intends to say about you now:

> I'm in the process of looking for a new job, and I'd like to determine just how I stand with you. If you are asked as part of a pre- or post-employment reference check, how would you describe the circumstances of my leaving the company? Would you say that I was fired? Would you say that I was laid off? Would you

say that I resigned? My problem is that, every time I tell a prospective employer about my termination, I blow another shot at a paycheck.

Perhaps you can persuade your former employer to use nonpejorative language in describing your termination.

"I'm Not Sure You Fit In ..."

Depending on who you are and the state of your ego, this objection can be truly devastating or merely offensive. It may also be illegal.

Making the Most of Diversity

If the interviewer tells you that he has doubts about how you would "fit in," respond with a probing question expressed in as neutral a tone as you can manage: "I don't understand that. Can you explain what you mean?"

If the employer's response touches on issues of gender, race, or age, you are well within your rights to remind him of the law. But do you want to initiate a lawsuit, or do you want to get a job? The more immediately effective alternative is to sell the employer on the value of diversity: "It's true that I bring a unique perspective with me—the perspective of the streets, of the working class, of the (African American, Hispanic, Polish, Italian, Asian, whatever) community. You do business with these people and this community. I offer firsthand experience. Don't worry. I'll fit in here. More important, I can help to ensure that the Smith Company will 'fit in' with all the people it serves."

You should also think about whether you want to work for someone to whom race, gender, or age is such a source of contention. Hopefully, no one at your workplace will have to be sold on the values of diversity.

Hiring and the Law

Strong federal legislation bars employers from discriminating against any person on the basis of sex, race, age, national origin, or religion (Civil Rights Act of 1964, Title VII); nor can an employer discriminate against workers age 40 or older (Age

Discrimination in Employment Act of 1967); nor can persons be barred from employment because of disabilities that do not prevent them from doing their assigned tasks (Americans with Disabilities Act of 1991, Title I). These are wonderful laws. The problem is that proving the occurrence of discrimination is often extremely difficult, time-consuming, and costly. When you are looking for employment, you probably don't want to take on any additional burdens, don't have much time, and certainly can't afford a protracted legal battle. Know what your rights are, but realize that, confronted by objections that reflect prejudices and even illegal discrimination, you have to choose whether to enforce your legal rights or overcome the objection in order to press the interview to a successful conclusion. Remember, you can always decide to turn down an offer. But first you must get the offer.

The Least You Need to Know

◆ Examine your resumé carefully in order to identify the "red flags" that will wave before the eyes of a potential employer.

◆ Based on your employment history, make a list of potential employer objections; before you go into an interview, prepare strategies to overcome each of these.

◆ Learn to view objections not as rejections, but as the employer's request that you help him make it possible to hire you.

◆ Know your rights to protection from discriminatory hiring practices, but be aware that discrimination is difficult to prove and that you may choose to make certain compromises in order to secure a job offer.

Part 6

To Follow Through, Follow Up

Think you can kick back and relax now that the interview is over? Better think again. What you do after the interview can be very important to "closing the sale." For one thing, you may find that your interviewing chores aren't quite finished. Employers are being increasingly careful these days—hiring the wrong person can be a very costly mistake—so you may be subjected to one or even more follow-up interviews. Read on for a chapter on making the most of this special interview situation.

But even if all the interviews are behind you, you have work to do. Your most important task is writing a thank-you message—one that is not merely courteous (although that's important), but that actually helps close the sale. The final chapter tells you how to write such an e-mail or letter.

Chapter 25

Nailing the Follow-Up Interview

In This Chapter

- ◆ Why a follow-up interview is a good thing
- ◆ Preparing for the follow-up
- ◆ Convincing the interviewer that you "belong"
- ◆ Closing the follow-up on a positive note

Let's begin by making sure we all know what we're talking about here. We've already discussed the common interview scenario—a screening interview (see Chapter 18) followed by an in-depth or selection interview. It has been on the selection interview that most of these chapters have focused.

There is yet another possible interview scenario. Sometimes even the selection interview is not the final interview. It may be standard practice for a particular employer to follow up an in-depth interview with yet one more, or it may be that the earlier interview has left some questions unanswered, and the employer feels that a follow-up is necessary.

This chapter gives you some suggestions for handling such close encounters of the third kind.

You've Made the Cut—Now What?

First, convince yourself of this: if getting called to a selection interview following a screening interview is a good thing, being asked to a final *follow-up interview* after the selection interview is even better. Go into the follow-up interview confident that the employer is highly interested in you, and that his purpose in asking you to the follow-up is mainly to confirm his decision.

def•i•ni•tion

A **follow-up interview** may take place after an in-depth, or selection, interview. It is often the venue in which unresolved issues are discussed. Sometimes its main purpose is to deliver the offer and negotiate salary and other matters.

Prepare for the Follow-Up Interview

If you are told, following the selection interview, to expect a follow-up, begin preparing for it immediately. While the interview just concluded is fresh in your mind, jot down a list of …

- ◆ Major issues raised.
- ◆ Topics the interviewer mentioned more than once.
- ◆ Issues the interviewer told you were key.
- ◆ Issues you feel remain unresolved.
- ◆ Questions you expected to be asked, but weren't.
- ◆ Questions you were asked, but wish you had answered more effectively.
- ◆ Mistakes you made: errors in information, inadequate information, and so on.
- ◆ Questions you still have.

Indeed, it's a good idea to make such a post-interview list, even if you *haven't* been advised of a follow-up. There are two reasons for this: first, a follow-up interview may be sprung on you unexpectedly, giving you little time for preparation; second, all interviews have valuable lessons to teach, and analyzing your performance will be helpful in subsequent interviews with other employers. And if you get hired as a result of the selection interview, you will find notes valuable to help you hit the ground running in the first days and weeks of your new job.

Study your list. Try to find or formulate answers to unresolved issues. Prepare discussion points for the topics that are clearly of greatest interest to the employer.

Clincher _____

If the salary issue was left untouched in the screening or selection interview, it's certain to be a principal subject of the follow-up. As a matter of fact, the main purpose of some follow-up interviews is salary negotiation (see Chapter 13).

Anticipate the Issues

Compile and review your list. Expect that the follow-up interview will focus on some or all of the issues either emphasized in the previous interview, left unresolved in that interview, or conspicuously absent from it.

Your Entrance

Feelings of resistance or even resentment at being made to jump through yet another set of hoops are normal and to be expected. Acknowledge these feelings, and then set them aside. Exert whatever effort it takes to put yourself into a high-energy, positive frame of mind *before* you walk through the hoop—er, *door.*

Like an Old Friend

Make your entrance like an old friend. Smile. Greet the interviewer or interviewers warmly and with firm handshakes all around. Your objective is to deliver the impression that this follow-up visit is a great pleasure for you—a step along the road to becoming a full member of the team.

The Name Game

The single most impressive demonstration of your enthusiasm sounds simple. For some people, it *is* simple. For others, it requires a singularly strenuous exercise of memory.

When you make your entrance and exchange greetings, call everyone by their name. The name game takes effort, especially when you have so much on your mind. In a high-stress situation, you're lucky if you can manage to remember your own name.

Don't Call Us ...

Unless you were specifically invited during the previous interview to use an interviewer's first name, don't do so now. Use surnames, and don't ask for permission to use first names.

Yet the effort is very much worth it. Of course, no one's memory is perfect. If you can greet four out of six interviewers by name, you're doing very well. As you greet an interviewer whose name you cannot recall, keep the handshake warm, look the person in the eye, and say, "Nice to see you again. I'm sorry, I can't recall your name ..." The other person will respond—"Bill Reynolds"—and you should then repeat the name: "Of course! Mr. Reynolds."

Connect a Face with a Concern

Connecting a face with a name challenges your memory; you may really have to stretch to associate an issue with the person who raised it. But, again, the effort is worth it. At the selection interview, try to take mental note of who raised what issue. Immediately after the interview, jot this down. Review your list of who said what before going into the follow-up meeting. People enjoy being given ownership credit for their ideas: "Ms. Kelly, I remember from our first meeting that cash flow is a particular concern of yours. As I said before, I agree that it's a key issue, which I would address with a special incentive program. May I share my ideas with you?"

You're Already There

Inertia is the tendency of a body in motion to keep moving at a constant velocity and of a body at rest to remain motionless. Inertia, in short, is resistance to change, and it is as operative in the realm of human behavior as it is in physics. A key to overcoming inertia is to *imagine* change. If you can get interviewers to see you as a member of the team, it will be that much easier for them to say yes. Your mission during the follow-up interview is to pull off a kind of balancing act. Without creating the impression that you believe the job is "in the bag," you should behave as if you are already part of the team.

- Using the interviewers' names will help achieve this impression.

- Speak about the long-term future whenever possible, as if you believe that you will have a stake in the company.

- While you should use *would* instead of *will*, avoid *if*.

Let's linger over that last point for just a moment. It would be presumptuous to say "I *will* start a new incentive program in this position," but it is effective to offer: "I *would* start a new incentive program." Do *not*, however, feel obliged to add, with modesty, the qualifying conditional phrase: " ... *if* I am hired." The interviewers are well aware that your employment is still an "if" proposition. You need not remind them.

Choose Your Pronoun

One of the most effective means of stimulating the employer's collective imagination to envision you as one of the team is simply, whenever possible, to use the pronouns *we, us,* and the possessive *our* in place of *I, you,* and *your:* "*Our* concern has to be cash flow" is a far more effective statement than "*Your* concern has to be cash flow." It demonstrates common cause and your wholehearted engagement with the prospective employer's enterprise.

Engage Problems

Speaking of engagement, you should address as aggressively and as enthusiastically as possible any problems or difficult issues raised in the course of the follow-up. Adopt and broadcast the attitude that this company's concerns are now—*already*—your own. Demonstrate an ownership interest in all issues raised: "We need to tackle that. I've given it considerable thought since we last met, and I have a few suggestions. Would you like to hear them?"

Be Positive

Don't shy away from any problems or doubts the interviewers may express. Review the tactics for overcoming objections, discussed in Chapter 24, and take to heart the advice given there to learn to regard interviewer's objections not as potential reasons for rejection, but as the employer's request that you help him to make the decision to hire you. As important as it is to create a positive impression and maintain a positive tone during the selection interview, it is even more crucial to establish a positive atmosphere in the follow-up meeting. Do not brush aside or downplay any doubts or concerns that may be expressed, but accept

> **Don't Call Us ...**
>
> If asking obvious or basic questions is bad in the first-round interview, it is fatal at the follow-up stage. Also avoid questions to which you should already have the answer: "What does Acme Widgets make, anyway?"

them as challenges—that is, as opportunities to excel, to show that you are precisely the kind of problem solver the firm needs.

By the same token, you should not introduce any markedly negative questions or concerns at this point: "Since the first interview, I've heard some terrible things about your company." By all means, ask questions, but postpone discussion of any potentially negative issues until *after* you have received an offer.

Wait Until They "Gotta Have You"

If salary is one of the issues raised at the follow-up interview, don't let go of your grip on the negotiating principles discussed in Chapter 13, the most important of which is to try to delay the discussion until you are confident that the interviewer or interviewers have reached the *gotta-have-you point*. The employer will be willing to shell out more money to someone in whom he has confidence and in whom he has invested time and attention.

def•i•ni•tion

The **gotta-have-you point** is that stage in the interview when the candidate senses that the interviewer or interviewers have decided to make an offer.

Making Your Exit

Ideally, the follow-up interview will conclude with a job offer, a salary discussion, joyous concord, and hearty congratulations all round.

But it may not end this way.

If it doesn't, don't be alarmed. But do try to push the meeting to a positive conclusion.

Do's and Don'ts for Bringing It to a Close

It is the responsibility of the interviewer or interviewers to bring the follow-up meeting to a close. If the closing signal comes—"Well, I have no further questions"—without an offer having been made, that's your cue to help out:

◆ "I've enjoyed our meeting. Is there anything else—any additional information I can provide that will help you make your decision?"

◆ "These have been exciting meetings. What more do you need to know in order to make your decision?"

If you feel highly confident about the interview, you might close with a question that pushes the interviewers to act: "Based on all that you've learned about me, wouldn't you agree that I am fully qualified for this position?" However, avoid asking such questions as the following:

◆ "Did I get the job?"

◆ "Am I hired?"

◆ "Well, how about it?"

◆ "What are my chances?"

◆ "How does it look?"

Do I Shut Up Now?

If the follow-up interview does not conclude with an offer, do, at the least, push for closure: "When do you expect to reach your decision?" Once you have an answer to this, the meeting is over. You've either made the sale, and that means—as all sales veterans know—that it's time to shut up, or you haven't. And if you haven't made the sale at this point, you need to leave the decision at long last in the hands of the employer. But although it is time now to be silent, your work is not done, as we shall see in the final chapter.

The Least You Need to Know

◆ Make a special effort to remember the names of multiple interviewers when you first meet them, so that you can greet these people by name at the follow-up interview.

◆ Prepare for a follow-up by jotting down notes—important concerns, unresolved issues—*immediately* after the first selection interview.

◆ Speak and act as if you already have a long-term stake in the company; make its concerns your own.

◆ Whenever possible, use the pronouns *we* and *us* (and the possessive form *our*) instead of *I*, *you*, and *your*.

◆ If the interview closes without an offer, ask the interviewers if they need any additional information to facilitate a decision.

Chapter 26

The Morning After

In This Chapter

- Why you *must* write a thank-you letter or e-mail
- Using the thank-you message to "close the sale"
- Finishing unfinished business
- Conducting a useful interview self-review
- Helping the employer reach a decision
- Accepting an offer

A sigh of relief. The interview's over. Nothing to do now but wait for the employer's decision. It's out of your hands now. Waiting is hard, but at least you don't have to *do* anything else.

Well, you *should* feel relieved. The interview may be over, but your interview work is not finished.

More to Do

Your most important post-interview task is to write a thank-you letter or e-mail. Which is better? If you have been communicating regularly via

Clincher

Some interview experts suggest that you send a thank-you message to *everybody* you spoke with during your interview. This is not always practical. What if you accidentally leave one person out? If you are confident that you can send letters or e-mails to all the interviewers, do so. Otherwise, target the lead interviewer only.

e-mail, use this medium. If not, the more traditional snail mail alternative is called for. Send your e-mail or mail your letter within one day of the interview.

A thank-you message is a courtesy that no employer demands, but most expect. Failure to send an e-mail or letter will almost certainly be noticed. Courtesy in and of itself is an important enough reason to write, but you have an even more pressing motive. The thank-you message is an opportunity to keep your candidacy in the forefront of the employer's mind, to address one or two issues left unaddressed or unresolved in the interview, and, most important, to push the "sale" to a successful conclusion.

Four Steps to Thank-You Messages That Mean Business

Your thank-you message should be more than a mere note. A single-sentence note fails to take maximum advantage of this opportunity for follow-up communication. Write a four-paragraph message, with each paragraph devoted to a separate "selling" step:

1. Begin by thanking the interviewer and saying how much you enjoyed meeting with him or her.

2. Tell the interviewer how excited you are by the prospect of working in the target position at this particular company.

3. Review interview highlights and selling points.

4. Establish closure: reiterate your understanding of when you expect to hear from the employer again.

Address the letter to the lead interviewer—if there was more than one interviewer—and be certain to ask the addressee to convey your regards and thanks to the others with whom you spoke. If it's impossible to identify a single lead interviewer, write to more than one of the people with whom you met. Don't send copies of the same message to multiple addresses. Each should receive a different message.

The following is an example of an effective thank-you message—in this case, a traditional snail-mail letter:

Jane Smith
1234 East 56th Street
Eden, New Jersey 01234
Telephone: 201-555-5555
Fax: 201-555-4444
Email: jsmith@compunerd.com

(Tip: Include full communications information in your letterhead. Make it easy for the employer to communicate with you.)

Mr. Kent Bromide
Executive Vice President
Acme Widget Company, Inc.
5678 Regal Street
Pine Barren, New Jersey 02345

(Tip: Address the letter to the lead interviewer, if you met with more than one person. Be certain to include his or her full and correct title.)

Dear Mr. Bromide:

(Tip: Unless you were invited to use the addressee's first name during the interview, don't use it now. Surname only, please.)

Thank you for the opportunity to interview for the position of assistant sales manager. I was greatly impressed by the intelligence and energy of everyone with whom I spoke at your offices, and I was very grateful for the warm reception and the sincere interest shown in me.

(Tip: Begin with thanks. Be sure to remind the reader of what position you interviewed for. A liberal dollop of praise and flattery doesn't hurt, either.)

The prospect of working at Acme is very exciting. You have forged a great team, and I would be thrilled to become part of it.

(Tip: Convey enthusiasm for the job.)

I was delighted by our conversation, particularly by the prospect of creating a special incentive program. As I mentioned, I was instrumental in designing just such a program for Smith Widget, which resulted in a 26 percent increase in order volume within two quarters after its introduction. That experience taught me a great deal, which I hope I will have the opportunity to apply at Acme.

(Tip: Gracefully hit a highlight or two of your qualifications, emphasizing what you can do to benefit the employer's company, not what you want from the company.)

Thanks again for the interview. I look forward to hearing from you, as you mentioned, before the end of the month.

(Tip: Reiterate whatever closure you have been promised. This serves not only as a reminder to the employer, but lets him know that you are expecting action.)

Sincerely,

Jane Smith

(Tip: End with a conventional polite "complimentary close." Don't repeat thanks or "hoping to hear from you," or anything of the kind. This is a friendly but businesslike communication.)

Pursue the Issues

At the beginning of this chapter, I painted a picture of relief and relaxation following the interview. Actually, if you're like most job candidates, you'll spend at least part of the post-interview period fretting over the important information you *forgot* to convey to the interviewer. Read on to find out what to do.

Those Unanswered Questions

The thank-you message is not the place to include questions *you* forgot to ask. A request for additional information should not be disguised as thanks. However, if you are aware of having left unanswered one or two of the interviewer's more significant questions, you could include the answer here: "I have given additional thought to your question concerning XYZ, and I'd have to conclude that, while there is no single right way to carry out this type of operation, the ABC method is probably the most efficient and cost-effective. I'd be quite pleased to discuss this further with you."

"I Forgot to Mention ..."

The thank-you message can also be used as a vehicle to convey one or two significant items of information that failed to find their way into the interview. Again, keep these comments brief. If an item merits detailed discussion, invite an additional meeting.

 Don't Call Us ... _____

Although you should not hesitate to correct an important omission or error with a phone call, don't make more than one phone call of this kind. You can't afford to give the impression that you make a lot of mistakes, which you then correct by dribs and drabs in a series of afterthought calls.

Zapping Doubt

You've dutifully written and mailed or e-mailed your thank-you message, but this still isn't reason enough to call a halt to your post-interview thought processes. As objectively as possible, review the interview in your mind. Did you say anything that might have created—or might have reinforced—doubt in the employer's mind? If you believe that you have, ask yourself what you could say to counteract this unwanted impression.

This is no exercise in idle self-criticism, let alone futile "shoulda-woulda-coulda." While you don't have the entire interview to do over again, no law bars you from making a telephone call. Let's say that you were asked to furnish the interviewer with a start date. You were a bit surprised by the question—you *shouldn't* have been, but you were—and you quickly calculated that you wanted to give your current employer a month's notice and you wanted another month's worth of vacation time for yourself. "I could start in two months," you replied.

The corners of the interviewer's mouth turned down. His eyes narrowed. But then the interview went on, and you thought nothing of this verbal and nonverbal exchange—until now.

Of course! The interviewer's body language was telling you something. Two months is too long. Rather than risk losing the offer, you recalculate. Your current employer can do with two weeks' notice, and you can do with a week off. Pick up the phone and make a call: "Hello, Mr. Thomas. This is Jane Smith. I just realized that I made a mistake during our meeting. You asked me when I would be available to begin work. I'm afraid I miscalculated when I told you that I couldn't start for two months. I'm very excited about the position and wouldn't want to wait that long. I could start as soon as three weeks from the date of offer."

The Silent Treatment

Silence in and of itself is neither a positive nor a negative sign. Don't be afraid that you are being too pushy or overanxious by checking in with the employer. You can be certain that passivity will not influence the employer's decision positively and may even make a negative impression. Checking in and asking if the employer needs further information will not make you look like an overanxious pest, but will be seen as enthusiasm and a desire to make the sale and get the offer. For this reason, too, it is preferable to make a follow-up phone call rather than send a follow-up e-mail; however, if you have been instructed to communicate by e-mail, do so. Just be aware that, in the face of silence, a proactive approach has a greater chance of eliciting an offer than a passive attitude.

That said, don't devote the rest of your professional life to calling the silent employer. Get on with your job search. Bid for more interviews with other companies.

Briefing Your References

Another way to use the interval between interview and offer is to contact your *reference network*, especially anyone you specifically mentioned in your application materials or at the interview as a reference. Brief them. Bring them up to date on your interview: "It went really well with Acme Widget. You remember that I interviewed for a slot as assistant sales manager? I'm waiting for word from them. You might get a call from them. Do you have a few moments now to go over some points I'd like you to reinforce concerning my background and qualifications?"

def•i•ni•tion

Your **reference network** is the set of colleagues, clients, supervisors, and others whose names you have furnished as references.

It's important that you take nothing for granted. Fully prep your references. Make sure they know …

◆ Who may be calling them.

◆ What position you interviewed for.

◆ What points about yourself you would like emphasized.

You should be as specific as possible about these points. Spell them all out for your reference.

What to Do with Success

Don't decide whether to take a job until you get an offer. Your goal should always be to get an offer. The more offers you get, the better you'll feel about yourself, your qualifications, and your ability to communicate effectively in an interview. Moreover, it's never wise to burn bridges. Treat each interview and offer seriously and graciously as items of great value. You can never tell with whom you may be doing business at a later time.

Unless you are 100 percent certain that you want the job, you need not leap to accept the offer. If you need 24 hours to reflect and ponder, ask for it. If you do accept the offer, do so graciously and with enthusiasm: "Great! I'm really eager to begin."

Nice Save!

What if the employer calls to tell you that one of your references gave a negative report about you? This is not likely to happen (if for no other reason than the reference's fear of slander litigation), but it's not impossible.

Respond by expressing surprise: "I'm very surprised to hear that, and I really don't understand. There must be some misunderstanding." Next, express your thanks to the target employer: "I'm very grateful that you are taking the time and effort to inform me of this." Finally, tell the target employer that you will speak to the reference immediately, and that you will report back: "Let me discuss this with _____ and see what's going on. I'm sure this can be resolved to your satisfaction. I'll call back with a report of what I discovered."

You must not jump to conclusions or take rash action. Do speak with your reference to determine just what went wrong. Assuming some misunderstanding occurred and the reference had intended to give a positive report concerning you, you should ask him or her to call the target employer immediately. If, however, the reference tells you that he or she cannot be positive about you, don't argue. Try to get the whole story, and report it yourself to the target employer. Put the situation in the best light possible and offer at least two alternative references: "This is, of course, very awkward. I was unaware that Mr. Smith had these feelings about this particular issue. May I ask you to call Mr. Josh Johnson and Ms. Clara Rappaport, who will give you a more accurate and objective appraisal of my qualifications?"

Be certain that you call these alternative references, informing them completely of the situation, before you mention their names to the target employer. It's usually not a good idea to have the alternative references call the target employer. Such a move smacks too strongly of frantic "damage control"; just furnish the names to the employer and invite *him* to make the call.

Obviously, the best way out of this disagreeable situation is to prevent it. Don't use references about whom you have even the slightest shadow of a doubt.

The Least You Need to Know

- Never fail to write a thank-you message to the interviewer. It should be sent, either by e-mail or snail mail, within one day following the interview.

- If the employer fails to contact you after the interview within the length of time promised, don't hesitate to call.

- Keep your reference network informed of your status following the interview. Brief them on what you would like them to say to the prospective employer.

- Your goal in the interview process is not to get a job; it is to get an offer. Only after you have secured the offer can you choose whether or not to take the job.

Talk the Talk Glossary

baby boomer   Anyone born during the sharp increase in birth rate following World War II, that is, between 1947 and 1961.

behavior-related questions   Questions aimed at assessing a candidate's character, attitude, and personality traits by asking for an account of how the candidate handled certain challenging situations.

benefit (of a product)   Something good a product or its features do, or are perceived to do, for the buyer; for example, the high-speed processor on that new notebook computer makes you feel more productive. The *benefit* of the processor—a perceived increase in productivity—may justify the buyer spending more money for it. *See also* feature.

bona fide occupational qualification (BFOQ)   An employment criterion that permits discrimination based on personal attributes in certain cases; for example, a women's bathing suit manufacturer needs to hire models for its catalog. No men need apply. A delivery company needs drivers capable of lifting 80 pounds. The applicant who is disabled by a chronic bad back and is therefore incapable of repeated heavy lifting may legally be rejected.

buy signal   A term, borrowed from the sales profession, meaning a verbal or nonverbal cue that suggests the prospective employer is responding positively to what the candidate is saying.

cold call   An unsolicited employment query/application usually made via telephone. The target employer doesn't know the caller and hasn't asked for the call.

dynamic listening   Listening with the mind and imagination, not just the ears. It is based on the listener identifying the interests he or she has in common with the speaker and responding to the speaker's themes in such a way that the conversation is energized by active give and take.

executive briefing   A condensed summary, no more than a half-page long, in narrative paragraph form, of the candidate's resumé.

feature (of a product)   An attribute of the product; for example, a high-speed microprocessor that makes one computer faster than another. *See also* benefit.

flex time   An arrangement that allows employees to adjust their morning start and evening quitting times to suit their preferences and family schedules, and even evade rush-hour traffic congestion.

follow-up interview   An interview that may take place after an in-depth, or selection, interview. It is often the venue in which unresolved issues are discussed. Sometimes its main purpose is to deliver the offer and negotiate salary and other matters.

freelancer   A person who offers services for hire, independently of a regular or permanent employer. *See also* independent contractor.

golden parachute   A liberal severance compensation package that is agreed to, by contract, at the time of the job offer. A golden parachute usually includes several months or more of severance pay and other goodies, such as stock or stock options and outplacement assistance.

gotta-have-you point   The stage in the interview when the candidate senses that the interviewer or interviewers have decided to make an offer.

group dynamics   The systematic study of how groups operate, how members persuade one another and fail to persuade one another, how conflicts develop, and how consensus is reached.

independent contractor   A person or company hired by another firm to perform certain services. The independent contractor is not a regular, permanent employee of the hiring firm. Whereas a freelancer works independently of an employer, an independent contractor may be a company or an employee of a company (other than the hiring firm). *See also* freelancer.

informational interview   An interview the *job hunter* requests in order to gather information about a particular company or an entire industry. The purpose of such an interview is to enlarge the job hunter's business network, to meet potential employers, and to learn from them. Immediate employment is not an objective of the informational interview.

jet lag   A temporary disruption of bodily rhythms caused by high-speed travel over multiple time zones. Symptoms include drowsiness, headache, and even flu-like symptoms.

layering   An interrogation technique that rapidly builds, piles, or "layers" one question on top of another.

layoff   Termination of an employee for reasons unrelated to his or her performance or behavior. Layoffs are usually the result of economic reversals or mergers (in which certain departments or individuals become "superfluous").

line extension   A new product or service that is a continuous, logical development of the products or services a firm currently offers. For example, a maker of breakfast cereal may introduce a line of snack foods (such as chewy bars) based on the cereal.

mission   The more or less concise formulation of the purpose, goals, and objectives of an entire organization or department.

network   An informal set of business and personal contacts the job hunter develops in order to acquire information and employment leads.

overqualified   Having too much experience or too much education to "fit into" a given position. The employer's assumption is that the overqualified employee will become bored with the job and soon quit.

panel interview   An interview in which (typically) 5 to 12 interviewers, assembled at one time and in one room, ask the employment candidate questions. The purpose of this mass interview is to expose the candidate to as many decision makers as possible in a short time. Also called a *group interview.*

portable skills   Skills specific to the individual rather than to a particular job. Portable skills describe a function—that is, how the individual works with people, data, or things. For example, knowing how to write computer programs in the Java programming language is a job-specific skill, whereas the ability to analyze and synthesize information is a skill that can be carried from job to job.

positive visualization   A mental exercise in which one imagines what success in a given context will look and feel like. A runner might prepare for a race by *seeing* herself successfully leaping the hurdles. A job candidate might visualize herself successfully answering the most difficult questions or accepting a congratulatory handshake at the end of a great interview.

problem-solving question   Poses a hypothetical scenario or sets a hypothetical task and asks the candidate to formulate solutions and procedures.

reference network   The colleagues, clients, supervisors, and others whose names you have furnished as references.

screening interview   A preliminary interview, typically conducted by a junior-level Human Resources staffer, for the purpose of screening out unqualified job candidates, so that (theoretically) only qualified candidates are interviewed by the supervisors who are actually authorized to hire.

selection interview   The in-depth interview conducted by the person (or persons) who has the authority to hire. Especially in larger organizations, this interview is often preceded by a screening interview. *See also* screening interview.

sequential interview   An interview in which the candidate is passed from one interviewer to another. Also called a *serial interview.*

skills   The intellectual and creative tools the candidate can offer an employer. Skills that can be applied to a number of different jobs and work environments are called portable skills. *See* portable skills.

stress interview   An employment interview that uses harsh, high-pressure techniques—such as long silences, deliberately offensive questions, impossibly difficult questions, very brusque questioning style—to test the candidate's mettle. The stress interview is most often used to evaluate candidates for high-pressure jobs in which difficult or hostile customer contact is anticipated.

transferable skills   *See* portable skills.

upsell   To use the customer service function as an opportunity to offer customers accessories and other products related to their original purchase.

videoconferencing   Transmitting and receiving audio-video communication in real time via the Internet (or a dedicated system) so that conferences and meetings, including job interviews, can be conducted between or among two or more remotely stationed participants.

VoIP   "Voice over Internet Protocol" is a hardware or software (or combination) means of transmitting voice (such as telephone) or voice and video (for videoconferencing) over the Internet. It is typically required for conducting online interviews.

Resources for Job Searches and Interview Preparation

General Information Sources

Burwell World Directory of Information Brokers. Houston: Burwell Enterprises. (Updated frequently.)

Directories in Print, 26th Ed. Detroit: Gale Research, Inc., 2006.

Encyclopedia of Business Information Sources, 22nd Ed. Detroit: Gale Research, Inc., 2007.

Reader's Guide to Periodical Literature. Bronx, NY: H. W. Wilson, Co. Available in most libraries. (Updated continuously.)

InfoMine (http://infomine.ucr.edu)

Librarian's Index to the Internet (http://lii.org)

Open Directory Project (www.dmoz.org)

Resource Discovery Network (www.rdn.ac.uk)

Career Forecasts and Outlook

Farr, J. Michael, and Laurence Shatkin. *200 Best Jobs for College Graduates.* St. Paul, MN: JIST, 2005.

————. *Enhanced Occupational Outlook Handbook.* St. Paul, MN: JIST, 2006.

U.S. Department of Labor. *Occupational Outlook Handbook 2008–2009.* St. Paul, MN: JIST, 2008.

America's Career InfoNet (www.acinet.org)

Bureau of Labor Statistics (www.bls.gov)

Career Converter (http://content.monstertrak.monster.com/tools/careerconverter)

Occupational Outlook Handbook (www.bls.gov/oco)

O*Net OnLine (http://online.onetcenter.org)

Vocational Information Center (www.khake.com/page5.html)

Industries and Fields (General)

Dictionary of Holland Occupational Codes, Dictionary of Occupational Titles, and *Standard Industrial Classification Manual.* These three reference works, available in public libraries, list virtually every occupation imaginable.

Encyclopedia of Associations. Detroit: Gale Research, Inc. (Frequently updated.) Lists 25,000 organizations, associations, clubs, and other nonprofit membership groups, many of which are rich sources of industry and employment information.

National Trade and Professional Associations of the United States. Washington, D.C.: Columbia Books, Inc. (Updated annually.)

Newsletters in Print. Detroit: Gale Research, Inc. (Updated frequently.)

Addresses.Com (www.addresses.com)

Bizjournals (www.bizjournals.com/search.html)

Business.com (www.business.com)

Chambers of Commerce Directory (http://clickcity.com/index2.htm)

Entry Level Employers Search (www.collegegrad.net/employers/search/agree.asp)

Hoovers (www.hoovers.com/free)

Thomas Global Register (www.tgrnet.com)

ThomasNet (www.thomasnet.com/home.html)

Vault (http://vault.com/companies/searchcompanies.jsp)

WetFeet Company Profiles (www.wetfeet.com/research/companies.asp)

Yahoo! Company Directories (http://dir.yahoo.com/Business_and_Economy/ Directories/Companies)

Yahoo! Finance (http://finance.yahoo.com/search)

Yellow.com (www.yellow.com)

Communications Industry

Telecommunications Directory. Detroit: Gale Research, Inc. (Updated frequently.)

Google Directory (www.google.com/Top/Business/Telecommunications/)

Computer Industry

Computers and Computing Information Resources Directory. Detroit: Gale Research, Inc. (Updated frequently.)

Computer Industry Almanac Information, 8th Edition. Arlington Heights, IL: Computer Industry Almanac Information, Inc., 2007.

Information Industry Directory. Detroit: Gale Research, Inc. (Updated frequently.)

Silicon Valley Web Directory (http://gocee.com/valley/s1_compi.htm)

Government Employment

United States Government Manual. Washington, D.C.: U.S. Government Printing Office. (Updated annually.)

United States Government Manual (www.gpoaccess.gov/gmanual/index.html)

Sources of Information on Specific Companies

The Adams Jobs Almanac. Holbrook, MA: Adams. (Updated annually.) Also consult this publisher's *JobBank* series, which lists jobs in specific cities, metropolitan areas, and regions.

Corporate and Industry Research Reports. New Providence, NJ: R.R. Bowker/ Martindale-Hubbell. (Frequent editions.)

Hoover, Gary, et al., eds. *Hoover's Handbook of American Business.* Austin, TX: The Reference Press. (Issued annually.)

Job Seeker's Guide to Private and Public Companies. Detroit: Gale Research, Inc.. (Updated frequently.)

People with Clout (Contacts)

Contacts Influential: Commerce and Industry Directory. San Francisco: Contacts Influential, Market Research and Development Services. (Updated frequently.)

Standard and Poor's Register of Corporations, Directors and Executives. New York: Standard and Poor's. (Updated frequently.)

The *Who's Who* series. Consult these volumes in the reference section of the public library.

Skills Inventories

A People Skills Inventory

Rate your skill levels from 1 to 4, with 4 being the strongest. Notice that the skills are arranged in approximate order of complexity, from lowest to highest. For example, "following instructions" (the first item listed) is a simpler skill than "coaching and mentoring" (the last item).

I am good at …

WITH PEOPLE AS INDIVIDUALS:

Following instructions	1	2	3	4
Serving	1	2	3	4
Listening	1	2	3	4
Communicating verbally	1	2	3	4
Communicating in writing (letters, memos)	1	2	3	4
Diagnosing, evaluating, and analyzing	1	2	3	4
Persuading	1	2	3	4
Recruiting and motivating	1	2	3	4

Selling	1	2	3	4
Instructing and training	1	2	3	4
Coaching and mentoring	1	2	3	4

WITH PEOPLE IN GROUPS:

Communicating	1	2	3	4
Representing	1	2	3	4
Guiding group discussion	1	2	3	4
Persuading and motivating	1	2	3	4
Formal public speaking	1	2	3	4
Performing and entertaining	1	2	3	4
Managing and supervising	1	2	3	4
Consulting and advising	1	2	3	4
Negotiating and resolving conflict	1	2	3	4
Pioneering (leading innovation)	1	2	3	4

A Data Skills Inventory

Here's a list for data skills. As in the people-skills inventory, the transferable skills are listed from least complex (lowest level) to most complex (highest level). In addition, they are gathered into more-encompassing groups.

I am good at …

SORTING:

Copying	1	2	3	4
Data entry	1	2	3	4
Record keeping and filing	1	2	3	4
Retrieving information efficiently	1	2	3	4

Helping others retrieve information	1	2	3	4
Memorizing and paying attention to detail	1	2	3	4

GATHERING:

Compiling	1	2	3	4
Searching and researching	1	2	3	4
Observing (in order to gather data)	1	2	3	4

MANAGING:

Comparing (similarities? differences?)	1	2	3	4
Computing	1	2	3	4
Analyzing	1	2	3	4
Organizing, systematizing, prioritizing	1	2	3	4
Step-by-step, goal-oriented planning	1	2	3	4
Visualizing (drawing, creating graphics, etc.)	1	2	3	4
Synthesizing, developing, improving	1	2	3	4
Problem solving	1	2	3	4
Developing the "big picture"	1	2	3	4

CREATING:

Daydreaming	1	2	3	4
Imagining	1	2	3	4
Improving	1	2	3	4

Designing	1	2	3	4
Inventing and innovating	1	2	3	4

A Things Skills Inventory

Ditto for "things" skills, except that here, the larger groupings (WORKING WITH MACHINERY AND VEHICLES, WORKING WITH MATERIALS, etc.) are not necessarily hierarchical; that is, each grouping is its own ladder, so that the skills involved in working with machinery and vehicles are not necessarily less complex than those you use in working with materials or working in construction.

I am good at …

WORKING WITH MACHINERY AND VEHICLES:

Operating	1	2	3	4
Controlling (including driving)	1	2	3	4
Maintaining	1	2	3	4
Repairing	1	2	3	4
Assembling	1	2	3	4

WORKING WITH MATERIALS:

Sewing, weaving, basic woodworking, etc.	1	2	3	4
Finishing	1	2	3	4
Carving	1	2	3	4
Sculpting	1	2	3	4
Precision hand work	1	2	3	4

CONSTRUCTION WORK:

Rough carpentry, framing, etc.	1	2	3	4
Finish carpentry	1	2	3	4
Remodeling	1	2	3	4

WORKING WITH LIVING THINGS:

Gardening	1	2	3	4
Farming	1	2	3	4
Caring for animals	1	2	3	4
Training and handling animals	1	2	3	4

BODY SKILLS:

Strength	1	2	3	4
Endurance	1	2	3	4
Dexterity	1	2	3	4
Athletics	1	2	3	4

Index